REVEAL

A CREATIVE EXPLORATION REVEALING LIVERPOOL'S CONNECTION WITH AN GORTA MÓR

First published in Great Britain in 2025 by ***Liverpool Irish Festival*** following a peer review by ***Liverpool University Press.***

First published in softback and ebook.

Liverpool Irish Festival asserts the moral right under the *Copyright, Designs and Patterns Act* of 1988 to be identified as the author of this work. Lead author and editor: Emma Smith (***Liverpool Irish Festival***, **ORCID** reference 0009-0009-7873-6759). *History Research Group* leader and second author: John Maguire (***ArtsGroupie CIC***). The *History Research Group*'s 2025 active contributors include Kieran Daly, Steven Garnett, Vicki Caren, Catherine Leen, Tricia Mackin and Flora Small.

A CIP catalogue record for this title is available from the ***British Library*** (Legal Deposit Office, Wetherby; ***Bodleian Library***, Oxford and ***Cambridge University Library***), ***National Library of Scotland*** and ***Trinity College Dublin***.

ISBN-978-1-7396640-2-2 - *Liverpool Irish Famine Trail*: *Reveal*
- A creative exploration revealing Liverpool's connection with An Gorta Mór (physical version)
ISBN-978-1-7396640-3-9 - *Liverpool Irish Famine Trail*: *Reveal*
- A creative exploration revealing Liverpool's connection with An Gorta Mór (eBook)

Thema NH-1QF-3M
BISAC ARC024010 SOC007000 HIS015060
BIC HB-1DBK-1DBR-3J-4Y-5AX

liverpoolirishfestival.com | liverpoolirishfaminetrail.com | info@liverpoolirishfestival.com

Liverpool Irish Festival is a registered charity (1100126) and company (04800736).

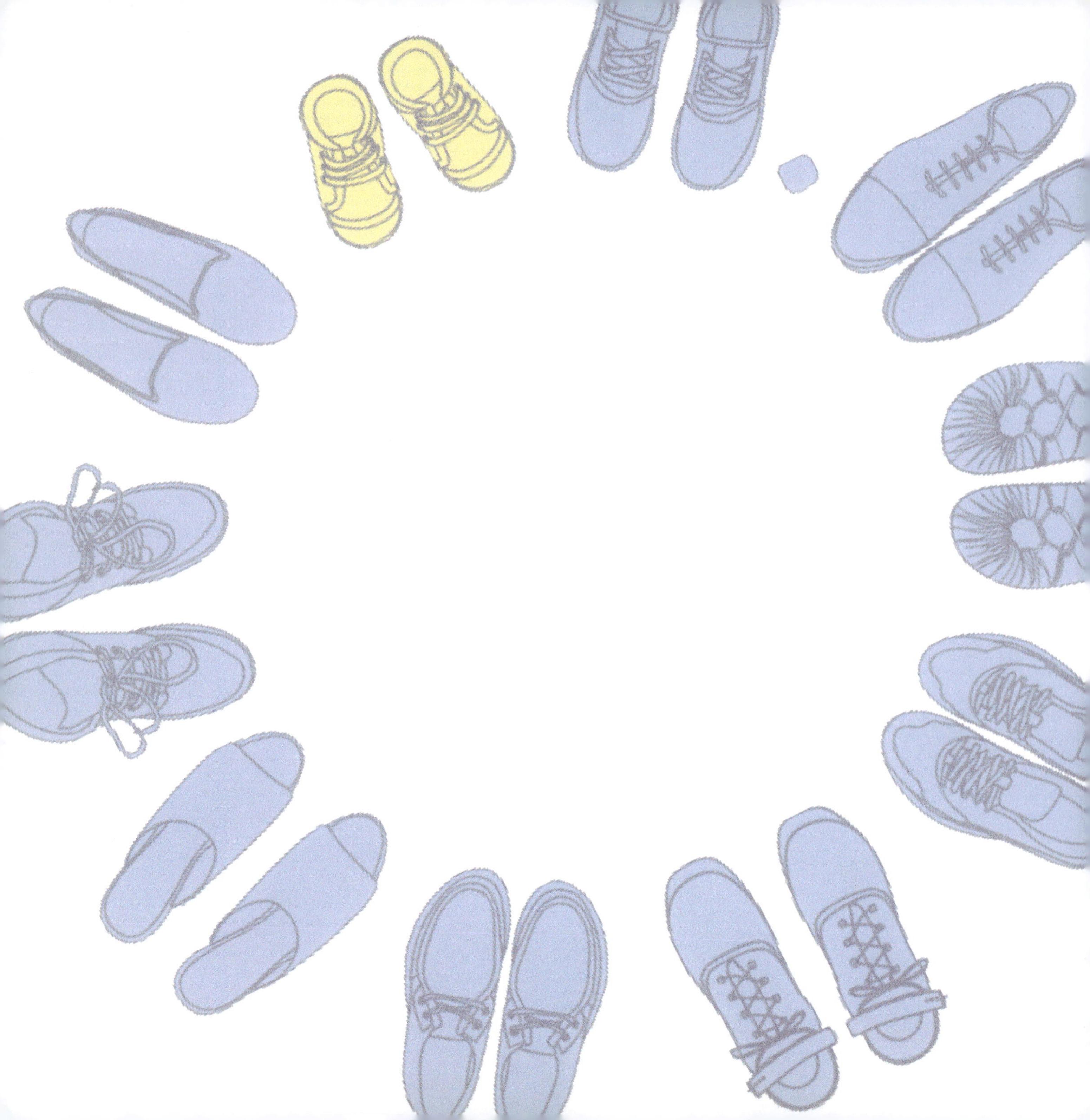

REVEAL

A creative exploration revealing Liverpool's connection with An Gorta Mór

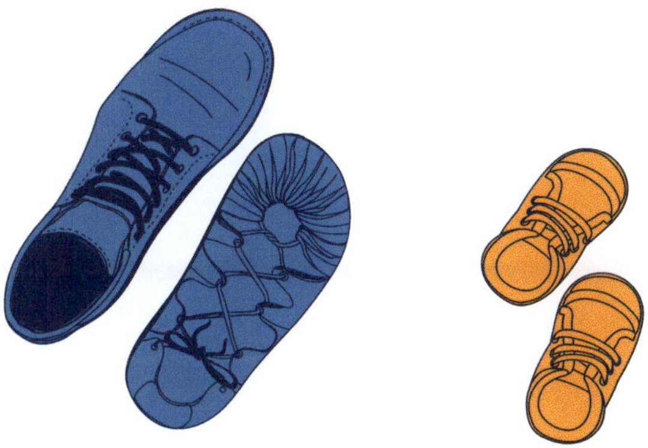

CONTENTS

Strokestown's bronze shoes in front of the famous Liverpool Dock wall. If one brick represented the life of each person fleeing from An Gorta Mór through Liverpool (thought to be 1,241,410 when we wrote *Revive*), between 1845-1852, an eight-foot wall like this would be 34-miles long. Using the new figures on page 40, it would be over 43 miles long or 69.3kms representing over 1.5m lives!

Strokestown's bronze shoes meet the Liverpool Irish Great Hunger commemoration memorial for the first time, 27 May 2004.

1/ INTRODUCTION

You only leave home
when home won't let you stay

Warsan Shire (b.1988-d–), *Home*[1]

This is the Festival's second book about An Gorta Mór (The Great Hunger, often known as 'The Irish Famine') whose dates are widely understood to be 1845-52. Our work considers Liverpool's role and function, within the wider historical story, and our regional connections then and now.

When we released our first book on the *Liverpool Irish Famine Trail* (*Revive*, 2022) it was a fast turnaround project that came about by accident. Another fund – designed to support a cross-Festival and Trail position – failed. This left the Festival with a portion of its ***National Lottery Heritage Fund*** without an allocated action. "Let's ask for a change-of-use and write a book" said the Festival's Director and within six-months we had!

It was a remarkable process that helped us to explain our intentions and share recently uncovered information. It became a meaningful way to recognise the hundreds of hours our *History Research Group* had undertaken. Additionally, it naturally expanded the Trail leaflet the ***Liverpool Great Hunger Commemoration Committee*** had been re-printing and sharing since the 1990s. We were thrilled to communicate that this book would sit in ***Oxford University***'s *Bodleian Library*, and other ***National Archives***, as a demonstration of the shared work we had accomplished. Nevertheless, we acknowledge it was written quickly and without the academic or editorial peer review it could have benefited from. As time has passed, research has advanced and errors have been noted. A new ***National Lottery Heritage Fund*** project has allowed us time to reflect, grow and reveal new information we have uncovered.

[1] We began *Revive* with a quote from Warsan Shire's poem and it felt fitting to do so again. Here is ***Amnesty International***'s publication of the poem this quote is taken from **https://www.amnesty.ie/wp-content/uploads/2016/06/home-by-warsan-shire.pdf** accessed 7 Mar 2025

STORYTELLING

The Liverpool Irish Great Hunger story is not the Festival's to tell – it is Liverpool's and Ireland's. The Festival is a conduit for helping collect and share stories and we aim to do this with energy, honesty and authenticity.

It has been exciting to collaborate with people, for people, and we hope that this is a document of those conversations, experiences and learning. We aim to continue to operate in this way. Whilst we are trusted to — and can bring our expertise to the project meaningfully — we will do all we can.

WHY ARE WE DOING THIS NOW?

2025 marks 180-years since the start of An Gorta Mór. This suggests we are between 7-9 generations away from this international tragedy. Whilst others might wait to mark 200-years, we fear not sharing the information before another generation is lost.

At a time when we are watching wealth inequality rise in the UK[2] we are concerned we are missing the lessons of the past. 'An Drochshaol' ('The Hard Times') does not suitably cover the experiences of the bombed, the displaced or the fallen created by today's ongoing wars. As we write this book, Myanmar is going through civil war; the Arab Israeli conflict is damaging lives in Israel, Palestine, Lebanon, Syria, Iraq, Iran and Yemen; the ongoing Russian Ukrainian conflict has killed over 608,000 people; insurgency in the Maghreb has killed 22,000 people in the last two years, with a further 19,000 dead in the Sudan. In the first months of 2025 over 630 people have been killed in the Ethiopian civil conflict. In Yemen half the children under 5-years old are facing malnutrition[3].

[2] Wealth inequality in the UK **https://www.jrf.org.uk/narrative-change/changing-the-narrative-on-wealth-inequality#:~:text=Wealth%20inequality%20is%20high%20and%20rising%20and%20more%20marked%20than,World%20Inequality%20Lab%2C%202022** accessed 12 Feb 2025

[3] Yemen's children **https://www.savethechildren.net/stories/what-happening-yemen** accessed 12 Feb 2025

Plaque for the former *Brownlow Hill Workhouse*, now close to Liverpool's ***Metropolitan Cathedral***

Whilst these places rage, class and protected characteristics in The West are having their protection removed, too. This is being witnessed in ***Amazon***, ***Google***, ***Meta*** and other global companies, who are removing their diversity, equality and inclusion (DEI, often EDI in the UK) policies after President Trump used executive orders to rescind policies in the federal government[4]. As social media moguls remove fact-checkers[5] from their platforms, the rise in hate speech is further isolating marginalised people. Freedom of speech versus hate speech arguments are rife. Language is once again being used to punish those fleeing life-threatening danger or those with the least commercial assets. We have seen this before with 'soupers' and 'taking the soup' (see chapter 10) and continue to fight narratives that suggest indentured servitude and slavery are the same.

Speaking of language, whilst we were undertaking *The Walk of the Bronze Shoes* in 2024 (see chapter 7), we were told about Strokestown's estate owner — Major Denis Mahon (b.1787-d.1847) – who referenced his tenants as "surplus population". This was a phrase first used in 1798 in *An Essay on the Principle of Population*[6] by economist Thomas Malthus (b.1766-d.1834) and was pivotal in garnering support for what eventually became the *Census Act*[7] (1800), also known as the *Population Act*. The Census became a critical instrument, fundamental to research, documenting identity as it does.

Interestingly, the first census was spurred by crop failure[8], which created a manufacturing recession, mass unemployment, food price increases and riots 45-years ahead of An Gorta Mór, echoing certain conditions in the UK now. The phrase "surplus population" was reused by Charles Dickens (b.1812-d.1870) in *A Christmas Carol* in 1843, just two-years before The Great Hunger began. On hearing it in Strokestown we gasped at the pomposity of the term, yet in 2025 we are watching world leaders force the displacement of people they see as collateral, using language that has become normalised through the erosion of compassion.

[4] *Ending Radical and Wasteful Government DEI Programmes and Preferencing* **https://www.whitehouse.gov/presidential-actions/2025/01/ending-radical-and-wasteful-government-dei-programs-and-preferencing** accessed 12 Feb 2025

[5] ***Meta*** removes fact checkers **https://www.theguardian.com/technology/2025/jan/07/meta-facebook-instagram-threads-mark-zuckerberg-remove-fact-checkers-recommend-political-content** accessed 12 Feb 25

[6] Thomas Robert Malthus's *Essay on the Principle of Population* asserting that population growth higher than agrarian capabilities will harm the poorest **https://oll.libertyfund.org/titles/malthus-an-essay-on-the-principle-of-population-1798-1st-ed** accessed 12 Feb 25

[7] *The Population Act* (1800) **http://www.histpop.org/ohpr/servlet/AssociatedView?path=Browse&active=yes&mno=4001&assoctitle=Census%20of%20England%20and%20Wales,%201801&assocpagelabel=** accessed 12 Feb 2025

[8] 1799-1800 crop failure **https://journals.ametsoc.org/view/journals/bams/73/2/1520-0477_1992_073_0187_ghetws_2_0_co_2.xml** accessed 12 Feb 2025

At the Festival we see these factors – war, removal of rights, erosion of compassionate language — as interconnected. Linking our work to a desire to change a global narrative may seem grandiose. However, our research has taught us that times that allow leaders to choose how they treat their most vulnerable citizens will often wreak havoc for generations.

Noting all the above, we can see how today reflects the atmosphere and environment of the 1840s. Cynicism around class and migrants in our politics, media and society began riots here in the UK in summer 2024. We must use our voice where we have built space to enable the change we want to see.

We have a history we should be using to help us make informed decisions. We have a heritage that continues to affect our bloodlines and populations today. Ireland's diaspora is a global success story now, but it should be remembered that many of their communities stem from the tragedy of An Gorta Mór.

We have, in our gift, a tangible link to the past that could inform our future. As Dr Eleanor Lybeck[9] states

> The history of the Great Famine is full of gaps and silences; of lives lost and stories left unrecorded. That history of lack and absence, passed down from generation to generation and carried across the world by the diaspora, is part of Ireland's intangible cultural heritage (ICH). ***UNESCO*** defines ICH as being at once community-based and inclusive, striking a balance between past traditions, contemporary practices, and future aspirations. In Liverpool, the work of the ***Great Hunger Commemoration Committee*** throughout the 1990s brought that heritage to the attention of a city whose own course through history has been shaped by the Famine.
>
> The original *Liverpool Irish Famine Trail*, which wove its way across the Mersey from Birkenhead to the docklands and city centre, encouraged people to stop and contemplate the ordinary, human reality of suffering that had once played out on the streets around them. The revival of the trail in recent years has clearly shown – through film and visual art, poetry and music, craft and textile design, and simple acts of ritual collectively performed – how that heritage might be made to live again, and flourish.
>
> It has fostered understanding between individuals and communities who are, at first glance, distant in time, space, and experience from the refugees who arrived in Liverpool in the mid-nineteenth century. But in them, and in their own cultural practices, the history of the Famine will continue to bear meanings which adapt and resonate with new people, in new contexts.
>
> Dr Eleanor Lybeck, Senior Lecturer in Literature, *Institute of Irish Studies* and *Department of English*, ***University of Liverpool***

So, for us, now is the time. We must share this knowledge to try and spread compassion in the world and share the knowledge that An Gorta Mór has given us. On a micro level, we have — and will — deeply affect a handful of people, who connect with the story and feel their history is better explained. They might be from Liverpool, Ireland or another shore. On a macro level we are telling over 76-million Irish diaspora community individuals something of their past. In a utopic way, we would hope learning the lessons of the past may improve life chances elsewhere, but we will settle for the knowledge that we have developed a credible and interesting document to help celebrate Liverpool's relationship with Ireland, yesterday and today.

[9] Quote provided to ***Liverpool Irish Festival*** by Dr Eleanor Lybeck for this publication **https://www.liverpool.ac.uk/people/eleanor-lybeck** accessed 12 Feb 2025

2/ UNDERSTANDING FAMINE POLICY AND APPLYING IT TO THE LIVERPOOL IRISH EXPERIENCE

Back in the 1840s, The Great Hunger was not declared in the sense of a formal, internationally recognised pronouncement, which would happen today, though it is universally recognised now as having been one. To break this down, we're going to share how famine is determined, assessed and communicated today.

In the 2020s famine is understood to occur based on the following primary drivers or combinations thereof:

- conflict/war and related displacement
- chronic poverty and food insecurity
- natural disasters and climate change
- lack of humanitarian access
- political hegemonies.

These drivers mirror many conditions that exacerbated An Gorta Mór. Political hegemonies especially played a devastating role when British administrative responses — such as Charles Trevelyan's — prioritised ideological commitments to free market principles over immediate humanitarian need. Conflict — though not military in nature — manifested through deeply entrenched class, and colonial tensions, which prevented effective relief measures.

When famine is "declared" a combination of authorities and principles combine, which include:

- The government of the country experiencing severe food insecurity
- 'Integrated (Food Security) Phase Classification' also known as 'The *IPC*'
- and the ***United Nations***, supported by a raft of aid organisations who monitor and analyse food security by applying *IPC* phases to the conditions being experienced making recommendations for aid, policy change and intervention.

These organisations can include (but are not limited to) ***Action Against Hunger***, ***Disasters Emergency Committee***, ***World Health Organisation***, ***UNICEF*** and ***Oxfam***, ***International Rescue Committee***.

The *Integrated (Food Security) Phase Classification* is a five-phase classification system:

- Phase 1 – Minimal/none
- Phase 2 - Stressed
- Phase 3 - Crisis
- Phase 4 - Emergency
- Phase 5 – Catastrophe/famine.

To be declared as having "famine status", at least 20% of a population must face extreme food shortages and global acute malnutrition (GAM). This is determined by the thinness of individuals and/or presence of oedema (swellings caused by severe protein deficiency). GAM rates must exceed 30%. In practice this means that 1 in 500 people in the country die of starvation daily, despite applying a full range of coping and management strategies. If we reverse engineer these facts and apply them to Ireland's population in 1845, Ireland would have been declared as being in famine.

To understand the scale: Ireland's population in 1845 was approximately 8.2 million people. We know 1.8m came through Liverpool (more on this later) and over a million died, totalling 34% of Ireland's population directly affected by An Gorta Mór. Today's global hunger crisis affects around 733 million people from a world population of 8 billion (9%). This means proportionally, Ireland's famine was almost three times worse than today's entire global hunger crisis but compressed into a single small nation.

Considering figures globally today, we looked at ***Action Against Hunger***[10] figures, as shown on their website (June 2025). It shows that today, 1 in 11 people go to bed hungry along with other statistics that seem hard to fathom in a world of supermarkets, bed stores and international logistics:

- 2.83bn or 35% of the global population are unable to afford a healthy diet
- 85% of those people facing hunger crises live in conflict-affected countries
- Almost 45% of deaths in children under-five globally are hunger linked
- 148m children are missing meals and health and nutrition services
- In 2023, ***Action Against Hunger*** helped 21m people in 56 countries.

Thinking in these terms, we felt we needed to think about where in the world famine is happening. The ***World Food Programme*** provides an international hunger hotspots report[11] which tells us the world's hungriest countries, presented in order of need: Haiti; Sudan; Mali; South Sudan (this country was the last country declared as in famine in 2017); occupied Palestinian territories and Gaza; Somalia; Kenya; Zimbabwe; Ethiopia; Namibia; Burkina Faso; Zambia; Lesotho; and Niger. It also shows the seven countries in severe risk of being declared as hungry atop those above: Lebanon, Nigeria, Myanmar, Syria, Mozambique, Chad and Yemen.

Backing up statistics like these is an international *Food Security Index*, released periodically by ***The Economist***[12]. To date there have been 11 such reports, the last being published in 2022.

The index is based on 18 metrics, including diet diversification, corruption, farmer financing and the percent of any population below the poverty line.

At the time of writing this book, Ireland has the second-best food security in the world, whereas the UK is ninth. Here are the top 20 most food secure countries:

1. Finland
2. Ireland
3. Norway
4. France
5. Netherlands
6. Japan
7. Sweden
8. Canada
9. United Kingdom
10. Portugal
11. Switzerland
12. Austria
13. United States
14. Denmark
15. New Zealand tie in 14th
16. Czech Republic
17. Belgium
18. Costa Rica
19. Germany
20. Spain.

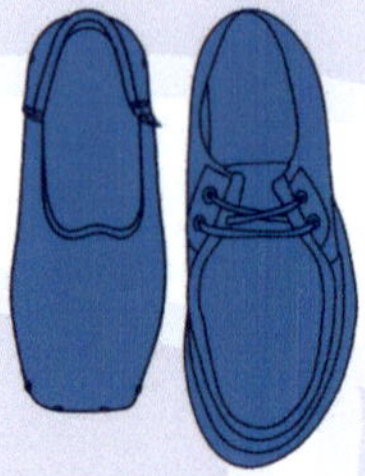

Why does the UK rank ninth, despite being the fourth most powerful country? The UK imports significant food, particularly fruits, vegetables and seafood, making us vulnerable to supply chain disruptions and price volatility. Recent events like COVID-19, the Russia-Ukraine war and climate change have highlighted these vulnerabilities. While we have high food availability, affordability and access remain issues for low-income households. The UK's ninth-place ranking reflects our reliance on global food systems, climate vulnerabilities, and affordability challenges.

Ireland has reversed its fortunes through abundant natural resources, robust agriculture, and EU membership providing access to diverse markets. As a net exporter of meat and dairy with temperate climate and fertile soils, Ireland focuses on high-quality

---

[10] ***Action Against Hunger*** *Global Impact Report* from Jun 2024 **https://www.actionagainsthunger.org.uk/publications-and-reports/global-impact-report-2023** accessed 27 Jun 2025

[11] ***World Food Programme*** **Hunger Hotspots report (Nov 2024) https://docs.wfp.org/api/documents/WFP-0000162510/download/?_ga=2.115420806.1607968960.1748018771-691832007.1748018771** accessed 27 Jun 2025

[12] ***The Economist's*** international *Food Security Index* **https://impact.economist.com/sustainability/project/food-security-index** accessed 27 Jun 2025

products with strong regulatory standards. Combined with effective farming policy, governance, research investment, and food safety nets, this ensures broad accessibility.

Conversely, Liverpool struggles. While the UK ranks ninth in food security, Liverpool ranks third most deprived of 317 UK local authorities. Such a national ranking masks significant internal local and national disparities. Liverpool faces what researchers call "food desert" conditions in many neighbourhoods, where residents lack access to affordable, nutritious fresh food despite living in one of the world's most food-secure nations. The legacy of deindustrialisation, combined with historical patterns of disinvestment, has created areas where corner shops selling processed foods are more accessible than supermarkets with fresh produce.

The *Index of Multiple Deprivation and Poverty*[13] shows that Liverpool *now* has the

- third most deprived health deprivation and disability
- fourth most deprived income ranking
- fifth most deprived employment figures and living environment
- 22nd most crime
- 29th most deprived education, skills and training
- 17% of households are in in fuel poverty, compared to 13% nationally
- almost 21% of Liverpool children (under 16s) are in low income (absolute poverty) families, compared to 16% nationally, with 32% of Liverpool's children (under 16s) are in low income (relative poverty) families, compared to 20% nationally.

This doesn't happen overnight. This is centuries of class struggle, hugely affected by the impact created during, by and after An Gorta Mór.

Recent austerity measures have pushed harder at an already damaged system in which Liverpool's authority pays out twice in benefits what it can earn in taxes, sustaining the 'managed decline' transit.

Emerging research on epigenetic trauma suggests that the biological effects of severe stress and malnutrition can be passed down through generations, altering gene expression in ways that affect descendants' stress responses, metabolism and mental health - for instance, affecting how the body processes stress hormones. While the Festival does not have the scientific evidence to draw direct lines from 1840s trauma to today's challenges, the combination of historical displacement, ongoing socioeconomic marginalisation and inherited stress patterns may help explain why some communities struggle to break cycles of deprivation, despite individual resilience and effort.

Various administrations have treated Liverpool harshly for its anti-establishment behaviours and voting history, with national treasury arrangements being shockingly out of kilter with the rest of the country. Liverpool's pro-European stance and Irish connections continue to separate it from London.

A 2017 ***Joseph Rowntree Foundation***[14] reporting on how poverty affects decision making found that people who grow up in poverty "make decisions focussed on coping with present stressful circumstances, often at the expense of future goals". It also proved that those who are in and have grown up in poverty are less likely to

- perform well cognitively
- to see themselves as able to learn or succeed at tasks
- to create links between their actions and life attainments, affecting positive health or achievement decisions or target setting
- or to take risks.

[13] Liverpool City Council's deprivation headline indicators **https://liverpool.gov.uk/council/key-statistics-and-data/headline-indicators/deprivation** accessed 27 Jun 2025

[14] ***Joseph Rowntree Foundation*** supported report by Dr Jennifer Sheehy-Skeffington and Jessica Rea from the ***London School of Economics and Political Science*** **https://www.lse.ac.uk/PBS/Research/Research-Articles/How-poverty-affects-peoples-decision-making-processes** accessed 27 Jun 2025

Props from Strokestown featuring Liverpool maps.

In turn this makes people more likely to

- feel excluded, which increases aggressive and protective tendencies
- follow stricter parenting styles
- make choices for today rather than tomorrow.

Those who know Liverpool well may see how these figures play out across the city, in different boroughs and in different communities. However benevolent a person might want to be, being held in poverty lessons your capacity to provide direct help, sustain amenability or sustain 'good moral thinking' and decisions that might help your neighbour before you.

We believe this sets an interesting framework for how we look at famine – contemporary and historic – when we can see what the effects of it can manifest as today. When we delve into archives and read about the bloated bodies of the famine poor, we begin to understand that these oedemas occur because of deficiencies. When we think about how people were locked into single-produce farming, we are reminded of how being held in poverty reduces your choices, life chances and access to aspiration. Many of the factors that shaped lives in the 1840s exist today and whilst a person may have access to a television, they may not have access to nutritious food or anything to watch on that device. Keeping these reminders front and centre helps us to understand how locked into a type of life the people fleeing hunger were and how few decisions they could make to prevent what would happen.

3/ UPDATES TO REVIVE AND READER HOUSEKEEPING

UPDATES TO WORK UNDERTAKEN

Keen readers will note that ***Liverpool University Press*** have joined us in releasing this book, providing a peer review that gives an additional layer of professionalism and insight. In 2019 we set ourselves an aspirational development plan. We would have a completely renovated, internationally linked Trail by 2025-2026. This work was outlined in *Revive*'s *What's Next?* chapter (pages 84-87). We are pleased to say that – whilst it may not have happened in the order we envisaged when writing our first successful ***National Lottery Heritage Fund*** bid – most of the activities suggested have been completed. In short, we have

- built a meaningful *Liverpool Irish Famine Trail* brand
- created downloadable and printable maps for those who prefer paper-based orienteering
- contributed to the formation of the ***Global Irish Famine Way***, connecting Liverpool (UK) with 30+ sites along the ***National Famine Way*** (Ireland) and 15 sites across North America, details of which can be found in chapter 7. At the outset, we could not have imagined the intensity of this connection, nor the journey we would travel together
- grown a broad community of people and organisations who know about the *Liverpool Irish Famine Trail*, its walks, tours, vigils and memorials and are positive advocates for our work
- developed a deep connection with ***Strokestown National Famine Park and Museum*** and the ***Irish Heritage Trust*** having completed a pilgrimage to bring a marker from Strokestown to Liverpool, which links us all to the ***Global Irish Famine Way***. Not only are there opportunities to travel with our story, but we have hosted visits from peers in Strokestown and Quinnipiac (USA), as well as generating a treasury of shared press and photographic archives

- generated a browser-based app – with GPS and geo-caching functionality – that provides information and interactive assets for each of the Trail's physical sites. The app is full of rich content, developed by local voices. Hosted on its own server and serviced by ***European Space Agency*** partner – ***Gazooky Studios*** – the app is easy to use. It is protected from degradation by being a 'live site' rather than a software download that goes out of date as devices develop
- made points of contact with all our physical sites and have a plan in place for how to amplify their whereabouts, recondition hardware and link to 'sibling' Trail sites
- secured in-app digital space to populate with new information as research develops. Though we may not have expanded our plaque count *yet*, new sites are under consideration to build a fuller picture of the history on the ground (see chapter 5). In the meantime, our app allows us to share new and interesting locations without need of plaques or hardware in the streets
- constructed an array of creative assets that allow us to share the Liverpool Irish Great Hunger story and history with others. This comprises of art works and films, presentations and music and more besides.

In our *Revive* 'to do list' reconditioning the plaques remains our only incomplete item. Though they have not yet changed, it would be unfair to say there has been no progression. We have undertaken considerable consultation and understand

- what we need to do
- how the plaques need to speak to one another
- how they must link with resources we have built
- and what their benefit is.

Aware of their significance in telling the Liverpool Irish Great Hunger story for almost 30-years, it is imperative we treat them with respect. Full of history, individual and public contributions and timely authenticity we may wish for them to work harder or be more accessible, but we are indebted to them.

Since their installation, they have collectively provided the most public Gaeilge in a city outside of Ireland and they matter to us. Accordingly, we have discussed their future with members of the public and Trail stakeholders throughout the project's development. Our plans for their future will be released later, when all parties have reviewed and agreed the principles and we can deliver them. The plaque and memorial conditioning are linked to locating a permanent home for a pair of bronze shoes – an addition not dreamed of in 2019 – which requires further thinking and consents. Readers will learn more about these in the coming chapters.

Making links with ***Liverpool Biennial***, ***Venice Biennale*** or developing our own conferences, as we suggested back in 2022, are still running. However, building in to and adding value to the ***Global Irish Famine Way*** seems a more beneficial activity in the immediate term.

Strokestown's bronze shoes meet Liverpool's Dock Road, 27 May 2024.

COLLECTIVE VOICES

We spoke about politicising words and voices in *Revive*, in our piece *Who has a Voice?* (pages 13-14). Reflecting on this a couple of years later we continue to feel the term 'history is written by the victors' must be readdressed. We have done our utmost to incorporate as many voices into our research as we have in sharing it. We hope, across the resources presented, you will see lots of names and hear various accents and brogues, ages and disciplines speak. It is the connected history we hope most to share; the stories between places and people that went unchecked, unthanked and unrecognised. We hope to bring light to what was dark and provide a case for better decision-making in future.

Our *History Research Group*, led by ***ArtsGroupie CIC*** Director and valuable Festival friend John Maguire, are a group of 10-members, local to Liverpool, who have thrown themselves headlong into their research. Through to today, they have undertaken thousands of hours reading articles, processing figures and analysing information to create connected narratives that help us to understand Liverpool's history and its relationship with Ireland and The Great Hunger.

It should be remembered that spending prolonged periods of time in archives associated with An Gorta Mór is hard. The reading is heavy going and the details are sad. Repeatedly. To overcome this emotional complexity, the group have set targets and moved with purpose, finding satisfaction in the achievement of discovering a looked-for item.

To counter the sadness, the group have developed deep friendships through positive feedback sessions. The group's members constantly review and critique each other's findings, talking through different points of view and contextualising experiences. They collaborated with artists, our artist's groups, site managers, ***Liverpool Great Hunger Commemoration Committee*** members, the public, archivists, friends and families. Our group members have shared their understanding, learned and strengthened their research methodologies and outputs.

We have tried to show this here in *Reveal* and in *Revive*, but also by sharing their voices with recordings in the app, providing presentations and leading tours.

LANGUAGE

Language can be overtly political and with a subject as emotive as this we are mindful of multiple sensitivities.

We have actively avoided the term 'The Potato Famine' in both books, finding it to be reductive. *Phytophthora infestans*[15] (blight) was one factor among scores that escalated The Great Hunger's global impact. Without blight we would still have been considering widespread poverty with Irish citizens — held in British subjugation — under laws and acts that penalised the poor. 'The Potato Famine', a term primarily used by non-Irish people, glosses over the socio-political actions of the British Government, which we now understand within the context of its colonial power and relationship with the island of Ireland.

Knowing what we know now, we don't believe 'The Potato Famine' is a credible term. That suggests something 'external' or 'outside' as responsible for the famine, rather than a set of decisions and hardships imposed on an oppressed group in a system that went on for over a century. In a time of post-colonial inquiry, we hope to revise the common belief that *any* famine is caused solely by one factor and remind people that famine is never inevitable.

Throughout *Reveal* you will see that we use 'An Gorta Mór' (meaning The Great Hunger) and 'The Great Hunger' interchangeably. We are very aware that 'Great' can be read with multiple meanings. In our usage, as with 'The Great War', we use the word 'great' to communicate the notion of large-scale and profound rather than 'great' meaning 'excellent'. As a direct translation of An Gorta Mór (sometimes written as An Ghorta Mhóir), Ireland's chosen term from the Gaeilge, it would be dismissive of us (here in Liverpool) to force a different name as if suggesting we know better.

[15] Phytophthora infestans **https://www.rhs.org.uk/disease/potato-blight** accessed 10 Feb 25

Additionally, our use is based in an inherited language we feel unable to alter, such as from our forebears ***Coiste Chuimhneachan An Ghorta Mhóir Learpholl/Liverpool's Great Hunger Commemoration Committee***. By retracting the term 'Great' we may reduce or politicise their name and actions, whereas we hope to embrace, amplify and progress their efforts.

In *Revive*, we used the term 'The Irish Famine' to reflect a famine that affected Ireland. We use this less now, having recognised the global impact and the implication it was by Ireland's design. This had never been the intention. If we do use this term, it is the imposition of British leadership decisions, actions or inactions *on* Ireland's people and land that we refer to. It was not solely an Irish issue; blight was first discovered in North America before being identified in Belgium in 1845, after which it devastated crops across Europe, not only in Ireland.

In 2025 we were introduced to the phrase 'An Drochshaol' or 'The Hard Times'. We have concerns about our using this, though value hearing it said in Gaeilge and in context. Akin to reducing a century+ of Ireland's civil unrest to 'The Troubles' we are concerned that our use of it perpetuates more of a colonial gloss-over than is helpful.

We have tried not to use 'the famine'. Again, we hope not to reassert reductive terminology or to diminish other global famines by suggesting that An Gorta Mór was the only one worthy of remembrance. In Scotland alone, during the decade 1846-1856, it is believed 150,000 people died – with a further 83,000 dying in Indonesia in 1849-50 – all attributable to a forced reliance on a type of colonised agrarian system.

HONESTY AND CORRECTIONS

As acknowledged earlier, *Revive* was released quickly, with few external fact and sense checks. This meant there were a handful of small, but meaningful errors in it. To address these, we would like to share them with readers in a spirit of honesty and growth. We will try to address them more fully where they intersect with *Reveal*, but in the meantime, this is the information we are providing with every other outgoing copy of *Revive* as it sells:

- **Page 22**: the 1821 timeline entry should be moved to 1849
- **Page 25**: Josephine Butler's birthdate should read 1828, not 1928
- **Page 30**: Site 13 ('Dandy Pat's' memorial) on the map should indicate Scotland Road, not Great Homer Street, which is close. Please use L5 5BD to locate
- **Page 32**: coordinates for ***Pleasant Street School*** should have read: 53.404809812164833, -29731960258411685
- **Page 56**: An editing error means the first sentence of the final paragraph is factually incorrect. The sentence should read 'One witness, writing at the time, recalls "I remember coming to the pro-cathedral and saying hurriedly…"'. What should have read 'pro-cathedral' was mis-edited to 'Pro[testant] Cathedral'. A 'pro-cathedral' is a church nominated to serve as a cathedral, often while another is being built or identified. For a time, we believed ***St Patrick's*** in Liverpool (Park Place) was such a church but have since learned this was, in fact, ***RC St Nicholas Church*** on Copperas Hill (not to be confused with ***Our Lady and St Nicholas Church*** on the waterfront), which was demolished once the ***Metropolitan Cathedral*** was built
- **Pages 29, 35 and 75**: Although technically correct, people looking to visit the Clarence Dock gates would be better using the following address and coordinates: 10 Regent Rd, Liverpool L3 7DS and 53.418957, -3.000072.

4/ UPDATED AND EXPANDED LIVERPOOL/IRELAND/GLOBAL TIMELINE

In the Festival's 2022 book *Revive*, we created Irish and Liverpool/Great British timelines (pages 22-29). Since publication, we have found it beneficial to amalgamate these, with the addition of pertinent dates. This has provided a far richer, deeper context that explores the atmosphere, conditions and environment of the time. This expanded history feels important to share in *Reveal*, both as a demonstration of our improved research methodologies since *Revive*, but additionally as a contextual analysis for how the world's political climate allowed An Gorta Mór to take hold. By providing this here, we intend to provide a quick reference to actions impacting decisions and vice versa, which readers can return to as they advance through other chapters. It is not and cannot be a full history, which would require historians far greater than us to complete! Nevertheless, these pointers allow the reader to see how actions and conditions contributed to the political, societal and economic environments that permitted The Great Hunger's advance, affecting populations across the world.

We ask readers to recognise this is not a full timeline of global history. We have prioritised a focus on Liverpool and Ireland. We have added in a selection of globally historic moments to provide a backdrop to the context of The Great Hunger and Ireland's relationship with Britain. For the evenness of storytelling and completeness of the timeline (1750-2025), we have included the monarchs and leaders of Ireland and Britain, indicating aspects of the politics at play.

As custodians of a Great Hunger related story, it is important to us to highlight the multiple factors that converged enabling *this* famine to occur. Famine is never inevitable. It takes multiple actions and permissions to enable it to occur. It is this we must remember if we are to avoid such tragedy again, so it bears repeating, famine is never inevitable.

That said, we have not given a full outline of Na Trioblóidí — meaning 'The Troubles' — as its dates are acknowledged as being between the late 1960s and 1998.

We recognise that calls for Home Rule existed from before The Great Hunger and throughout Ireland's history, but this is not the focus of the *Liverpool Irish Famine Trail*'s work. If readers are interested in the story of Ireland's independence, the ***Imperial War Museum***[16] has a substantive timeline if you follow the story links.

1750 Liverpool is a Lancashire coastal town, already incorporating Irish migrants. Its population, including its maritime community, is estimated to be 22,000[17]. Please note this is a revision to *Revive*, which stated 5,000 from the 1701 Census, which is incorrect

1760 George III (b.1738-d.1820) becomes King of Great Britain and Ireland

1763 Great Britain took possession of Canada from France following the Seven Years War[18]. George Grenville (b.1712-d.1770) is Whig Prime Minister in Britain

1766 Wiliam Pitt the Elder, First Earl of Chatham (b.1708-d.1778) runs the Whig Government in Britian. *Liverpool Pilot Services*[19] established via the *Liverpool Pilotage Act*[20], which made it compulsory for a pilot (navigator) to be aboard all vessels in the Mersey, to steer vessels safely through the sand bars and around the coastline.

[16] ***Imperial War Museum***'s *What you need to know about the Troubles* (use links from the page to access more details) **https://www.iwm.org.uk/history/what-you-need-to-know-about-the-troubles** accessed 4 Mar 2025

[17] Fiona Lewis, *The Demographic and Occupational Structure of Liverpool: a study of parish registers 1660-1750* **https://livrepository.liverpool.ac.uk/3175743/1/318931.pdf** accessed 12 Feb 2025

[18] History of the Seven Years War **https://www.nam.ac.uk/explore/seven-years-war** accessed 24 Feb 2024

[19] Context for Liverpool Pilot Services **https://www.liverpoolmuseums.org.uk/edmund-gardner/pilotage-service-mersey** accessed 12 Feb 2025

[20] *Liverpool Pilotage Act*, 1766 **https://www.pilotmag.co.uk/250-years-of-the-liverpool-pilotage-service-1766-2016-part-1-geoff-topp** accessed 12 Feb 2025

The Pilotage Building (a site on the *Liverpool Irish Famine Trail*) was built in 1883 for the pilots to operate from. *The Pilotage Building* is owned by ***National Museums Liverpool*** and bears one of our plaques

1768 Augustus Henry Fitzroy, Third Duke of Grafton (b.1735-d.1811) becomes British Prime Minister (Whig)

1770 Lord Frederick North (b.1732-d.1792) leads a new Tory government in Britain. His *Tea Act*[21] of 1773 sparks the Boston Tea Party of the same year

1772 The construction of the *Brownlow Hill Workhouse* (also called the *Brownlow Hill Infirmary*) was completed, with a further six houses added by 1777. It was built to accommodate around 1,000 people, but it is known to have had over 5,000 in its walls in the mid-1800s. It would be at this site that Agnes Jones would take Florence Nightingale's lessons and train a generation of nurses. It was demolished in 1930-1931, becoming the site of the ***Metropolitan Cathedral***[22]. They bought the site for £110,000 then, the equivalent of £6.1million today[23]. A Trail plaque marks the site on Mount Pleasant

1776 *The Declaration of Independence*[24] split the American colonies from Great Britain

1782 William Petty, Secord Earl of Shelburne (b.1737-d1805), leads the Whig party in Britain for a year following a short stint by Charles Watson-Wentworth, Second Marquess of Rockingham (b.1730-d.1782), also a Whig

[21] Context and information about the *Tea Act* of 1773 **https://www.jyfmuseums.org/learn/research-and-collections/essays/the-tea-act-and-the-boston-tea-party#:~:text=The%20British%20Parliament%20passed%20the,the%20colonies%20from%20other%20places** accessed 24 Feb 2025

[22] ***Metropolitan Cathedral***'s Workhouse Site page **https://liverpoolmetrocathedral.org.uk/the-workhouse-site** accessed 12 Feb 2025

[23] ***Bank of England*** inflation calculator, based on calculation from 1931 to Dec 2024 **https://www.bankofengland.co.uk/monetary-policy/inflation/inflation-calculator** accessed 12 Feb 2025. All future monetary calculations that review costs 'then' and 'today' will use this calculator

[24] Transcription of *The Declaration of Independence* **https://www.archives.gov/founding-docs/declaration-transcript** accessed 24 Feb 2025

1783 William Cavendish-Bentinck, Duke of Portland (b.1738-d.1809), becomes British Prime Minister, representing the Whigs. The signing of the *Treaty of Paris*[25] the same year leads to the end of the American War of Independence. This year, William Pitt The Younger (b.1759-d.1806) became British Prime Minister, representing both the Tory and Whig parties. He will lead again between 1804-1806

1785 Catherine "Kitty" Wilkinson (née Seaward, b.1785 (see note below)-d.1860)[26] — who became known in Liverpool in the 1830s as "Saint of the Slums" for her ceaseless work to eradicate cholera — was born in Derry. Though this is in Northern Ireland now, at the time of her birth it was Ireland. Whilst 1785 is the birthdate given in certain notable listings, her gravestone states she "died 1860-aged 73" making her birthyear 1786 or 1787, depending on her birthday

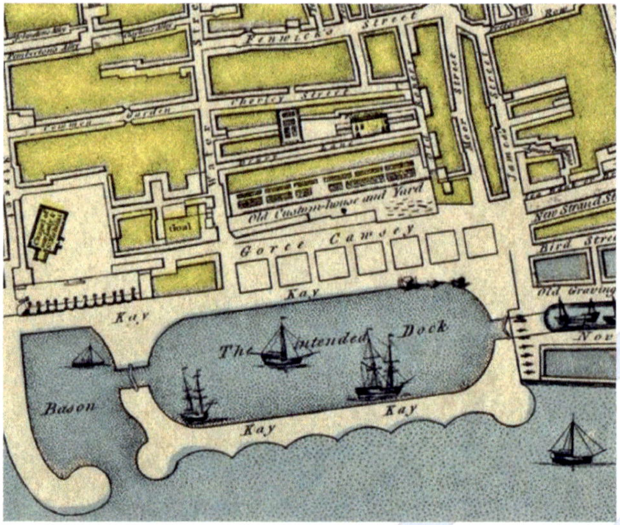

Above: A detail from John Eyes's 1775 map of Liverpool's waterfront (c) ***Liverpool Records Office*** courtesy of *Liverpool Central Library and Archives.*

[25] *Treaty of Paris* overview **https://2001-2009.state.gov/r/pa/ho/time/ar/14313.htm#:~:text=The%20Treaty%20of%20Paris%20was,the%20U.S.%20significant%20western%20territory** accessed 24 Feb 2025

[26] Kitty Wilkinson biography **https://www.stjamescemetery.co.uk/index/category/kitty-wilkinson** accessed 12 Feb 2025

1800 The *Census Act*[27] (1800), also known as *The Population Act* is passed

1801 In *Revive* we reported Liverpool's population as 77,653 following online searches. Further researching has shown that the census returned a value of 82,430 that year[28]. Henry Addington, First Viscount Sidmouth (b.1757-d.1844) is Tory Prime Minister. *The Act of Union*[29] is passed. Under *The Act of Union*, the Kingdom of Ireland unites with Great Britain, forming the United Kingdom of Great Britain and Ireland. An accidental result of this union means passenger names are not required to be listed on ships between Ireland and Britain. This will cause issues for researchers later! There are 1,000 people in Liverpool's *Brownlow Hill Workhouse*

1804 William Pitt The Younger returns to power as Prime Minster, representing Tories and Whigs, for the United Kingdom of Great Britain and Ireland

1805 William Henry Duncan[30] (later Dr Duncan) is born in Seel Street, Liverpool on 27 January (d.1863). He will become Britain's first Medical Officer of Health, during An Gorta Mór

1806 ***St Mary's Cemetery*** (Liverpool) opens. This cemetery would eventually inter 2,600 paupers from the *Brownlow Hill Workhouse* (see *Names and Numbers* section in chapter 6) the majority of which were An Gorta Mór poor. In 1848 it would close its cemetery and finalise its burial lists. In 1882, ***St Mary's*** became a public garden. In 1949, all the burials are disinterred and moved to ***Walton Park Cemetery*** to provide space to build a new wing for the ***Myrtle Street Children's Hospital***. William Wyndam Grenville, First Baron of Grenville (b.1759-d.1834) takes over the reins of Prime Ministerial office for the UK, leading the Whigs

1807 *The Slave Trade Act*[31] abolished the transportation of enslaved people throughout the British Empire. Though transporting enslaved people was illegal in English law, and therefore on English soil, it barely addressed what was happening away from England's shores and did not criminalise enslavement itself. Arriving at this act had taken from 1787 and it would take until the 1833 *Slavery Abolition Act* to make the purchase or ownership of 'slaves' illegal (except in ***East India Company*** territories). Though progressive, this does not close the matter of transatlantic – or other – enslavement practices. William Cavendish-Bentinck, Duke of Portland (Whig) returns as UK Prime Minister

1809 Spencer Perceval (b.1762-d.1812) ascended to be UK Prime Minister for the Tories. He was assassinated on 11 May 1812 by John Bellingham (b.1769-d.1812), who was himself executed on 18 May after his trial just three days earlier

---

[27] *The Population Act* (1800) **http://www.histpop.org/ohpr/servlet/AssociatedView?path=Browse&active=yes&mno=4001&assoctitle=Census%20of%20England%20and%20Wales,%201801&assocpagelabel=** accessed 12 Feb 2025

[28] *A Vision of Britain* **https://www.visionofbritain.org.uk/datavalue/11449257** and *Chapter 7: Liverpool* from *Vision of Britain* **https://images.liverpoolmuseums.org.uk/2020-01/Liverpool-Part-2.pdf** accessed 12 Feb 2025

[29] *The Act of Union* (1801): a ***UK Parliament*** overview **https://www.parliament.uk/about/living-heritage/evolutionofparliament/legislativescrutiny/parliamentandireland/collections/ireland/act-of-union-1800** accessed 12 Feb 2025

[30] ***BBC*** *KS3 History: Transforming the Health of Liverpool – Doctor Duncan* **https://www.bbc.co.uk/teach/class-clips-video/articles/znfp382** accessed 12 Feb 2025

[31] Wording of *An Act for the Abolition of the Slave Trade* **https://web.archive.org/web/20230711152759/https://www.pdavis.nl/Legis_06.htm** accessed 12 Feb 2025

1811 *The Regency Act*[32] put The Prince of Wales (b.1762-d.1830; later George IV) into office as regent in place of George III whose mental and physical health was seen to be dangerous and unstable

1812 Robert Banks Jenkinson, Earl of Liverpool (b.1770-d.1828), was asked to form a new party after the assassination of Spencer Perceval. He formed a 'Conservative' party. His leadership would last until 1827, riding out the Napoleonic War and instating the 1815 *Corn Laws*[33]. Designed to improve domestic prices of flour for landowners, the effect was increased cost to the poor

1818 *Pleasant Street School*, Liverpool – founded by the ***Benevolent Society of St. Patrick*** for the education of Irish children, regardless of religion – opens in Liverpool. It cost £2,681 then, equivalent to £194,860 today. This is a site on our Trail, but it is not presently marked with a plaque. Its connection to The Great Hunger is by virtue of its shared Catholic and Protestant pupils, taught together in mixed classes of children, with predominantly Irish funders and parents

1819 The UK's Prime Minister officially returns Britain to the Gold Standard having been on a de facto gold standard before. Britain would remain on the Gold Standard model until 1931. The future Queen of England, Victoria (b.1819-d.1901) is born

1820 Antarctica is discovered[34] and George IV is coronated King of the United Kingdom of Great Britain and Ireland and King of Hanover, having served as prince regent for his father George III since 1811. The United States began to require passenger lists from the 1820s onwards forcing new conditions on international passenger sailings. After 1825 ship captains were required to provide passengers with food and water and the minimum quantity of food per passenger was stipulated by law, increasing journey fares. Additionally, ship masters were obliged to have a physician and medicine chest aboard ship to address immediate medical needs

1822 Father James Nugent (d.1905)[35] is born on 3 March in Hunter Street, Liverpool. Education for Catholic children is sparse, so James is privately educated under the patronage of Reverend James Picton (b.1805-1889) of Christ Church. His story is important in Liverpool as he is described "the friend of all in poverty and affliction" and contributed to helping the Irish poor with housing, education, savings plans and abstinence. ***The Nugent Care Society***[36] continue his efforts today

1823 Daniel O'Connell (b.1775-d.1847) establishes the ***Catholic Association***[37] to campaign for equal rights for Catholics. As a famed abolitionist and liberal, Daniel O'Connell[38] was posthumously honoured when Dublin's main thoroughfare was named after him in 1922

---

[32] ***Royal Collection Trust*** overview of 1811 *The Regency Act* **https://www.rct.uk/collection/royal-archives/collections-and-catalogue/george-iv-and-princess-charlotte-of-wales/official-papers-of-george-iv-as-regent-and-king** accessed 6 Mar 2025

[33] An overview of the 1815 *Corn Laws* by ***History Extra*** **https://www.historyextra.com/period/victorian/corn-laws-guide-what-impact-why-repealed-benefit** accessed on 6 Mar 2025

[34] ***Royal Museums Greenwich*** *Exploring Antarctica – a Timeline* **https://www.rmg.co.uk/stories/topics/history-antarctic-explorers#:~:text=January%201820%3A%20Antarctica%20is%20'first,Russian%20expedition%20to%20the%20Antarctic** accessed 12 Feb 2025

[35] Father James Nugent biography **https://www.liverpoolmuseums.org.uk/father-james-nugent-1822-1905** accessed 12 Feb 2025

[36] ***Nugent***'s website **https://wearenugent.org** accessed 12 Feb 2025

[37] *The Act of Union* created further concerns about Catholic representation for the British Government **https://www.parliament.uk/about/living-heritage/transformingsociety/private-lives/religion/overview/emancipation/#:~:text=Although%20Catholics%20made%20up%20most,full%20public%20and%20political%20rights** accessed 12 Feb 2025

[38] Daniel O'Connell biography **https://www.nottingham.ac.uk/manuscriptsandspecialcollections/learning/biographies/danieloconnell(1775-1847).aspx** accessed 12 Feb 2025

1827 ***St Patrick's Chapel***, Park Place, Liverpool — a Roman Catholic parish church — is built. It is believed to have been completed by 1832. With records from 1827-1841 showing there to be 7,466 An Gorta Mór dead in its grounds and crypt, innovative studies[39] are taking place there. It is now believed, based on an understanding of how The Great Hunger progressed, that it is highly likely there are more than double the known figure of Famine dead there, potentially making it one of the largest mass graves for An Gorta Mór poor in the world.

As a piece of social history — from its 1816 inception, fundraising, 5,000-year lease, Irish donations, Gaeilge speaking priests and original ambition — ***St Patrick's Chapel*** is hugely significant. The Tories are returned to power in the UK with George Canning (b.1770-d.1827) becoming Prime Minister for just five-months, being replaced by Frederick Robinson, Viscount Goderick (b.1782-d.1828) who also only held office for a brief time for the Tories

1828 Arthur Wellesley, First Duke of Wellington (b.1769-d.1852; Tory) became Prime Minister of the UK, managing the subject of Catholic Emancipation — via the *Roman Catholic Relief Act* (1829)[40] — to allow Catholic MPs. Sometimes known as 'The Iron Duke' he is better remembered today for his military service than as a politician. A memorial was built in Liverpool in his honour, which is listed in chapter 8

1828 Josephine Butler (b.1828-d1906) is born in Northumberland. Butler's campaign against the *Contagious Diseases Acts*, which disproportionately affected women (particularly in British military towns), had a significant impact on Irish women's lives. Josephine moves to Liverpool in 1864, where she becomes known for her social reform work and successful campaign to repeal the *Contagious Diseases Act* (1886)[41]. We acknowledge an error in *Revive*, which stated Joesphine was born in 1928[42]

1830 *Clarence Dock* (Liverpool waterfront) — designed by Jesse Hartley (b.1780-d.1860)[43] — opens. It becomes the berthing dock for Irish Steamers carrying goods and passengers to England. It will also become the dock and set of gates through which over 1.3-million Irish An Gorta Mór migrants will pass either on their way to new shores or to stay on Merseyside. The gates are marked with a Trail plaque. William IV (b.1796-d.1837) is crowned King of the United Kingdom and Great Britain and King of Hanover

1830s In Liverpool, Kitty Wilkinson invites neighbours to use her boiler to wash their laundry to stave off cholera. She goes on to establish the first public washhouses, saving thousands of lives, earning her the moniker "Saint of the Slums". In London, Charles Grey, Second Earl Grey (b.1764-d.1845) leads the Whigs, overseeing *The Representation of the People Act* (aka *The Reform Act* (1832))[44] and *Slavery Abolition Act* (1833)[45]

[39] *Department of Archaeology*, ***University of Liverpool***, paper *Collaborating with the Community: Applying Non-Invasive Archaeological Methods in the Crypt and Churchyard of* ***St Patrick's Roman Catholic Church***, *Toxteth, Liverpool* **https://livrepository.liverpool.ac.uk/3165913/1/Mytum%20et%20al%202022%20Collaborating%20Community%20St%20Patricks%20Heritage-05-00169.pdf** accessed 12 Feb 2025

[40] *Roman Catholic Relief Act* (1829) **https://www.parliament.uk/about/living-heritage/evolutionofparliament/2015-parliament-in-the-making/get-involved1/2015-banners-exhibition/rachel-gadsden/1829-catholic-emancipation-act-gallery/#:~:text=In%20the%201828%20County%20Clare,Irish%20peasants%20entitled%20to%20vote** accessed 24 Feb 2025

[41] A history of the *Contagions Diseases Act* and its detractors **https://archiveshub.jisc.ac.uk/search/archives/06cf0698-1f6f-3e61-b592-b3620ddbd825** accessed 12 Feb 2025

[42] Josephine Butler **https://www.english-heritage.org.uk/visit/blue-plaques/butler-josephine-butler/#:~:text=Josephine%20Butler%20was%20a%20social,Contagious%20Diseases%20Act%20in%201886** accessed 11 Feb 2025

[43] ***ICE Virtual Library: Essential Engineering Knowledge*** obituary (including biography) of Jesse Hartley **https://www.icevirtuallibrary.com/doi/pdf/10.1680/imotp.1872.22902?download=true** accessed 12 Feb 2025

[44] *The Reform Act* **https://www.parliament.uk/about/living-heritage/evolutionofparliament/houseofcommons/reformacts/overview/reformact1832** accessed 24 Feb 2025

[45] *Abolition of Slavery Act*, 1833 **https://beta.nationalarchives.gov.uk/explore-the-collection/explore-by-time-period/georgians/1833-abolition-of-slavery-act-and-compensation-claims/#:~:text=In%20August%201833%2C%20Parliament%20passed,owners%20over%20the%20compensation%20process** accessed 24 Feb 2025

1832 Agnes Jones (b.1832-d.1868)[46] is born on 10 November, in Cambridge to a military family whose seat was in Fahan, County Donegal. Agnes would become the *Brownlow Hill Workhouse* infirmary's first trained Nursing Superintendent. In Liverpool she is remembered with a building named in her honour, on Catharine Street, close to several sites that are important to our Trail. Not far away, the *Church of St Luke* is built at the corner of Berry and Leece Streets. Deconsecrated now, the church and grounds are a memorial to peace[47], hosting five memorials, including the Liverpool Irish Great Hunger commemoration memorial, commemorating those lost and displaced between 1845-52 and after

1833 ***St Anthony's Church***[48] is built and opened on Scotland Road (Liverpool) to accommodate the growing number of migrant communities flocking to Liverpool. It is believed over 2,000 An Gorta Mór[49] dead are buried here. Though not yet marked with a plaque, plans are afoot to mark this piece of history especially as the memorial to 'Dandy Pat' (also see 1845 entry) is also kept here. *The Abolition of Slavery Act*[50] is passed

1834 *The Poor Law Amendment Act* or *New Poor Law* is passed[51]. Ultimately, it is supposed to end vestries administering *The Poor Law*, but in Liverpool few changes occur. The Duke of Wellington is briefly returned to British Prime Ministerial duties for the Tories before William Lamb, Second Viscount Melbourne (b.1779-d.1848) was installed for the Whigs. He had been Secretary of Ireland (1827-28) and Home Secretary 1830-34, during which time he had done his utmost to quash agricultural unrest. He was mentor to a young Queen Victoria. Soon power would be given to the Conservatives under Sir Robert Peel, Second Baronet (b.1788-d.1850)[52]

1835 Revising previous laws, *The Passenger Act*[53] is passed. It stipulated that enough food and water be stored and provided onboard emigrant merchant ships to last 10 weeks, down from the previous 12. Only vessels transporting more than 100 passengers would be required to supply the services of a surgeon. To help the newcomers, the act allowed passengers to remain aboard ship, after reaching port, for up to 48-hours so that further travel arrangements could be made. William Lamb is returned as Whig Prime Minister

1836 Major Denis Mahon brings a motion against his uncle, Maurice Mahon, Third Baron Hartland (b.1772-d.1845) to whom the Strokestown Estate had been bequeathed following the death of his brother Thomas (b.1766-d.1835). Denis declared Maurice to be unstable and incapable of commanding of the Strokestown Estate, having permitted it to fall into considerable debt (the majority of which was inherited). This was passed and Maurice was declared a lunatic. To clear the debt, Major Mahon renewed the estate's lease with the crown, issued debt recovery letters and began collecting arrears. Maurice becomes his legal guardian, too, dying a decade later

[46] Agnes Jones biography by ***Ulster University*** **https://www.ulster.ac.uk/news/2020/march/ulster-universitys-nurses-of-the-future-take-inspiration-from-a-local-heroine-of-the-past** accessed 12 Feb 2025

[47] The story of ***St Luke's 'Bombed Out' Church*** **https://www.slboc.com/the-story** accessed 12 Feb 2025

[48] ***St Anthony's Church*** website **https://stanthonyscotlandroad.wordpress.com/about** accessed 12 Feb 2025

[49] Article about ***St Anthony's Church*** in ***Liverpool Echo*** **https://www.liverpoolecho.co.uk/news/liverpool-news/secrets-crypt-thousands-buried-23491149** accessed 12 Feb 2025

[50] *An Act for the Abolition of Slavery throughout the British Colonies* **https://beta.nationalarchives.gov.uk/explore-the-collection/explore-by-time-period/georgians/1833-abolition-of-slavery-act-and-compensation-claims** accessed 12 Feb 2025

[51] ***UK Parliament*** provides an overview of *The Poor Law Amendment Act* (1834) **https://www.parliament.uk/about/living-heritage/transformingsociety/livinglearning/19thcentury/overview/poorlaw/#:~:text=The%20Poor%20Law%20Amendment%20Act,all%20the%20commission's%20main%20recommendations** accessed 12 Feb 2025

[52] ***UK Government*** biography of Sir Robert Peel 2nd Baronet **https://www.gov.uk/government/history/past-prime-ministers/robert-peel-2nd-baronet** accessed 12 Feb 2025

[53] *Hansard* transcript of the passing of the *Passenger Act*, 1835 **https://api.parliament.uk/historic-hansard/commons/1835/mar/19/passengers-act** accessed 24 Feb 2025

1837 Victoria is crowned Queen of the United Kingdom of Great Britain and Ireland, becoming Empress of India in 1876

1837-39 Charles Dickens's *Oliver Twist* is published in monthly instalments. Another social comment on the disparity between the wealthy and paupers, it is believed by certain of Dickens's fans that a trip to *St James's Cemetery* (Hope Street, Liverpool; where Kitty Wilkison is also buried) may have provided Dickens with his namesake for the book. However, as this child died in 1861 it seems unlikely! Nevertheless, Dickens was a visitor to Liverpool[54], with known visits in 1838 and 1842 and public readings given in 1858 and 1862[55]

1838 *The Irish Poor Law Act*[56] divided Ireland into 130 'Poor Law Unions' with a workhouse in each district. It was set up to assist with the level of destitution in Ireland

1839 Herman Melville (b.1819-d.1891) – American author of *Moby Dick* (1851) – visits Liverpool

1839-1842 British Indian forces fight in the first Opium War, sending a naval expedition to China to pay reparations[57]

1841 The population of Ireland is at 8,175,124 (source: 1841 Census)[58]. In *Revive* we stated, "it will not rival this figure again until 2016", but – in truth – we had misinterpreted the figures. For the avoidance of doubt, in 2022 Ireland's census returned a population of 5,149,139[59] with mid-year reports showing Northern Ireland's population as 1,910,500[60]. This gives the island of Ireland a total population of 7,059,639, still lower than the 1841 figures at just 86%. Further to his previous Prime Ministerial term (1834-1835), Sir Robert Peel (b.1788-d.1850) forms a Conservative government, which will last until 1846

1842 The *Brownlow Hill Workhouse* is enlarged. It now houses 3,000 people. By 1900 it houses 4,000 people, over half of them Catholics and mostly Irish born. The world's first public wash house was opened on Upper Frederick Street (Liverpool), after the tireless work of Kitty Wilkinson (also see 1785 and 1830s entries)

1844 Samuel Finley Breese Morse (b.1791-d.1872) dispatches the first telegraphic message on a line from Washington DC to Baltimore beginning a new world of communication[61]. In Britain, Sir Robert Peel sees in *The Factory Act*[62], improving working conditions for women and children

1845 In June the potato blight – *Phytophera Infestans* – was noticed in Belgium[63]. Over the next two-years 44,000 Belgians die from hunger and disease

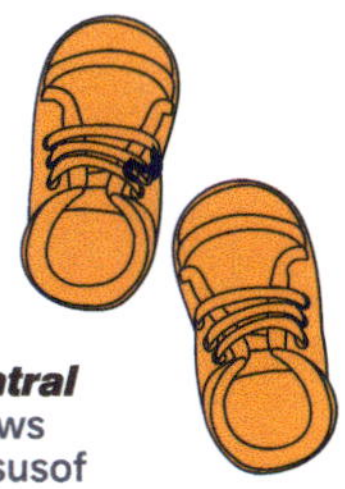

54 *The Story of Charles Dicken and his links with Liverpool* by ***The Guide*** **https://theguideliverpool.com/the-story-of-charles-dickens-and-his-links-with-liverpool** accessed 12 Feb 2025

55 A photograph of the gravestone that 'may' have inspired Dickens to name his book *Oliver Twist* **https://www.facebook.com/photo.php?fbid=1914225055397483&id=677401399079861&set=a.752061751613825** accessed 12 Feb 2025

56 Ireland's ***National Archives*** overview of the 1838 *Irish Poor Law Act* **https://nationalarchives.ie/help-with-research/research-guides/poor-law-records/#:~:text=SHARE,were%20closed%20to%20cut%20costs** accessed 12 Feb 2025

57 ***National Army Museum*** overview of the *First China War* **https://www.nam.ac.uk/explore/first-china-war-1839-1842** accessed 12 Feb 2025

58 ***History Ireland*** on census figures for Ireland **https://historyireland.com/the-1841-census-do-the-numbers-add-up** accessed 12 Feb 2025

59 Statement on Ireland's population in 2022 from their ***Central Statistics Office*** **https://www.cso.ie/en/csolatestnews/pressreleases/2023pressreleases/ressstatementcensusofpopulation2022-summaryresults** accessed 12 Feb 2025

60 Mid-year population estimates for Northern Ireland from the ***Northern Ireland Statistics and Research Agency*** **https://www.nisra.gov.uk/system/files/statistics/MYE22-summary.pdf** accessed 12 Feb 2025

61 ***Library of Congress*** overview *Today in History – May 24* **https://www.loc.gov/item/today-in-history/may-24** accessed 12 Feb 2025

62 Updated reform to *The Factory Act* in 1844 **https://www.parliament.uk/about/living-heritage/transformingsociety/livinglearning/19thcentury/overview/laterfactoryleg** accessed 24 Feb 2025

63 ***Canon Van Laanderen*** explore Belgium's potato crop failures **https://www.canonvanvlaanderen.be/en/events/the-potato-crisis/#:~:text=In%20Belgium%20the%20potato%20blight,them%20in%20the%20two%20provinces** accessed 12 Feb 2025

1845 Patrick Byrne[64] — also known as 'Dandy Pat' — is born in Tinnashrule, County Wexford, eventually settling in Liverpool's Vauxhall where he took ownership of ***The Tichfield*** (late 1860s/early 1870s). Also see 1833 ***St Anthony's Church*** entry

1845-1852 Generally described as the period of The Irish Famine, The Great Hunger or An Gorta Mór. 'Potato Blight' is reported in the Irish press in September[65]. In November, a *Relief Committee* is appointed. In1845 approximately 50,000 Irish sea passengers enter Liverpool, which is deemed an ordinary year. The UK's Sir Robert Peel ordered £100,000 of 'Indian corn' (maize) from the USA[66]

1846 After potato crop failures in Ireland, approximately 90,000 Irish enter Liverpool, between January and March. Numbers requiring poor relief are unprecedented and overwhelming. In March, Peel extends relief methods by passing a *Public Works Act*[67] to assist employment and to relieve distress followed by county relief works in England. He reduced the price of corn by managing the release of the crop onto the market by repealing the *Corn Laws*[68]. On 26 June, Prime Minster Robert Peel resigns. On 30 June, Lord John Russell, First Earl (b.1792-d.1878)[69] forms a new Whig administration. Crops continue to fail in Ireland and migration to Liverpool, and its environs, continue to rise

1846 In July the blight reappears. 75% of Ireland's potato crop is destroyed. Emigration and mortality begin to rise. In August, Russell introduces a change to the policy of distributing corn, saying they would not interfere with the regular operations of merchants for the supply of food to the country. After members had joined together to send support from 1846, in November the ***Central Relief Committee of the Society of Friends*** was formed by Quakers in Dublin[70]. The *Liverpool Sanitary Act*[71] 1846 was the first piece of public health legislation in Britain, and the city created the first medical officer of health post and awarded it to Dr Duncan. That private legislation was subsequently incorporated into the national *Public Health Act* 1848[72].

In contrast with the destruction caused by An Gorta Mór, in the same year, Liverpool's *Albert Dock*[73] opens. It is the first British building to use cast iron, stone and brick, making it a fire safe structure. Two years on, hydraulic cranes were added. The ability to load directly in to warehouses from the docks made it an important stronghold for premium cargo. Despite the city's work on providing relief for the poor, it did not lose sight of the infrastructure needed to bring commercial gains.

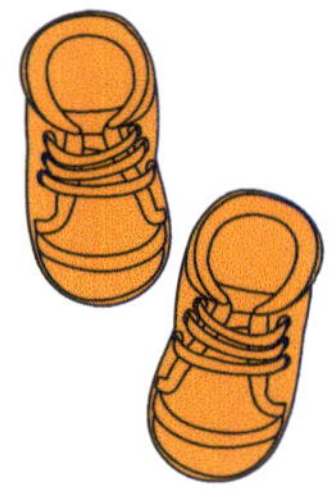

[64] Patrick 'Dandy Pat' Byrne biography **http://www.liverpoolmonuments.co.uk /drinking/dandypat11.html** accessed 12 Feb 2025

[65] First broadcast of the Irish Famine in Ireland **https://www.irelandxo.com/ireland-xo/history-and -genealogy/timeline/arrival-potato-blight-reported-dublin-evening-post** accessed 10 Feb 2025

[66] ***RTÉ*** *Peel's brimstone: the Temporary Relief Commission* **https://www.rte.ie/history/the-great -irish-famine/2020/1117/1178730-the-temporary-relief-commission/#:~:text=The%20arrival 20of%20Indian%20corn,relief%20to%20the%20destitute%20poor** accessed 12 Feb 2025

[67] ***Irish Statute Book*** *Public Works (Ireland) (No.2) Act* **https://www.irishstatute book.ie/eli/1846/act/86/enacted/en/print.html** accessed 12 Feb 2025

[68] Analysis of the *Corn Laws* by ***History Extra*** **https://www.historyextra.com/period /victorian/corn-laws-guide-what-impact-why-repealed-benefit** accessed 12 Feb 2025

[69] ***UK Government*** biography of Lord John Russell, First Earl **https://www.gov.uk/government /history/past-prime-ministers/lord-john-russell-1st-earl-russell** accessed 12 Feb 2025

[70] Detail of the formation of the ***Central Relief Committee of the Society of Friends*** in 1846: **https://www.jstor.org/table/30099847** accessed 24 Feb 2025

[71] *Liverpool Sanitary Act*, 1846 **https://publications.parliament.uk/pa/ld200506 /ldhansrd/vo050720/text/50720-20.htm** accessed 10 Feb 2025

[72] ***UK Parliament*** overview of the 1848 *Public Health Act* **https://www.parliament.uk/about /living-heritage/transformingsociety/towncountry/towns/tyne-and-wear-case-study /about-the-group/public-administration/the-1848-public-health-act** accessed 12 Feb 2025

[73] ***Albert Dock*** website and history **https://albertdock.com/history** accessed 12 Feb 2025

Starving tenants in Cloonahee (part of the Strokestown Estate) petition Major Denis Mahon in a letter, begging for assistance, stating:

"Our families are really and truly suffering in our presence and we cannot much longer withstand their cries for food. We have no food for them, our potatoes are rotten and we have no grain".

This letter can be seen at the ***National Famine Museum***, Ireland. A reading of the original Cloonahee Petition can be found on ***YouTube***[74]

1847 On 1 January Dr William Henry Duncan is appointed as Liverpool's first Medical Officer of Health. He orders the closure of unhealthy cellars, many of which were reopened by those in need. Between 4-9 January the *Select Vestry* relieves 7,146 Irish families, consisting of 29,417 persons.

This year becomes known as 'Black '47', having the highest number of An Gorta Mór fatalities in a year than any other. Reported in *The City of Liverpool's: A Century of Progress 1847-1947*[75] the life-expectancy of a child born in Liverpool was just 19-years (lifting to 55-years a century later). Between 13 January and 13 December Magistrate Rushton asks police to count the numbers of Irish entering Liverpool at Clarence Dock, understanding that the majority would require relief on arrival. They learn that between 13-25 January 10,724 people arrived in Liverpool from Irish Ports. By the end of January, 370,359 Irish people had received poor relief at Fenwick Street. Liverpool ratepayers paying for the relief of the Irish migrants, with no help from the London government, start to become disgruntled. The ***Liverpool Mercury*** reports 35,000 people are living in cellars without light or ventilation.

Liverpool hits the height of the typhus epidemic. In Ireland, in March-April, the numbers on relief work pass 700,000. The relief works begins to be phased out to be replaced by soup kitchens. The continued spread of the fever epidemic leads to the *Fever Act*[76].

In essence, this transferred responsibility for fever treatment from poor law guardians to local relief teams. On 19 May a public meeting is held in Liverpool by principal ratepayers who organised a protest on the cost of Irish immigration. In June, a law is passed that shipowners must accommodate passengers below decks in inclement weather.

In the same year, the *Irish Poor Law Extension* Act[77] or *Poor Relief Ireland Act*[78] only allowed outdoor relief to those with less than quarter of an acre of land in their names, forcing some to give up the last asset they had remaining. Known as the 'Gregory Clause', it was introduced by Sir William Gregory (b.1816-d.1892), who became a despised figure. The bill allowed guardians to provide outdoor relief to those who could not work or those more able, but where workhouses were full or infected with disease. By August, three million people were in receipt of soup kitchen support in Ireland.

There was less blight, but because of the shortage of seed potatoes only 25% of the normal crop was harvested. In October relief is restricted and Ireland's soup kitchens close and from August to December cholera turns into an epidemic

In May, landlord Major Denis Mahon pays for the assisted passage of 1,490 of his 'surplus population' otherwise understood to be his poorest tenants.

[74] Reading of the Cloonahee Petition **https://www.youtube.com/watch?v=Fpf99hvMe4k** accessed 28 Feb 2025

[75] An online reference or version of *The City of Liverpool A Century of Progress 1847-1947* cannot be found, but it is referenced within the film shown on ***BBC*** *KS3 History: Transforming the Health of Liverpool – Doctor Duncan* **https://www.bbc.co.uk/teach/class-clips-video/articles/znfp382** accessed 12 Feb 2025

[76] Analysis of the 1847 *Fever Act* by ***RTÉ*** **https://www.rte.ie/history/famine-ireland/2021/0128/1193691-how-the-temporary-fever-act-failed-to-stop-an-epidemic/#:~:text=In%20the%20face%20of%20the,guardians%20to%20local%20relief%20committees** accessed 12 Feb 2025

[77] Analysis on the *Poor Law Extension Act* of 1847 by ***RTÉ*** **https://www.rte.ie/history/famine-ireland/2020/0810/1158380-this-land-of-sorrows-the-poor-law-extension-act-1847** accessed 12 Feb 2025

[78] ***Hansard***'s capturing of *The Poor Relief Ireland* bill, 1847 **https://hansard.parliament.uk/Commons/1847-03-12/debates/3cc8f39d-901b-4e35-af4c-c037b3aed099/PoorRelief(Ireland)Bill** accessed 24 Feb 2025

The Estate he removed from his uncle two years prior was already £30,000 in debt (equivalent to over £2,637,655 today) and over-crowded with subletters totalling over 11,000 people. Of the 1,490 evictees it is understood that over 600 were children. Whilst a quarter of the original group would die at sea, only half the 1,490 would make it all the way to Canada, after their walk to Dublin, sail to and wait in Liverpool (some for as long as two weeks)and on-ward sailing to Grosse Île on the coffin ships *Erin's Queen*, *Naomi*, *The Virginius* and *The John Munn.* Whilst riding home with a colleague, from a Famine Relief meeting on 2 Nov 1847, Major Denis Mahon was shot and killed, leaving behind him his wife Henrietta Bathurst and daughter. The Estate would pass to the Mahon's daughter and husband — Grace Catherine Mahon and Henrey Sandford Pakenham — who took 'Pakenham Mahon' as his surname to assist with inheriting the estate. Thought to be the first of The Great Hunger's retaliatory murders, his murder was followed by other attacks on landlords and celebratory bonfires were lit across Roscommon

1848 ***The Royal Liverpool Children's Hospital***, the world's first purpose-built children's hospital, is constructed in Myrtle Street. Ireland's small harvest seen the previous year, fails once more. In Europe there is a cholera epidemic ravaging its people. Against the backdrop of uprisings and revolutions across Europe, An Gorta Mór added considerable weight to anti-monarchy and middle-class growth arguments, with the poor continuing to suffer at the hands of poor industrialisation and agrarian plans alongside limited social welfare reform.

On 1 December, *The Londonderry*[79], a steamer — Liverpool bound from Sligo — is hit by a storm off Donegal (northwest Ireland) with 180 passengers and 26 crew on board. The passengers, most fleeing An Gorta Mór, are sent below to the hold.

73 suffocated in the enclosed space. 67 of the 102 surviving passengers continue to Liverpool.

[79] Further exploration of *The Londonderry* tragedy **https://seamusdubhghaill.com/2018/12/01/the-londonderry-tragedy** accessed 12 Feb 2025

An inquest held into the deaths found Captain Alexander Johnstone (b. unknown-d. unknown) — and two of his crew — guilty of manslaughter. Meanwhile the Mexican American War unfolds. Eventually, the USA will gain California, Nevada, Utah, New Mexico, Arizona and parts of other states from Mexico

1849 Herman Melville writes *Redburn: His First Voyage*, a fictional account of experiences at sea, with reference to his time in Liverpool. In Ireland, blight affects areas already hit by the agrarian disease in the south and west of Ireland. In Liverpool, Dr Duncan moves to close all the overcrowded graveyards in the city and open new ones to the north (Ford) and the south (Allerton). He works to change the law to allow cremations (please note, this was mis-inserted in *Revive* as 1821). Father Nugent returns to Liverpool after his training in the priesthood, as curate of ***St Nicholas's Parish Church***. He opens *The Ragged School* on Copperas Hill, a boarding school for homeless children. The *Encumbered Estates Act*[80] is passed. Between 2 -12 August Queen Victoria makes a royal visit to Ireland after Westminster declared An Gorta Mór officially over[81]. Despite this, a further 240,923[82] migrants arrive in Liverpool. It is understood that by August 800,000 are on outdoor relief in Ireland whilst — by December — there are estimates of 250,000 people living in workhouses and suggestions that 210,000 people have emigrated

1850 ***Irish Tenant Right League***[83] forms in Ireland against a backdrop of estate clearances, happening under assisted emigration schemes.

[80] *Encumbered Estates Act*, 1849 **https://hansard.parliament.uk/lords/1849-06-11/debates/e64ee548-5ea9-4118-bde8-2971f4e40b71/IncumberedEstates(Ireland)Bill** accessed 10 Feb 2025

[81] Queen Victoria's first visit to Ireland **https://irelandxo.com/ireland-xo/history-and-genealogy/timeline/queen-victorias-first-visit-ireland**; **https://www.rmg.co.uk/collections/objects/rmgc-object-12123** accessed 10 Feb 2025

[82] Frank Neal's 1987 doctorate *Sectarian Violence in Nineteenth Century Liverpool: A Study of the Origins, Nature and Scale of the Catholic-Protestant Conflict in Working Class Liverpool, 1819-1914* **https://salford-repository.worktribe.com/preview/1500415/Neal.pdf** accessed 12 Feb 2025

[83] ***Britannica***'s explanation of ***The Irish Tenant Right League*** **https://www.britannica.com/event/Home-Rule-Great-Britain-and-Ireland** accessed 12 Feb 2025

251,001 migrants are registered as arriving in Liverpool over the year[84]. Across this year, and next, more Irish estates will be cleared of their tenants

1851 283,503[85] migrants arrive in Liverpool across the year. Ireland's population is recorded as 6,552,385 in the 1851 Census[86]. This suggests 20% have either left or died; a total of 1,622,739 people. In Hyde Park (London), *The Great Exhibition* showcases the best of Victorian industrialisation and invention

1852 An Australian emigration depot is established in Birkenhead[87] (Wirral, UK). After a short term by Edward Smith Stanley, 14th Earl of Derby, George Hamilton Gordon, Earl of Aberdeen (b.1784-d.1860)[88] — also known as Lord Aberdeen — becomes Prime Minster of Great Britain following a general election, gaining considerable support from the Irish "tenant interest" MPs.

232,331 Irish migrants are reported as arriving in Liverpool[89]. It is commonly understood that 1852 marks the end of The Great Hunger, but in 1853 a further 233,652 Irish migrants are shipped to Liverpool[90]

1854 ***Great Western Railway*** opened a through-route from Birkenhead to London enabling people, migrants included, to mobilise for the capital. Additionally, begun in 1841, Liverpool's *St George's Hall* opens in St George's Place on the site of the former (and first) *Liverpool Infirmary*

[84] F Neal, *Sectarian Violence in Nineteenth Century Liverpool*, 1987

[85] Ibid

[86] ***Irish Genealogy Toolkit*** exploration of Irish census fragments 1821-1851 **https://www.irish-genealogy-toolkit.com/irish-census-fragments.html#:~:text=What%20the%201851%20Irish%20census,flax%20plant%20into%20Irish%20linen** accessed 12 Feb 2025

[87] ***Australian National Maritime Museum of the Sea archive*** engraving of the Birkenhead emigration depot **https://collections.sea.museum/en/objects/43373/emigration-depot-at-birkenhead** accessed 12 Feb 2025

[88] ***UK Government*** biography of George Hamilton Gordon, Earl of Aberdeen **https://www.gov.uk/government/history/past-prime-ministers/george-hamilton-gordon-earl-of-aberdeen** accessed 12 Feb 2025

[89] F Neal, *Sectarian Violence in Nineteenth Century Liverpool*, 1987

[90] Ibid

1855 In June, Henry John Temple, Third Viscount Palmerston (b.1784-d.1865) leads a Liberal government in Great Britain. *The Carriage of Passengers Act* (full name: *An Act further to regulate the Carriage of Passengers in Steamships and other Vessels*[91]) was passed by the United States federal government on 3 March, replacing the previous 1819 *Steerage Act* (also known as the *Manifest of Immigrants Act*) and others passed between 1847 and 1849 provide new regulations on the conditions of sea transportation used by passenger ships landing in the United States

1858 *Birkenhead Docks* are transferred to ***Mersey Docks and Harbour Board***

1859 33 drinking fountains are inserted into Liverpool's Dock Wall by the ***Mersey Docks and Harbour Board*** suggesting an amount of societal and/or industrial compassion

1860 On 11 November Kitty Wilkinson dies aged 73 (also see 1785 and 1830s entries)

1860s Agnes Jones becomes a Superintendent Nurse in the *Brownlow Hill Workhouse*, training others in nursing care. Agnes contracts typhus fever and dies aged 35 (1868). Also see her 1832 entry

1861 Liverpool's population stands at 429,881 according to *Vision of Britain*'s census list[92], rather than 555,000 as we reported in *Revive.* Ireland's population has further reduced to 5,798,967 (source: 1861 Census)[93] a decrease of 2,376,157 lives in 20-years. This puts the population at just 71% of its 1841 figure, showing it has lost over a quarter of its people.

[91] *Passenger Act* 1855 **https://law.resource.org/pub/us/case/reporter/F.as/0018.f.cas/0018.f.cas.1283.6.pdf** accessed 24 Feb 2025

[92] *A Vision of Britain* **https://www.visionofbritain.org.uk/datavalue/11449257** accessed 12 Feb 2025

[93] *Census of Ireland 1861: Part I, Area, Population, and Number of Houses, by Townlands and Electoral Divisions Provinces of Ulster and Connaught* **https://archive.org/details/op1248751-1001/page/n589/mode/2up** accessed 12 Feb 2025

Whilst Liverpool and Ireland do their best to recover, the America Civil War begins in April[94], fighting over the right to enslave others and territory. This will last until 1865. *The Offences Against the Person Act*[95] makes abortion illegal in the United Kingdom of Great Britain and Ireland

1862 A serious fire breaks out at the *Brownlow Hill Workhouse*; 21 children and two nurses burn to death

1863 17-year-old Patrick Byrne ('Dandy Pat') arrives in Liverpool from Ireland (also see 1845 entry). On 23 May Dr William Duncan dies in West Park, Elgin (Scotland). The same year, the *Brownlow Hill Workhouse* (also known as the *Brownlow Hill Infirmary*) adds an infectious diseases hospital

1864 Based on the *Sanitary Amendment Act*[96] of the same year, building (new) court-houses was banned. 3,073 courts existed at this time, in which 17,825 homes contained an estimated 110,000 people

1865 Lord John Russell, First Earl Russell leads a Whig government in Britain for a year before Edward Smith Stanley 14th Earl of Derby brings the Conservatives back to power

1867 Following a series of conferences the British Parliament formed the Canadian Confederation[97], whilst in the same year the US purchases Alaska from Russia

1868 After Benjamin Disraeli's (b.1804-d.1881) short spell as Conservative Prime Minister, William Gladstone (b.1809-d.1898)[98] — a Liberal — becomes Prime Minister for the first time

[94] ***History*** shares information on the American Civil War **https://www.history.com/topics/american-civil-war/american-civil-war-history** accessed 12 Feb 2025

[95] *The Offences Against the Person Act* (1861) **https://www.legislation.gov.uk/ukpga/Vict/24-25/100/contents** accessed 21 Feb 2025

[96] *Sanitary Amendment Act, 1864: report of the Medical Officer of Health on his second presentment to the grand jury* **https://wellcomecollection.org/works/zx3c2s93/items?canvas=3** accessed 12 Feb 2025

[97] ***The Canadian Encyclopedia*** gives an overview of the Canadian Federation **https://www.thecanadianencyclopedia.ca/en/article/confederation** accessed 12 Feb 2025

[98] UK Government biography of William Gladstone **https://www.gov.uk/government/history/past-prime-ministers/william-ewart-gladstone** accessed 12 Feb 2025

1874 Benjamin Disraeli (who would become Earl of Beaconsfield in 1876) retakes the lead of a Conservative British government

1874 (or **6**) James Larkin (b.1874/6-d.1947) was born in Liverpool to the Irish James Larkin and Mary Ann McNulty. There is confusion over his actual birth date, but his gravestone states 1876[99]. Larkin was heavily involved in the Dublin Lockouts of 1913 and did especially well espousing socialist values in America. Rising quickly through the socialist unions, Larkin was heavily involved in the Irish labour movement throughout his life, dying after falling through a floor in a terrible work accident

1875 Laurence Connolly was elected in Liverpool's Scotland Ward as the first ***Irish Nationalist Party*** (councillor in Liverpool, beginning a 47-year period (1875-1922) of Irish nationalist representation on the city council that would eventually include 48 councillors advocating for Irish Home Rule and local Irish community interests

1878 ***Everton Football Club***[100] founded

1880 Returning the Liberals to power in Britian, William Gladstone came back to power leading a Liberal party. Liverpool gains city status, becoming a borough independent from Lancashire eight years later[101]

1883 Liverpool's *Pilotage Building* is built for its pilots (navigators) to operate from. Although post-An Gorta Mór, the *Pilotage Building* is a site on our Trail because of the work earlier pilots did to guide in all the ships carrying the famine poor to Liverpool, primarily through Clarence Dock. They will have escorted each ship out on their onward journeys around the world, taking the An Gorta Mór poor with them

[99] James Larkin gravestone image **https://upload.wikimedia.org/wikipedia/commons/4/44/James_Larkin_gravestone.JPG** accessed 12 Feb 2025

[100] ***Everton Football Club*** history site **https://www.footballhistory.org/club/everton.html** accessed 12 Feb 2025

[101] *Chapter 7: Liverpool* from *A Vision of Britain* **https://www.visionofbritain.org.uk/datavalue/11449257** accessed 12 Feb 2025

1885 Robert Gascoyne-Cecil, Third Marquess of Salisbury (b.1830-d.1903) leads a Conservative government in the UK, from June this year until the following January, when he is unseated by William Gladstone, who returns as a Liberal Prime Minister until July 1886, when Robert Gascoyne-Cecil retakes his position. In Liverpool's Scotland Ward, T.P. O'Connor, an Irish nationalist politician and journalist, is elected as MP (the only English constituency ever to return an Irish Nationalist MP). He held this seat for 44 years until his death in 1929, becoming a prominent voice for the Irish community in Britain, though some dispute his ability to pay attention to his constituent's needs

1890 Patrick Byrne ('Dandy Pat') dies aged 45 (also see 1845 entry)

1892 ***Liverpool Football Club***[102] founded. In August William Gladsome becomes Prime Minister again. He would resign in 1894, succeeding the leadership to his colleague Archibold Primrose, Fifth Earl of Rosebery (b.1847-d.1929), who would lead for just 110 days before power shifted once more to the Conservative leadership of Robert Gascoyne-Cecil

1897 Chemist Felix Hoffmann (b.1868-d.1946), of ***Farbenfabriken vorm, Friedr, Bayer & Co***, succeeds in synthesising the agents needed for a safe aspirin

1898-1900 *The Philharmonic Dining Rooms* is built on Hope Street (Liverpool), by Irish Philanthropist and brewer Robert Cain (b.1826-d.1907)[103]. This remains known as 'the most ornate pub in England'[104]

1899 *George's Dock* is closed and filled in, to create Pier Head; a new site for Liverpool's *Dock Offices*

[102] ***Liverpool Football Club*** history **https://www.footballhistory.org/club/liverpool.html** accessed 12 Feb 2025

[103] Chris Routledge's *Social Mobility in Victorian England: The Case of Robert Cain* **https://chrisroutledge.co.uk/2009/01/06/social-mobility-in-victorian-england-the-case-of-robert-cain** accessed 12 Feb 2025

[104] ***The Philharmonic Dining Rooms*** website **https://www.nicholsonspubs.co.uk/restaurants/northwest/thephilharmonicdiningroomsliverpool#** accessed 12 Feb 2025

1901 Liverpool's population hits 711,030[105]. Queen Victoria dies. King Edward VII (b.1841-d.1910) ascends the throne of the British Empire, becoming King of the United Kingdom and the British Dominions and Emperor of India

1902 Continuing the Conservative leadership in Britain, Arthur James Balfour (b.1848-d.1930) becomes Prime Minister

1903 The Wright Brothers make their first flight the same year as the first narrative silent movie is released in America (*The Great Train Robbery*, directed by Edwin S Porter (b.1870-d.1841) and produced by Thomas Edison's (b.1847-d.1931) ***Edison Manufacturing Company***)

1905 Father Nugent dies. The following year, a statue was unveiled in his honour (also see 1822 and 1849 entries as well as our Trail site 11). In Britain, Balfour oversees *The Unemployed Workmen Act*[106], providing 'Distress Committee' grants to local authorities to decrease the number of unemployed persons before being replaced as Prime Minister by Liberal Henry Campbell-Bannerman (b.1836-d.1908). Known to peers as 'CB' Campbell-Bannerman was known to support social improvements, free trade and Irish Home Rule

1907 *The Probation Act*[107] is passed in Britain laying the foundation of the modern probation service

1908 After Campbell-Bannerman's resignation, Herbert Henry Asquith (b.1852-d.1928) became Prime Minister for Britain (Liberal)

1910 George V (b.1865-d.1936) becomes King of the United Kingdom, British Dominions and Emperor of India

[105] *Chapter 7: Liverpool* from *Vision of Britain* **https://images.liverpoolmuseums.org.uk/2020-01/Liverpool-Part-2.pdf** accessed 12 Feb 2025

[106] *The Unemployed Workman Act*, 1905 **https://discovery.nationalarchives.gov.uk/details/r/304a7d5a-1582-4357-acea-b281d3ffa74d** accessed 24 Feb 2025

[107] *The Probation Act*, 1907 **https://www.legislation.gov.uk/ukpga/Edw7/7/17/enacted** accessed 24 Feb 2025

1912 The Titanic sinks 370 nautical miles south-southeast of Newfoundland, Canada (coordinates 41°43'35" N, 49°56'54" W)[108]

1913 Major social and industrial unrest leads to the Dublin Lockouts, where police attacked a crowd gathered to hear James Larkin

1914-1918 World War I rages in international locations, delaying Ireland's independence negotiations to remove them from British dominion

1916 After seizing Dublin's General Post Office, Irish nationalists claim Ireland as an independent republic. The British execute 15* of the declaration's leaders at Kilmainham Gaol (Dublin) between 3-12 May and Roger Casement (3 August, London), crushing what became known as *The Easter Uprising*, causing outrage across Ireland. In December that year, David Lloyd George (b.1863-d.1945) took over as Prime Minister from Asquith, within a wartime coalition with the Conservatives

* Patrick Pearse, Thomas Clarke, Thomas MacDonagh, Joseph Plunkett, Edward Daly, Michael O'Hanrahan, William Pearse, John MacBride, Éamonn Ceannt, Con Colbert, Seán Heuston, Michael Mallin, Thomas Kent, Seán Mac Diarmada and James Connolly

1918 *The Education Act*[109] raised the school leaving age from 12 to 14 in the UK and made state elementary schools free, transferring that financial burden from local authorities to central government

1919 ***Sinn Fein***'s Éamon de Valera (b.1882-d.1975) forms a Dublin Assembly: the 'Dáil Eireann', proclaiming Irish independence. Cathal Brugha (b.1874-d.1922) becomes the first President of the Dáil Éireann (Irish Republic), swiftly followed by de Valera as Chair of the Provisional Government of Southern Ireland, both from ***Sinn Féin***. During this time, the ***Irish Republican Army*** (***IRA***) forms to fight British forces to maintain independence

1921 Signed on 6 Dec 1921, *The Anglo-Irish Treaty*[110] would take a year to take effect. When it did, fundamentally it created an Irish Free State within the British Empire. Comprising 26 counties, this new state would govern by an Oireachtas (parliament) of two houses, the Dáil Éireann (lower house) and the Seanad Éireann (upper house). Headed by a Governor-General, representing the British monarch, all members still had to swear an oath to the monarch to maintain governance of their domestic, fiscal and military affairs. It created a Northern Irish devolved parliament, which spurred a Boundary Commission to determine the borders of Northern Ireland, comprising the remaining six of the original 32 counties

1922 Despite the misgivings of de Valera and others, the Dublin Parliament accepts *The Anglo-Irish Treaty*, prompting civil war (June 1922-May 1923) and hundreds of killings. ***Sinn Féin***'s Arthur Griffith (b.1872-1922) becomes President of the Executive Council of the Fourth Ministry whilst Michael Collins – also ***Sinn Féin*** – becomes the President of the Executive Council for the First Provisional Government. William Thomas Cosgrave (b.1880-d.1965) takes over in August retaining ***Sinn Féin*** connections, whilst drawing on ***Cumann na nGaedheal*** (***Society of the Gaels***). In Britain, Andrew Bonar Law (b.1858-d.1923) takes the helm from David Lloyd George, forming a Conservative government at the behest of King George V

1924 In Britain, Stanley Baldwin (b.1867-d.1947) leads a Conservative government (May to January) when Ramsay MacDonald (b.1866-d1937) takes over with a Labour leadership (the first Labour Prime Minister ever), before being replaced in November 1924 by Baldwin

[108] Information on the location of *The Titanic*'s final resting place **https://expedition.discovertitanic.com/where-did-the-titanic-sink/#:~:text=The%20Titanic%20sank%20at%20the,was%20determined%20through%20various%20expeditions** accessed 24 Feb 2025

[109] ***UK Parliament*** overview of the 1918 *Education Act* **https://www.parliament.uk/about/living-heritage/transformingsociety/parliament-and-the-first-world-war/legislation-and-acts-of-war/education-act-1918** accessed 24 Feb 2025

[110] *The Anglo-Irish Treaty* **http://commonslibrary.parliament.uk/research-briefings/cbp-9260/#:~:text=The%20resulting%20Anglo-Irish%20Treaty,control%20of%20several%20military%20ports**) accessed 21 Feb 2025

1927 The ***BBC*** is founded. The same year, the first black and white televisions are released on the market and the first talking movie – *The Jazz Singer* (directed by Alan Crosland (b.1894-d.1936), produced by ***Warner Brothers***) – is screened

1929 In June this year, Ramsay MacDonald retook Britain's Prime Ministerial seat first with ***The Labour Party*** and then ***National Labour***

1932 Scientists John Cockcroft (b.1897-d.1967) and Irish physicist Ernest Walton (b.1903-d.1995) split the atom (lithium nucleus) using the Cockcroft-Walton generator, which pounded the atom with protons. Éamon de Valera returns as Taoiseach for the Irish Free State (for the First-Fourth Governments), this time leading ***Fianna Fáil***

1935 Stanley Baldwin retakes Britain's leadership

1936 The Spanish Civil war begins in July. Edward VIII (b.1894-d.1972) – who would become the Duke of Windsor – is crowned King of the United Kingdom, the Dominions of the British Empire and Emperor of India on 20 January. Having abdicated his throne the same year (10 Dec), George VI was made King of the United Kingdom, the Dominions of the British Commonwealth and Emperor of India

1937 Continuing the Conservative leadership of Britain, Neville Chamberlain (b.1869-d.1940) takes over command, soon following up the *Factories Act* with amendments to working hours for women and children, overseeing *The Holiday with Pay*[111] and *The Housing Acts* (1938), aimed to clear slums. A new constitution is formed in Ireland, abolishing the Irish Free State. Led by de Valera, Éire is declared independent, democratic and sovereign.

1939-1945 World War II rages. Éire remains neutral, though 130,000+ Irish people will serve for Britain (66,000+ from Éire and 64,000 from Northern Ireland)[112]

[111] *The Holiday with Pay Act*, 1938 **https://www.legislation.gov.uk/ukpga/Geo6/1-2/70/enacted** accessed 24 Feb 2025

[112] ***Four Courts Press*** on Irish and Northern Irish volunteers serving in World War II **https://www.fourcourtspress.ie/books/2021/irish-men-and-women-in-the-second-world-war#:~:text=In%20this%20updated%20edition%2C%20new,some%2064%2C000%20from%20Northern%20Ireland** accessed 24 Feb 2025

1940 In Britain, ***The Conservative Party*** lead an all-party coalition headed up by Sir Winston Churchill (b.1874-d.1965) in a bid to get through the war effort

1943 Austin Harford appointed as Liverpool's first Irish Catholic mayor. A successful cloth merchant who led the local Irish Party from 1903-1923, Harford championed innovative housing projects for working-class communities and was recognized for his commitment to religion, patriotism and civic welfare

1945 A general election in the UK sees Labour take the helm, with Clement Attlee (b.1883-d.1967) as Prime Minister

1947 Britain dissolves the British Raj and in 1949 used *The London Declaration*[113] to transition India to a republican constitution

1948 John A Costello (b.1891-d.1976) becomes the Taoiseach for the First Government representing ***Fine Gael***

1949 Éire becomes the Republic of Ireland and leaves the British Commonwealth

1951 The first colour television broadcasts are introduced. De Valera becomes Taoiseach of the Sixth Government of the Republic of Ireland (***Fianna Fáil***). Churchill becomes (Conservative)the British Prime Minister

1952 Elizabeth II becomes Queen of the United Kingdom and other Commonwealth Realms after the death of her father

1953 James Watson (b.1928-d.–) and Francis Crick (b. 1916-d.2004) discover DNA at the *Cavendish Laboratory* in Cambridge, England[114] and Britain hosts Queen Elizabeth's coronation

[113] *The London Declaration*, an overview by ***The Commonwealth*** of the 1949 agreements **https://thecommonwealth.org/london-declaration-1949** accessed 24 Feb 2025

[114] ***Cambridge University*** reflects on 70-years of DNA discovery **https://www.cam.ac.uk/stories/DNA-structure-discovery-cambridge-70th-anniversary** accessed 17 Mar 2025

Eamonn de Valera glass photography portrait by an unknown photographer, used under a creative commons licence from the ***Library of Congress***.

1954 Costello – still ***Fine Gael*** – returns as Taoiseach for the Seventh Government of the Republic of Ireland

1955 Sir Antony Eden (b.1897-d.1977) becomes Prime Minister for Britain, retaining the Conservative leadership

1957 De Valera (***Fianna Fáil***) leads the Eighth Government of Éire as Taoiseach, whilst in Britain Harold Macmillan (b.1894-d.1986) takes over from Anthony Eden

1958 ***National Aeronautics and Space Administration*** (***NASA***) is founded

1959 Seán Lemass (B.1899-1971) becomes Taoiseach for the Ninth, Tenth and 11th Irish government, maintaining a ***Fianna Fáil*** leadership

1963 John F. Kennedy (JFK)(b.1917-d.1963) is assassinated on 22 November and Martin Luther King Jr (b.1929-d.1968) makes his "I have a dream" speech (28 August). In the United Kingdom, Sir Alec Douglas-Home, 14th Earl of Home (b. 1903-d.1995), leads for two-days short of a year, after a general election saw Harold Wilson (b.1916-d.1995 and previously an MP for Huyton, formerly Lancashire, but now Liverpool) win a four-seat majority for ***The Labour Party***, the first time they had been in power for 12-years

1966 Jack Lynch (b.1917-d.1999) of ***Fianna Fáil*** becomes Taoiseach of the 12th and 13th Irish Governments

1968 Martin Luther King Jr is assassinated on 4 April in Memphis Tennessee, USA

1969 Neil Armstrong walks on the moon (20 July) whilst civil unrest in Northern Ireland, occasionally entering the Republic of Ireland and other parts of Britain, continues. Known broadly as 'The Troubles' great hardship would hit thousands of people

1970 Sir Edward Heath (b.1916-d.2005) won a UK general election to lead a Conservative government. Remembered for a controversial *Industrial Relations Act* (later repealed), Heath lasted for almost 4-years

1973 Ireland joins the European Economic Community and Liam Cosgrave (b.1920-d.2019) becomes the Irish Taoiseach, leading with ***Fine Gael***

1974 Reclaiming the UK's Prime Ministerial office, Harold Wilson resigned in March 1976, handing the reins of ***The Labour Party*** to James Callaghan (b.1912-d.2005). With only a small House of Commons majority and strike action across Britain threatened, this was a testing time

1977 Jack Lynch (still ***Fianna Fáil***) returns as Taoiseach for Ireland's 15th Government

1979 Charles Haughey (b.1925-d.2006) leads Ireland's 16th Government whilst in the UK Baroness Thatcher became Conservative Prime Minister after a general election. She would be the longest serving Prime Minister in 150-years

1980 John Lennon (b.1940-d.1980) is assassinated on 8 Dec in New York, USA

1981 Garret FitzGerald (b.1926-d.2011) leads the 17th Government of Ireland

1982 Charles Haughey and Garret FitzGerald – for ***Fianna Fáil*** and ***Fine Gael*** respectively – are Taoiseach within the year for the 18th and 19th Governments of Ireland, respectively. Meanwhile, The Falklands War rages between 2 April-14 June

1983 The Republic of Ireland's eighth constitutional amendment enshrines "the equal right to life of the pregnant woman and the unborn". This was repealed by referendum in 2018

1985 In an attempt to break 'The Troubles' a new *Anglo-Irish Agreement* was formed, allowing the Republic of Ireland a consultative role in Northern Irish politics

1987 Charles Haughey reclaims the role of Taoiseach for ***Fianna Fáil***, leading the 20th and 21st Governments of Ireland

1990 The Right Honourable Sir John Major KG CH (b.1943-d.–) takes the leadership of ***The Conservative Party*** in Britain. His administration will oversee the advent and roll out of ***The National Lottery*** (contributing later to the *Liverpool Irish Famine Trail*); the death of Lady Diana Spencer (b.1961-d.1997); the first Gulf War (1990-1991); peace negotiations with Ireland and surviving a 1991 ***IRA*** mortar attack on Number 10 (the official home and working office of the UK Prime Minister) during a Cabinet meeting

1992 Albert Reynolds (b.1932-d.2014) takes over as Taoiseach, running the 22nd and 23rd Irish Governments still under ***Fianna Fáil***. Despite their strict anti-abortion laws the Republic of Ireland is permitted to sign the *Treaty on the European Union*[115] at Maastricht. In Ireland, abortion laws are loosened slightly, granting people access to information and permitting travel abroad for the purpose of abortion

1993 Warrington (Cheshire, UK) suffered a shooting (PC Mark Toker, then 25[116]) and multiple ***Provisional Irish Republican Army*** (***IRA***) bombs in February and March. In the March bombings, Johnathan Ball (b.1990-d.1993) died at the scene and Tim Parry (b1981-d.1993) died later in hospital, whilst 50+ people were reported injured (reports vary between 54 and 56).

The deaths of two young children – and controversial ***IRA*** press statements – drew international media attention and caused widespread anger. The following year the event was memorialised by ***The Cranberries*** with their song *Zombie* and in 1996 a peace sculpture called *The River of Life* was opened in Bridge Street, Warrington (this is listed in chapter 8). The murdered boys are remembered by the ***Tim Parry Johnathan Ball Foundation for Peace***[117]

[115] *Treaty on the European Union* (1992) **http://europarl.europa.eu/about-parliament/en/in-the-past/the-parliament-and-the-treaties/maastricht-treaty** accessed 21 Feb 2025

[116] ***Cheshire Museum of Policing*** report on the Warrington shooting and aftermath **https://cheshirepolicemuseum.org.uk/facts-and-features/brave-police-officer** accessed 3 Mar 2025

[117] ***The Tim Parry Johnathan Ball Foundation for Peace*** website **https://timparryjohnathanballfoundation.org.uk** accessed 3 Mar 2025

1994 The 24th Government of Ireland elects John Bruton (b. 1947-d.2024) as Taoiseach, moving the leadership to ***Fine Gael***

1997 Bertie Ahern becomes Taoiseach for the 25th-27th Governments, bringing ***Fianna Fáil*** back to the leadership, whilst in the UK The Right Honourable Sir Tony Blair KG (b.1953-d.—) wins a landslide victory for ***The Labour Party*** forming a new government. At ***St Anthony's Church*** (in Liverpool, UK) a (150th) sesquicentennial anniversary is held, which reads aloud the names of everyone known to have died in connection with An Gorta Mór in Black '47, comprising of over 7,000 names

1998 Ireland signs the *Good Friday (Belfast) Agreement.* The Liverpool Irish Great Hunger commemoration memorial is erected and opened by Ireland's President Mary McAleese. The Trail as we know it today is laid out by the ***Liverpool Great Hunger Commemoration Committee***

2000 In March, the Rector of Liverpool deposits the burial records from ***St Mary's Cemetery*** with the ***Liverpool Records Office***, having been in the custody of ***Our Lady and St Nicholas Church***

2002 Ireland replaces its national currency — the punt (IR£) — with the Euro (€)

2004 In the UK *The Civil Partnership Act*[118] is passed granting legal recognition to people of the same or opposite sex marriage-like rights and responsibilities

2008 The 28th Government of Ireland elects Brian Cowen (b.1960-d.—) as Taoiseach, sustaining a ***Fianna Fáil*** leadership

2011 Enda Kenny (b.1951-d.—) becomes the Taoiseach of the 29th and 30th Governments of Ireland, transferring leadership to ***Fine Gael***

[118] *The Civil Partnership Act*, 2004 **https://www.legislation.gov.uk/ukpga/2004/33/contents** accessed 24 Feb 2025

2016 Britain holds a vote to leave Europe. A total of 33,577,642 votes are cast. 48.11% vote to remain and 51.89% vote to leave. This creates years of 'Brexit' negotiations and causes people to reappraise England's relationship with its united nations (Scotland, Wales and Northern Ireland). It would also cause considerable parliamentary hours to manage how new arrangements would impede or otherwise affect Ireland and Northern Ireland, including back stops for border policy, security controls and reappraisals of the *Common Travel Agreement*

2017 The ***Strokestown National Famine Museum and Park***[119] is opened, alongside the ***National Famine Way***[120] (Ireland), supported by ***Irish Heritage Trust***[121]. Meanwhile, Leo Varadkar becomes Taoiseach of Ireland's 31st Government

2019-22 ***Liverpool Irish Festival*** attempts to raise funds to secure custodianship of the *Liverpool Irish Famine Trail.* They are successful in April 2021, raising £46,500 (equivalent to £56,442.95 today) from ***The National Lottery Heritage Fund***

2020 Micheál Martin (b.1960-d.—) of ***Fianna Fáil*** takes command of the 32nd Government. On 31 December, the UK's transition period ended, formally separating it from the EU

2022 ***Liverpool Irish Festival*** release *Revive* and Leo Varadkar returns as Taoiseach for ***Fine Gael*** to run the 33rd Government of Ireland

2023 In August, ***Liverpool Irish Festival*** was awarded a further grant from ***The National Lottery Heritage Fund*** of £99,650, to deliver more assets for the Trail and develop an app.

[119] ***Strokestown National Famine Museum and Park*** website **https://strokestownpark.ie/national-famine-museum** accessed 12 Feb 2025

[120] ***National Famine Way*** website **https://nationalfamineway.ie** accessed 12 Feb 2025

[121] ***Irish Heritage Trust*** website **https://irishheritagetrust.ie** accessed 12 Feb 2025

Using a small grant of £3,194 from the Irish Government's *Strategic Diaspora Fund*, two contributors to the *Liverpool Irish Famine Trail* take a research trip to ***Strokestown Estate and National Famine Museum***. The funding also maintains the *History Research Group* leader role and group, research and Trail developments

2024 Simon Harris (b.1986-d.—) leads Ireland's 34th government, sustaining a ***Fine Gael*** leadership. The ***Global Irish Famine Way***[122] is formed when Ireland's Ambassador to Canada ships 15-pairs of shoes from Strokestown Ireland to North America and walks with members of the *Liverpool Irish Famine Trail* team to carry another pair of bronze shoes to Liverpool (see chapter 7).

During the year, as well as undertaking *The Walk of the Bronze Shoes*, the ***Liverpool Irish Festival*** secures £11,656 from the Irish Government's *Strategic Diaspora Funds* to underwrite a documentary film that will be released in 2025. The Festival released the *Liverpool Irish Famine Trail* app, produced in conjunction with ***Gazooky Studios*** and ***Second Stride***

2025 ***Liverpool Irish Festival*** publishes *Release* with ***Liverpool University Press***[123] and Micheál Martin is returned as Taoiseach for Ireland's 35th Government[124] with ***Fianna Fáil***.

5/ THE TROUBLE WITH NUMBERS

It is unlikely we will ever know the precise numbers of Irish who died, nor those who emigrated, during An Gorta Mór 1845–1852. Estimates range from 1million-1.3million for the number of deaths and 1.5million-2million emigrants, although these figures are almost certainly underestimated. Likewise, the dates of The Great Hunger are contentious, depending on which accounts you read. Although by 1852 the blight was no longer widespread throughout Ireland, it still prevailed in certain areas of the country.

The proximity of Liverpool — and its status as the major port of emigration — meant that it was the first step on the journey to Canada, the United States and other parts of Britain. Through *The Act of Union* (1801)[125], Ireland became part of the United Kingdom, meaning that the Irish were not emigrants (external) but migrants (internal) and, as such, could travel freely throughout Britain. This freedom of movement allowed for less onerous administration, but means some travel was undocumented, causing researchers trouble today. In 1841, four-years before the onset of the blight, the population of Liverpool was 255,492[126].

According to 1849 figures sent to parliament by Edward Rushton (b.1759-d.1814; a local magistrate in 1847, the worst year of The Great Hunger) 296,231[127] Irish men, women and children landed in Liverpool, which is more than the population of the town just six years previously. However, Dr Duncan — Liverpool's first Medical Officer of Health — reported that nearly 300,000 Irish had landed in Liverpool in the first six months of that year. So, how accurate are the figures for Liverpool and how were they compiled?

[122] Irish Government website about the ***Global Irish Famine Way*** **https://www.ireland.ie/en/canada/global-irish-famine-way-the-longest-heritage-trail-in-the-world** accessed 12 Feb 2025

[123] ***Liverpool University Press*** website **https://www.liverpooluniversitypress.co.uk** accessed 12 Feb 2025

[124] ***AP News*** confirm Micheál Martin as Ireland's Taoiseach **https://apnews.com/article/ireland-micheal-martin-taoiseach-return-eab53d572e0400715276f89b962d92d5** accessed 3 Mar 2025

[125] *The Act of Union* (1801): a ***UK Parliament*** overview **https://www.parliament.uk/about/living-heritage/evolutionofparliament/legislativescrutiny/parliamentandireland/collections/ireland/act-of-union-1800** accessed 12 Feb 2025

[126] *Chapter 7: Liverpool* from *A Vision of Britain* **https://images.liverpoolmuseums.org.uk/2020-01/Liverpool-Part-2.pdf** accessed 12 Feb 2025

[127] Confirmation of Edward Rushton's police counts of arrivals in Liverpool **https://drb.ie/articles/the-evaporation-of-hatred** accessed 24 Feb 2025

Strokestown's bronze shoes on the ferry towards Liverpool, May 2024.

In December 1846 Liverpool's 'Guardians of the Poor', the *Select Vestry*, were concerned by the numbers of Irish arriving daily in need of relief, that is, in need of food and often medical attention[128]. Alarmed by November's increases – and facing the prospect of an impending crisis – Magistrate Rushton ordered the police to count the number of Irish disembarking at Clarence Dock. They were to differentiate between businesspeople (men), (e)migrants with luggage and the 'destitute', who frequently arrived with just the clothes on their back, often in rags. This afforded the authorities an indication of the number of paupers who could potentially swell the already overburdened relief system.

A *Select Vestry* account shows 15,000 pauper's arriving in December 1846, but contemporaneous sources reported the arrival of 50,000 destitute Irish in the year. Other sources quoted 90,000 arrivals from Ireland during 1846. ***The Liverpool Journal*** reported 'immense numbers of Irish paupers were landing in Liverpool, escaping from the threat of death by starvation in Ireland'. Prior to The Great Hunger, Liverpool's Irish population was 49,639. Of 296,231 Irish who arrived in 1847, almost 50,000 were classed as businesspeople; 130,000 as migrants and 116,000 as paupers; the latter being dependent on the ratepayers of Liverpool.

Official police counts are available from 1849-1852 but – frustratingly – official figures for 1848 are not. Using a range of sources, including statistics from a report to Parliament in 1854, shipping returns and accounts from 1840s newspapers, Professor Frank Neal has calculated the numbers for 1848 as 252,722 arrivals, of which 94,190 were paupers. Neal also suggests that the numbers stated by Edward Rushton for 1847 are probably more feasible than those quoted by Dr Duncan, which are not substantiated by the reports documented in newspapers of the time.

Migration to Liverpool from Ireland did not start and end with The Great Hunger. An Irish community was already established in the town by the time of the 1841 Census, which records 49,639 Irish-born. By 1851 this number had increased to 83,813, 22.3% of the population. However, these figures do not include the Irish community, the children and grandchildren of those born in Ireland, who were ethnically Irish. There were more Irish in Liverpool than in most Irish towns, mainly in – but not restricted to – the north end.

We can only imagine the impact such vast numbers would have on both the destitute Irish fleeing starvation, and on the people of Liverpool, notably the ratepayers. Local officials asked the Government in London for help in December 1846, and again in April 1847, but none was forthcoming. The exodus from Ireland continued after 1852. For example, 233,652 arrivals were recorded in 1853 of whom 71,353 were classed as paupers.

Although the numbers are approximate, the police figures and Professor Neal's work enable us to gauge a reasonable 'best estimate'. This moves us from a figure of 1,241,410 in 2022 to 1,571,714 today. 71,353 were classed as paupers. Thousands of these desperate people died of starvation and disease in Liverpool and in towns and villages throughout Britain where they made their way in search of a better life. Many thousands stayed. In 2011 ***The Office For National Statistics*** estimated that Irish heritage in Liverpool was still growing, up 7.8% on its previous census.

Readers are invited to look at the table on the following page. The table evidences a further 300,000 in addition to the 1.27million migrants that ***The Liverpool Great Hunger Commemoration Committee*** established a figure for in the 1990s, covering the An Gorta Mór years1845-52 and more for the years following. It means that over 1.5m individuals are known to have come through Clarence Dock in The Great Hunger period of 1845-1852.

[128] ***National Archives*** for the *Liverpool Select Vestry* archives **https://discovery.nationalarchives.gov.uk/details/r/b69cd7a6-805c-40e4-b9a3-ac9b0de08b98** accessed 24 Feb 2025

Year	Jobbing emigrants	Paupers (P)	Total	%= P	Reference
1845			0		Figures not calculated
1846			15,000		*Liverpool Select Vestry* minutes for Dec 1846 only
1847	180,231	116,000	296,231	39	Magistrate Edward Rushton's figures
1848	158,532	94,190	252,722	37	Frank Neal's reported figures
1849	160,458	80,468	240,926	33	*Select Committee on Poor Removal*, 1854, as reported by Professor Frank Neal in *Sectarian Violence* thesis (1987)
1850	173,236	77,765	251,001	31	
1851	215,369	68,134	283,503	24	
1852	153,909	78,422	232,331	34	
1853	162,299	71,535	233,834	31	
Totals 1845-52	**1,041,735**	**514,979**	**1,571,714**	**33**	**N/A**
Inc.1853	**1,204,034**	**586,514**	**1,805,548**	**33**	**N/A**

In 2011 ***The Office For National Statistics***[129] estimated that Irish heritage in Liverpool was still growing, up 7.8% on its previous census. It should be noted that newspapers printed during The Great Hunger's early years claimed 50,000+ migrants from Ireland per year. This could add to the above numbers, if they could be verified. Such inclusions might push the total to over 1.9m migrants through Liverpool alone.

The trouble with numbers is that numbers only tell part of the story, especially when we look at who is undertaking the counting and why. Numbers can say that a government did more than they should, or not enough. They can show that money was put to good use, or that it was spent on malmanagement. From the Festival and Trail's point of view, we wish to ensure that people have access to their own histories by ensuring every life is recognised.

For us, numbers are not an instrument of blame, but a record of events. If they cannot be verified, people may not have access to their heritage and we may not know the extent to which people were lost. We always try to remember that within the enormity of these numbers, every 'one' is a name; a set of lived experiences and feelings. The trouble with numbers is they can mask these.

Facts compiled by *History Research Group*
member researcher Tricia Mackin, June 2024.

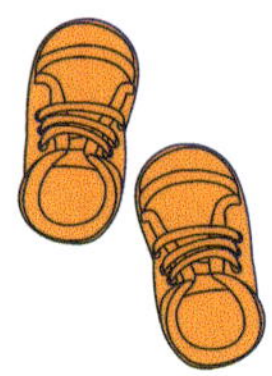

[129] Information on ***Office for National Statistics*** 2011 Census analysis **https://cairdeliverpool.wordpress.com/tag/irish-ethnicity-2/#:~:text=The%20Merseyside%20region%20as%20a%20whole%20has%20seen%20an%20increase,to%20prosper%20and%20grow%E2%80%A6** accessed 24 Feb 2025

The bronze shoes arrive at Woodside Ferry Terminal, Birkenhead, May 2024.

On the walk between Clondra and Abbeyschrule, along Ireland's ***National Famine Way***, a school group had placed hawthorn painted pebbles on one of the trail's markers (May 2024).

Pebbles are often used as a memorial marker at holocaust sites, using the Jewish tradition of leaving a stone when honouring the dead as a sign of rememberance and respect. It was witnessed several times along the journey. Guided exercises had taken place in schools. It is often believed hawthorn marks the graves of many who died during An Gorta Mór, as detailed in Marita Conlon-McKenna's seminal 1990 children's book *Under the Hawthorn Tree.*

6/ TRAIL MAP

Originally produced for *Revive*, this is an indicative map of the *Liverpool Irish Famine Trail*'s existing sites. A full site list and coordinates are given in the following chapter. To the map, we have added four prospective sites we are committed to investigating in 2025 and believe will be added to the Trail in the next year-to-18-months. These include:

- 13 - ***St Anthony's Church***, Scotland Road, Liverpool (church coordinates 53.42233301004717, -2.9814092869050337)
- 16 - 'The Simmy' (see orange map pin) at ***Silvester Street Park and Garden*** formerly the ***St Martin-in-the-Fields Churchyard*** (park coordinates 53.42101, -2.98779)[130].
  A poem reflecting on 'The Simmy' can be found here: **liverpoolirishfestival.com/lockdown-lights-the-simmy**
- 17 - (to be added) - New Brighton, to mark the catastrophic 1846 collision of *The Sea Nymph* and *The Rambler* (coordinates to be agreed)[131]
- 18 - (to be added) Livingstone Street (Birkenhead) marking one of the fever hospitals built in response to the escalating numbers of An Gorta Mór poor (coordinates to be agreed).

We recognise this is not a map for real orienteering! On our website you will find an enhanced ***Google*** map (individual site maps with information), which shows precisely where sites are. We have a print-at-home map, with the official coordinates on, which you can use with GPS systems. Additionally, you can access our app, which hosts a GPS-linked interactive map to navigate to any of the sites using a handheld device. Accessed through your browser, you will need to keep the window open for it to communicate with you about directions and provide you with site information. Visit **liverpoolirishfaminetrail.com**

[130] A short history of ***St Martin-in-the-Fields Church*** **https://www.findagrave.com/cemetery/2442087/st-martin-in-the-fields-churchyard** accessed 26 Feb 2025

[131] A description of the collision between *The Sea Nymph* and *The Rambler* **https://www.liverpool.ac.uk/~cmi/books/earlySS/collision.html#SN** accessed 26 Feb 2025

STANLEY PARK & GARDEN
ANFIELD
A5089
TOWNSEND LN
A5038
EVERTON
GREAT HOWARD ST
GREAT HOMER ST
REGENT RD
A5050
VAUXHALL
NEWSHAM PARK & GARDEN
A5049
LIVERPOOL
KENSINGTON
EDGE LANE
B5178
UNIVERSITY OF LIVERPOOL
ROPEWALKS
UPPER PARLIAMENT ST
UPPER PARLIAMENT ST
KINGSLEY RD
TOXTETH
SEFTON ST
PARK RD
SEFTON PARK
1
2
3
4
5
6
7
8
9
10
11
12
13
14
16

7/ LIVERPOOL IRISH FAMINE TRAIL SITES

The following chapter sets out the Trail's existing sites, long- and short-term plans and idea additions. We would also recommend readers and visitors read this in connection with chapter 8, which lists other known plaques and markers across the region, designed to acknowledge either The Great Hunger, peace and reconciliation or people with deep Irish connections and/or influence.

EXISTING SITES

For newcomers to the *Liverpool Irish Famine Trail*, it is worth recapping our existing sites. We currently have 15 sites, as identified by the ***Liverpool Great Hunger Commemoration Committee*** in the 1990s. The rationale for these sites is given in our first book, *Revive*, and the same detailed historical site information can also be found on our enhanced ***Google*** map on the *Liverpool Irish Famine Trail* website (**liverpoolirishfaminetrail.com**). Not all sites had green plaques; only those that specifically tell the story of An Gorta Mór. In the list below, these are indicated with the following symbol ●.

Post codes provide 'general' locational information. Though we have done our best to locate and share the most relevant post codes occasionally these are imprecise as sites are not necessarily at specific buildings. For example, Clarence Dock's gates do not provide a valid postal address, therefore the next best address has been sought, using the building opposite.

Similarly, ***St George's Hall*** provides the post code for Father Nugent's statue (located in the connected St John's Gardens), but a satellite navigation system would take you to the building not the statue. The coordinates we have given are as close to the sites as we have been able to pinpoint, but you may need to look up or around to find the object as the coordinates may be for a building, not its entrance; a cemetery and not the exact stone. You may need to explore a little.

In addition to the information provided in *Revive*, we have added ***What3Words*** descriptions. ***What3Words*** offers a global gridding system of 3m^2, identifiable by three unrelated words. Some global positioning systems (GPS) systems can navigate using this technology, so we hope these additions might prove beneficial.

Site 1: The Liverpool Famine Memorial (coordinates 53.40196 – 2.97482), located in the gardens at ***St Luke's 'Bombed Out' Church*** (corner Leece and Berry Streets, enter gardens from the Leece Street entry), L1 2TR. NB: This is a key site, but does not have a suited *Liverpool Irish Famine Trail* plaque. We hope to install one in the coming years. ***What3Words***: **choice. combining. vocab**

Site 2: *Pleasant Street School* (coordinates 53.40480981264833, -2.9731960258411685), Pleasant Street, L3 5TS. ***What3Words***: **maple. stem. adopt**

● **Site 3: The *Brownlow Hill Workhouse*** (coordinates 53.40556819487453, -2.9667444702188464), Hart Building, Mount Pleasant, L69 7ZX. ***What3Words***: **radio. odds. useful**

● **Site 4: The Paupers' Graveyard** (coordinates 53.4017950830834,-2.9671092599499955), Mulberry Street, L69 7SH. ***What3Words***: **always. song. shift**

Site 5: Agnes Jones House (coordinates 53.4000188937363, -2.9674296883117526), 1A Catharine Street, L8 7JZ. ***What3Words***: **packet. grid. relate**

Site 6: Kitty Wilkinson's grave (coordinates 53.39735, -2.97211), *St James's Gardens* at ***Liverpool Anglican Cathedral***, L1 7AZ. ***What3Words***: **fight. sizes. parade**

Site 7: *St Patrick's Chapel* (coordinates 53.39223128803399, -2.971767215300476), Park Place, Park Road, L8 5RA. ***What3Words***: **sounds. adding. scales** These coordinates take you to the Church entrance where you might find a custodian who can help you with crypt access and pit grave information

Site 8: James Larkin's birthplace (coordinates 53.389830256572886, -2.97055984460683), ***The Globe***, 44-46 Park Road, L8 6SH. (NB: This was marked as a plaque site in the 1990s, because there is a plaque, but it is not a *Liverpool Irish Famine Trail* plaque, thus we are no longer labelling it as a 'plaque site'). ***What3Words***: **system. bend. loyal**

● **Site 9: The Pilotage Building** (coordinates 53.40230261972989, -2.995353873442184), ***National Museums Liverpool***, Canning Pier, L3 1BY. ***What3Words***: **lower. shovels. violin**

● **Site 10: Relief Station** (coordinates 53.40594741449407, -2.9914153153000633), Fenwick Street, L2 0NZ. ***What3Words***: **output. dates. spark**

Site 11: Father Nugent's statue (coordinates 53.408639270899066, -2.9817393022778247), ***St John's Gardens*** (facing Old Haymarket and Tunnel entrance), L1 1JJ. ***What3Words***: **open. helps. pink**

● **Site 12: Lace Street**. The plaque is currently concealed from view within the ***Holy Cross Catholic School*** (Fontenoy Street, L3 2DU). We are working on relocating the plaque. ***What3Words***: Not available at the time of writing

Site 13: Dandy Pat memorial (coordinates for ***St Anthony's Church*** updated: 53.42229944446871, -2.98144415581237), ***St Anthony's Church***, Scotland Road, L5 5BD. ***What3Words***: **twin. slick. shop**

● **Site 14: Clarence Dock Gates** (coordinates 53.418957, -3.000072), Clarence Dock, Regent Road, L20 8DJ. ***What3Words***: **builds. struck. prefer**. Clarence Dock's gates are not a functional postal address therefore the next best address has been sought, using the building opposite. Of the two sets of gates to Clarence Dock, visitors should approach the ones closest to the town centre to see the plaque there

● **Site 15: Price Street** (coordinates updated from *Revive*: 53.3889024, -3.0343168/53.393313), Birkenhead, CH41 6DQ. ***What3Words***: **nest. yard. flips**.

St Patrick's Chapel, **Park Place Liverpool (c) AB 2022.**

Frederick Douglass portrait by an unknown photographer, used under a creative commons licence from the ***Smithsonian Institution***. Douglass is remembered in Liverpool.

SITES UNDER LONG-TERM CONSIDERATION

The *Liverpool Irish Famine Trail*'s sites, as outlined above, help to tell a deep story of the plight of the Irish in Liverpool, both during The Great Hunger and sometime around the major dates of 1845-52. Nevertheless, the story of the Irish in Liverpool began before then and continues to this day. The docks that connect the harbours; the economic migrations and family connections on either side of the sea, all contributed to Liverpool becoming a key port for those fleeing An Gorta Mór.

We identified various Liverpool (UK) sites that could be added in *Revive*, such as

- the former and present Irish Centres (the *Wellington Rooms* and ***St Michael's***)
- *The Institute of Irish Studies*, established in 1988 at ***University of Liverpool***
- the pubs and brewery of Irishman Robert Cain (b.1826-d.1907) who is buried in Liverpool's *St James's Gardens*
- a site for Michael James Whitty (Duncormick, County Wexford, b.1795-d.1873) Liverpool's first Chief Constable; founder of Liverpool's first fire service and founder of ***The Liverpool Post***
- Ballymena's Sir William Brown (b.1784-d.1864), a British merchant, banker, Corn Law abolitionist and benefactor of the 1860 *Derby Museum* (now *World Museum*) and *Liverpool Central Library*. Both buildings can be found on the eponymous street that now features an ***Eric Scott Lynch Slavery History*** plaque (installed April 2022) declaring Brown's ownership of enslaved people in America
- the Hope Street plaque marking famed African American social reformist Frederick Douglass (b.1818-d.1895), who sailed to Ireland from Liverpool in 1845 and recounted that two Irishmen inspired his self-emancipation from enslavement

- a marker for James Larkin's sister Delia (b.1878-d.1949), First General Secretary of the ***Women Workers' Union*** and columnist in James's *The Irish Worker and People's Advocate*
- a link to Sir James Sexton (b.1856-d.1938), the son of displaced Irish market traders, who defeated James Larkin as General Secretary of the ***National Union of Dock Labourers*** in Liverpool in 1893. Sexton was a founder member of – and MP within – the ***Independent Labour Party***
- a marker for MP Thomas Power (TP) O'Connor (b.1848-d.1929), an Irish nationalist who represented Liverpool's Scotland Road area for 40+ years. TP O'Connor became 'Father of the House of Commons' with an unbroken service of 49 years and 215 days
- resolving the rumours and marking that Liverpool's dock kerbstones are either Newry or Galloway granite
- ***The Wavertree Lock Up***, known to be an overnight dwelling for unfortunate migrants seeking out-of-town shelter during An Gorta Mór
- or Liverpool's ***Quaker House***, known to have provided support to The Great Hunger's poor.

As you can see, there are numerous ways in which the Trail *could* be expanded. What seems key to us is we must maintain a focus on An Gorta Mór and Liverpool's – or Merseyside's – role at the time and in Irish lives today. There is cross-over above with markers that already exist, so we recommend readers cross-reference this chapter with chapters 5 and 8.

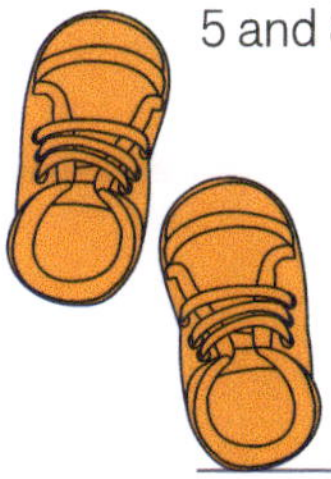

SITES UNDER SHORT-TERM CONSIDERATION (AND HOPEFUL ACTION)

Since writing *Revive*, we have committed to researching (and hopefully marking) the following sites:

- 'The Simmy' at ***Silvester Street Park and Garden*** formerly the ***St Martin-in-the-Fields Churchyard*** (park coordinates 53.42101, -2.98779)[132]. ***What3Words***: **sticky. slows. evenly**. A poem reflecting on 'The Simmy', by Liverpool-Belfast historian and poet Greg Quiery (b.1947-d–), can be found here: **liverpoolirishfestival.com/lockdown-lights-the-simmy**
- New Brighton, to mark the catastrophic 1846 collision of *The Sea Nymph* and *The Rambler* (coordinates to be agreed and followed with ***What3Words*** information)[133]
- ***St Anthony's Church***, Scotland Road, Liverpool (church coordinates 53.42233301004717, -2.9814092869050337). ***What3Words***: **twin. slick. shop**
- Livingstone Street, Birkenhead marking one of the fever hospitals built in response to the escalating numbers of An Gorta Mór poor (coordinates to be agreed and followed with ***What3Words*** information).

We are also keen to have a marker at ***Walton Park Cemetery***, where the 2,600+ workhouse burials from ***St Mary's Cemetery*** were reinterred in 1949.

At the time of writing, the Festival remains open to additions, suggestions and updates. If readers have any suggestions to add, we welcome you to contact us directly.

[132] A short history of ***St Martin-in-the-Fields Church*** **https://www.findagrave.com/cemetery/2442087/st-martin-in-the-fields-churchyard** accessed 26 Feb 2025

[133] A description of the collision between *The Sea Nymph* and *The Rambler* **https://www.liverpool.ac.uk/~cmi/books/earlySS/collision.html#SN** accessed 26 Feb 2025

6/ NEW FINDINGS

The Festival has developed an incredible *History Research Group* who have committed thousands of hours to the development of the Trail. For this book, we set research questions, such as:

- Can we name/locate the dead from Lace Street and ***St Mary's Cemetery***?
- How do people arrange their migration passage and what would their experience have been?
- What were the conditions onboard ships from Liverpool to the rest of the world?

This chapter provides the answers we have located.

RECEIVING HELP: LIVERPOOL'S SELECT VESTRY: POOR LAWS - AN OVERVIEW THROUGH TIME

The British *Poor Laws* of the 1830s and 40s hark back to medieval times. In 1351 the *Statute of Labourers*[134] required that everyone that could work should and tried to cap wage levels and food costs. This piece of law came in to try to address labour shortages following the Black Death. When workers tried to flee employers to become free men, Edward III (b.1312-d.1377) passed laws to punish fleeing workers. By 1388, the *Statute of Cambridge* restricted labourer and beggar movements.

In 1495, Henry VII (b.1457-d.1509) passed the *Vagabonds and Beggars Act,* punishing "vagabonds, idle and suspected persons" with days in stocks without sustenance and to be removed from that town. Instituting whipping as a just punishment, Henry VIII (b.1491-d.1547) amended *The Vagabonds Act* in 1530, which also stated that Justices of the Peace must assign a location in their jurisdiction for the purposes of licenced begging that they must administer. Licences would be given to the disabled, sick and elderly (terms of the time) and punishment awarded to those begging without licence or able to work.

In London in 1547, unable to raise enough money from voluntary contributions to pay for the maintenance of hospitals, whilst the number of poor people grew, Sunday collections were replaced with a compulsory *Poor Rate*. In essence, this formed a local/parishioner income tax that moved to a property tax over time. Failure to pay would result in a summons and Justices of the Peace (JPs) could seize assets from, award custodial time to or fine non-payers. As poor numbers increased, 'able bodied' workers were unable to locate employment, so Houses of Correction (workhouses) were built for cap-making, feather-bedmaking and wire drawing. This would be further expanded nationally in 1601.

The Vagabonds (*Vagrancy*) *Act* of 1547[135] further criminalised poverty, with two-year custodial sentences and branding subjects with a 'V' for a first offence (being out of work for more than three days) and death for a second (some historical references suggest an 'S' for 'Slave' rather than a 'V' for 'vagabond'). However, JPs were loath to enact the full penalty, so *The Poor Act* of 1551 designated a Collector of Alms in each parish to create a register of licenced poor, making parish collections responsible for the poor, with begging no longer acceptable at all.

The Vagabonds Act of 1572[136] ordered that a first-time beggar be burned through the ear whilst persistent beggars be hanged but did reclassify "professional beggars" versus no-fault beggars. Elizabeth I's (b.1533-d.1603) 1563 *Act for the Relief of the Poor/ Statute of Artificers* made most parishioners pay in to poor collection or be fined by JPs, whilst *The Poor Act* of 1575-6 stated that competent provisions be maintained by workhouses to give means of work for the poor.

By 1597 increased poverty forced considerable parliamentary discussion with another four acts passed, culminating in *The Poor Relief Act* of 1601. The new act paid for parish administrations (c.15,000 at the time)

[134] ***Yale Law School*** *The Statute of Labourers*, 1351 **https://avalon.law.yale.edu/medieval/statlab.asp** accessed 27 Feb 2025

[135] ***Intriguing History.com***'s overview of Edward VI and *Vagrancy Act* 1547 *Poor Laws* **https://intriguing-history.com/edward-vi-enacts-harsh-statute-against-vagabonds** accessed 28 Feb 2025

[136] ***UK Parliament*** on *The Vagabonds Act*, 1572 **https://www.parliament.uk/about/living-heritage/transformingsociety/livinglearning/coll-9-health1/health-06** accessed 27 Feb 2025

by levying local rates and instigating outdoor relief, consisting of bread or clothing provisions. It additionally made children responsible for their parents and vice versa. In 1607 a House of Correction was set up in each county, which distinguished between 'vagrants' and the settled poor.

The 1662 *Settlement Act/An Act for the better Relief of the Poor of this Kingdom*[137] redrew aspects of the *Statute of Cambridge*, removing offenders back to their 'place of settlement' (usually the parish of their birth). It additionally conferred settlements on children and wives as the same as their fathers and husbands, with illegitimate children being awarded the settlement of their birth location. This produced accidental loopholes and counterstrategies, including short-term employment contracts that invalidated poor relief eligibility and unfair relocations costing many parishes harshly.

Over the next 80 years, corporations constructed workhouses to deal with caring for the poor and petty criminals under private acts. Of course, people in workhouses were overworked, under nourished and frequently ill residents. Recognising that workhouses were not attractively profitable more regulation was needed. The 1782 act *For the better Relief and Employment of the Poor* (or *Gilbert's Act*)[138] put relief into the control of 'hundreds', administrative areas akin to counties. This allowed unions of parishes to build a common workhouse (applying new model rules), but limit their use to the old, sick, infirm or orphaned children. 'Able-bodied' paupers would be found employment near their homes, with employers receiving allowances drawn from the poor rates to improve wages in line with subsistence. These would be run by elected Boards of Guardians and appointed by magistrates.

Laws were tweaked again in 1795 with the *Poor Removal Act*, which had the effect of only being able to move someone to another parish if they had applied for relief. Struggling with the effects of The Napoleonic Wars (1803-1815), *Corn Laws* were passed to keep grain prices high (see our timeline in chapter 2 for more details of these). This made it difficult for poor people to buy certain products and allowed farmers to pass off a portion of their wage bill to the taxpayer.

A Royal Commission into the Operation of the Poor Laws was triggered by The Swing Riots (an agricultural uprising in 1830), delivering its report in 1832[139]. Its conclusion was that the existing system undermined its own objectives. The commission argued that current laws promoted immorality among women and encouraged laziness by effectively rewarding illegitimacy and unemployment. Additionally, the wage subsidy system enabled employers to deliberately keep wages low. The Commission made 22 recommendations, centred around reviving the "workhouse test," which utilised the assumption that the deserving and undeserving poor could be easily distinguished. The underlying principle was that anyone willing to accept relief within the harsh conditions of a workhouse must truly lack the moral determination to survive without assistance.

Thus the 1834 *Poor Law Amendment Act*[140] was born for England and Wales, though practically little changed in Liverpool due to the existing functions. In effect, it should have swept away all former laws, replacing them with a national system based on a Union workhouse model. Deemed to be a key piece of social reformatory law, 'able-bodied' paupers were now only able to claim relief from inside the workhouse, with new Poor Law Commissioners administering the law through and around Poor Law Unions, which brought small parishes together to operate. History has reviewed this move as both positive and negative, depending on the prevailing social model of the time.

Though this new structure reduced costs to rate payers, property owners were still forced to pay poor rates, which caused the law significant resistance, particularly in northern industrial areas.

---

137 Overview of many of *The Poor Laws* **https://www.workhouses.org.uk/poorlaws/oldpoorlaw.shtml#PoorRate** accessed 27 Feb 2025

138 An overview of *Gilbert's Act* by ***The Victorian Web*** **https://victorianweb.org/history/poorlaw/gilbert.html** accessed 11 Mar 2025

139 The 1832 Royal Commission outlined by ***The Victorian Web*** **https://www.victorianweb.org/history/poorlaw/royalcom.html** accessed 27 Feb 2025

140 The 1834 *Poor Law Amendment Act* **https://www.workhouses.org.uk/poorlaws/1834intro.shtml** accessed 27 Feb 2025

Workhouses were to be seen as shameful places. Strengthening eligibility for access to poor relief (e.g., making it harder to claim) came at the cost of starving paupers. Workhouses were not cheap to build, meaning outdoor relief was often a preferred option of the Unions, though with demand outstripping provision this became problematic. To counter this, the *Outdoor Labour Test Order* [141] of 1842 was brought in alongside the 1844 *Outdoor Relief Prohibitory Order*[142]. The first of these orders meant relief could only be given outdoors in exchange for an amount of labour, usually stone breaking, often in outdoor spaces attached to a workhouse. A minimum of half the relief had to consist of 'articles of necessity' (food, clothing) rather than money.

The second, attempted to rid the relief system of assistance to the able-bodied, making it necessary for any relief given to be retrospectively sanctioned by Poor Law Commissioners. In practice, these reforms caused problems. Applied in the industrial north, recession forced cyclical unemployment. The able-bodied and unemployed were reluctant to enter the shameful workhouses and sought alternative support, but ultimately the workhouses were the only places left providing any kind of support. Regulations tried to make the workhouse worse than the experience of pauperism, but this meant inhumane hardship beyond separation or embarrassment such as starvation, which undervalues the whole system of relief. Over the next 20-years, Victorians begin a philosophical repositioning on moral welfare and societal ills veering from one extreme to the other.

The burden of relief was found to be much harder on certain parishes than others and so *The Union Chargeability Act* of 1865 attempted to spread costs across unions of parishes, though this too was imperfect. Increased industrialism and mounting pressure by social activists brought about *The Reform Act* (1867, also known as the *Second Reform Act* and *The Representation of the People Act*), which granted voting rights to urban working-class males over a certain earning or asset threshold, doubling the existing voting population. It also restructured England's boroughs, changing the numbers of MPs to be elected or reducing their power due to corruption charges. As Liberal interests grew, trade unions mobilised, and friendly societies were established causing limited alleviation to the parish structures that had previously underwritten the burden of relief provisions. Belief in what caused pauperism also changed.

Acts such as *The Medical Relief Disqualification Removal Act* (1885) and *The Unemployed Workmen Act* (1905) followed, each supporting those in need, when needed, a little more than before. The introduction of old age pensions, national insurance and new voting structures mean that by the time of World War I *The Poor Laws* were under less pressure. They were refocussed again after 'Smash up the Workhouse' protests and increased unemployment following the war. *The Poor Laws* were eventually abolished altogether in 1948 when the *National Assistance Act*[143] was passed by government.

LIVERPOOL AND THE POOR LAW, 1840S

Who qualified for poor relief? Settled poor (not able to support themselves) who had at least five-years residence in the Parish qualified for 'poor relief'. In England, immediate relief was given to people in desperate need (casuals) at soup houses. Officials were not required to provide long-term relief for the casual poor and able-bodied paupers were required to be returned to their home parish to receive relief there. To pay for poor relief, rates were collected from those in the parish owning or renting a property over £10 rateable value a year. Comparing 1845 values with today's money draws an equivalent value of £1,030.

While Liverpool's *Select Vestry* worked within the existing *Poor Law* framework to provide relief, their efforts occurred against a backdrop of widespread

[141] *The Outdoor Labour Test Order*, 1842 **https://www.workhouses.org.uk/gco/outdoorlabourtestintro.shtml** accessed 27 Feb 2025

[142] *The Outdoor Relief Prohibitory Order*, 1844 **https://www.workhouses.org.uk/gco/outdoorreliefprohibitoryintro.shtml** accessed 28 Feb 2025

[143] ***UK Parliament*** on the *National Assistance Act* (1948) **https://www.legislation.gov.uk/ukpga/Geo6/11-12/29** accessed 11 Mar 2025

prejudice against Irish migrants. Contemporaneous newspapers and official discourse often characterised the Irish through negative stereotypes - portraying them as carriers of disease, disorder, and moral contagion. Local press references to Irish areas as 'fever nests' exemplified these beliefs, with at least 10 references in ***Liverpool Mercury*** publications in 1847. These attitudes influenced how aid was administered and received, with some Irish migrants feeling pressure to downplay their heritage to avoid discrimination. Despite these challenging social conditions, Liverpool's institutional response demonstrated remarkable humanity and scale.

Setting, collecting and administering *The Poor Law* rates in Liverpool was the duty of the *Select Vestry* Chairman, Rector of Liverpool and vicar of Childwall Augustus Campbell (b.1786-d.1870)[144]. A select vestry[145] is a small group, formed within a church or parish (usually elected), managing the administration of the church's property, assets and affairs. Usually chosen from the congregation, they serve as the governing body for that church. The first *Liverpool Select Vestry* was elected on 28 July 1842 and functioned for over 50-years.

Relief was provided in five forms: indoor and outdoor, industrial schools, soup houses and voluntary. Indoor relief was generally considered to be 'the workhouse'. In 1842-3, the workhouse at Brownlow Hill was enlarged to house 3,000 people. On occasion it housed 5,000, providing food, shelter and work for poverty-stricken people with no other means of support. Men and women in families were separated and slept in dormitories.

Industrial Schools were for children and known as 'Ragged Schools'. These provided industrial training and sometimes residential care for destitute and vagrant children. Young orphans, homeless children and those whose parents could not cope, learned a trade with the aim of preventing them falling into a life of crime.

[144] Entry on ***Gibbs Family Tree*** confirming the Rev Augustus Campbell's details **https://gibbsfamilytree.com/tng/getperson.php?personID=I5139&tree=gft1** accessed 27 Feb 2025

[145] Though not of the period, the following guidance outlines what a select vestry member would undertake today, providing a good outline for what was probably expected then ***Church of Ireland*** (2017). *Church of Ireland – Parish Handbook: Introduction To Serving On A Select Vestry.* [online] Available at: **https://www.churchofireland.org/cmsfiles/pdf/Resources/ParishResources/SelectVestry/Introduction-to-Serving-on-a-Select-Vestry-11-01-17.pdf** accessed 27 Feb 2025

'Industrial Schools' were sometimes given as the 'abode' for infants in the pauper burial records. The ***St Mary's Cemetery*** microfiche records at ***Liverpool Records Office*** show that often the date of death is not recorded, but their burial is, for instance: George Hulligan, aged 2, buried 17th March 1847 and Bridget Ryan, aged 12 months, buried 26th April 1847.

Outdoor relief consisted of paid work or food support. Soup houses were a short-term measure for desperate people to seek nutrition, however meagre. From February 1847, bread was provided in addition to soup. In Liverpool in 1846-7 such paid work might be described as stone breaking, stone carting and levelling land at Kirkdale. Other work included were crushing bones and picking oakum. Additional forms of relief were managed by volunteers, from charitable institutions, often from religious orders.

Relief obtained by the 'non-settled poor' was repayable, reclaimed from the parish or district from which they came, or they could be returned to their home parish. 'Casuals' — those newly arrived in the city needing immediate aid and those passing through — availed of the soup house. Such places were also called relief stations. We have commemorated one such relief station on Fenwick Street (Liverpool) where the Trail has a plaque. For the settled poor, there were soup houses at Gill Street (near *Brownlow Hill Workhouse*), Pickop Street (close to Lace Street) and Flint Street (south of the city centre and close to the docks). As well as food, the *Select Vestry* provided clothes, medical assistance, hospital facilities and extra Relieving Officers.

The Board of the *Liverpool Select Vestry Finance Committee* meeting minutes from 19 December 1846 recorded: "A discussion ensued relative to the great numbers of destitute poor daily coming from Ireland, (15,000 in December 1846 alone) becoming chargeable to the Parish…". The Committee resolved to transmit a memorandum to the *Home Office* asking for help to pay for the …. "supplying of soup to the poor to the extent that may be required under the present emergencies…". No help was forthcoming. The following meeting of 26 December 1846, recorded:

Liverpool's *Select Vestry* costs	Pounds (£)	Shillings (s)	Pence (d)	***Bank of England*** equivalent as of Jan 2025
Removal of 1,529 paupers to Dublin at 2s a head	152	18	0	£15,116
Removal of 672 to other parts of Ireland	81	9	0	£8,002
Removal of 79 to Scotland	15	3	6	£1,482
Removal of 2 to the Isle of Man	0	8	0	£40
Totals	**248**	**38**	**6**	**£24,640**

In old money, twelve pence (d) equalled one shilling (s) with a shilling being one-20th of a pound (£). There were 20 shillings (s) in an old pound (£) or 240 pence (d). **Right**: An 1847 Victorian shilling (accessed 19 Jun 2025, **coinsandtreasures.com**).

Lazarettos (quarantine ships) were introduced on the River Mersey to prevent those sick with fever from alighting at Clarence Dock. Fever sheds in the north and south of the town were set up to ease the overcrowded hospitals. The *Liverpool Select Vestry* provided 3,176 pauper burials in ***St Mary's Cemetery*** between 17 March and 15 July 1847, including 56 dead on the lazarettos.

In June 1847, *The Poor Relief Ireland Bill* was passed, which expected that Irish parishes would look after their own poor. Newspapers asked that people should stop sending the poor to Fenwick Street, instead they should direct paupers to a shed in Vulcan Street (close to Clarence Dock) for return to their own parishes. 15,008 paupers were removed for the whole of 1847, but over 100,000 remained. Migration to Liverpool continued at a similarly high rate until 1853, severely stretching *The Poor Law* system.

Not all Irish migrants could openly maintain their heritage. The pressures of discrimination affected migrants at all social levels. Robert Cain, who arrived from County Cork during the Famine years, built a successful brewing empire in Liverpool. Despite his Irish birth, he later may have represented himself as Liverpool-born in official records - a telling sign of the social pressures facing even successful Irish immigrants. His story illustrates how anti-Irish sentiment could push people to alter their identities, even as Liverpool's institutions provided practical assistance[146].

Facts compiled by *History Research Group* researcher Flora Small, June 2024.

[146] For more on Irish identity and discrimination in Victorian Liverpool, see Frank Neal's *Black '47: Britain and the Famine Irish* (1998) and John Belchem's *Irish, Catholic and Scouse: The History of the Liverpool-Irish, 1800-1939* (2007)

Detail from *The New Poor Law* poster, 1837 (EXT 6/1) depicting what it would mean for seekers of relief, taken from ***The*** (UK) ***National Archives***.

SUMMARY: GOVERNMENTAL AND LOCAL RESPONSES TO POOR RELIEF IN 1840S LIVERPOOL

NATIONAL GOVERNMENT RESPONSES

1. The Poor Law Amendment Act (1834)...

- established a national system of poor relief
- made workhouses deliberately unappealing
- created Poor Law Unions to administer relief
- aimed to discourage what was seen as 'undeserving' poverty.

2. The Poor Relief Ireland Bill (June 1847)...

- attempted to shift responsibility for Irish paupers back to Irish parishes
- intended to reduce the financial burden on English cities like Liverpool
- legally mandated that Irish parishes should manage their own poor.

3. Home Office involvement...

- demonstrated minimal direct intervention
- rejected Liverpool's request for additional support during the migration crisis
- maintained a hands-off approach to local relief efforts.

LIVERPOOL SELECT VESTRY'S LOCAL RESPONSES

1. Direct relief mechanisms

- Established forms of relief: 1) indoor relief (*Brownlow Hill Workhouse*) 2) outdoor relief (paid work, e.g., stone breaking) 3) industrial schools for children 4) soup houses 5) voluntary charitable support.

2. Migration Management

- tracked incoming Irish migrants (15,000 in December 1846 alone)
- implemented strategies to manage people, e.g.:
  - setting up lazarettos (quarantine ships)
  - building fever sheds
  - attempting to return migrants to their home parishes in Ireland.

3. Financial Burden

- collected poor rates from property owners
- managed relief within strict local budget constraints
- proactively sought government assistance (though unsuccessfully).

KEY DIFFERENCES IN APPROACH

- **Government**: Macro-level policy focused on discouraging dependency seeking to minimize financial responsibility
- **Liverpool's *Select Vestry***: Immediate, practical response to overwhelming human need, directly confronting the humanitarian crisis.

OUTCOMES

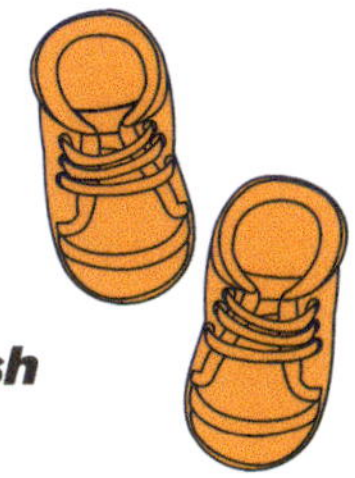

- 15,008 paupers removed in 1847
- Over 100,000 migrants remained
- 3,176 pauper burials between March and July 1847 by the ***Liverpool Parish***
- severe strain on local relief systems
- development of resilient Irish community networks that provided mutual support beyond official relief systems
- gradual formation of distinctly Liverpool-Irish identity that would become increasingly assertive in later decades.

CRITICAL OBSERVATION

The governmental response was largely systemic and detached, while the local Liverpool response was more immediate and humanitarian, despite limited resources. This humanitarian approach was all the more remarkable given the climate of ethnic prejudice that characterised Irish migrants as problematic and undeserving. Without Liverpool's *Select Vestry*'s intervention, even more death and disease would have spread, increasing mortality rates further. Whilst conditions were far from perfect, there is a lot to applaud their work for, especially with such little support from structural leadership or national taxation. The Irish community's response - maintaining cultural identity while building new forms of solidarity - would prove equally remarkable, laying foundations for the vibrant Irish-Liverpool identity that emerged in subsequent decades[147].

[147] For further reading on this, see Donal M MacRaild's *Irish Migrants in Modern Britain, 1750-1922* (1999) and Patrick O'Mara's *The Irish in Liverpool: A Social History* (2005)

PRE-EMBARKATION PROCESS AT LIVERPOOL

> Of all the seaports in the world, Liverpool most abounds in all the variety of land sharks, land rats and other vermin which makes the helpless mariner their prey. In the shape of landlords, barkeepers, clothiers, crimps and boarding house lodgers, the land sharks devour him limb by limb.
>
> Herman Melville, *Redburn: His First Voyage*, 1849

The above passage refers to mariners, but Professor Oliver MacDonagh (b.1924-d.2002)[148] argues that it can equally be applied to migrants. Melville visited Liverpool in 1839 as a merchant sailor and wrote a fictional account of his experiences in *Redburn His First Voyage* a decade later. *Redburn* is described by MacDonagh as being a dramatic and remarkably accurate account of conditions in Liverpool and on the North Atlantic emigrant ships in the mid-nineteenth century.

Outlined below is a summary of McDonagh's findings, which are supported by papers from the Colonial Office and House of Commons Select Committee reports. As noted elsewhere, ships used for passenger traffic were primarily cargo ships repurposed for passenger travel. Passengers took second place to the stowing of cargo and were not allowed to board until the last minute, which frequently resulted in scenes of wild confusion. Because of the uncertainty of embarkation time, emigrants were required to stay – on average – in dockside lodgings for two nights. The accommodation was – in MacDonagh's words – "invariably foul". Travellers were packed together on straw, often on cellar floors. MacDonagh is in no doubt that plenty of epidemics that ravaged those at sea had their origins here.

Leading scholar James S Donnelly Jr (b.1943-d.–) states Irish migrants stopping temporarily at Liverpool had to contend with a host of tricksters determined to relieve them of their money[149].

[148] MacDonagh, O. (1961). *A Pattern of Government Growth: The Passenger Acts and their Enforcement*. MacGibbon and Kee

[149] Biography of James S Donnelly **https://history.wisc.edu/people/donnelly-james** accessed 26 Feb 2025

A Select Committee identified runners employed by shipping agents as the main culprits in this process. The runners met the arriving migrants from Ireland at the dockside and frequently won their confidence, which led them into a system of exploitation and expropriation. Leading migrants to shops, lodging houses and liquor shops would provide the runners with a commission from each outlet.

Passenger payment and booking systems were subject to widespread abuse and fraud. Liverpool shipping agents had representatives in country towns throughout Ireland. On payment of a deposit, prospective passengers could book a sailing to Liverpool from an Irish port and pre-book a transatlantic sailing, to be paid for on arrival in Liverpool.

In an 1851 House of Commons select committee set up to review *The Passenger Acts*, Sir George Stephen QC (b.1794-d.1879, an anti-slavery campaigner and legal figure) reported to the committee that receiving prepaid fares and deposits under false pretences was the most common means of defrauding emigrants during this period and was on the increase with migrants leaving from North America and Australia. By 1854 such discussions were ongoing, where the experiences of migrants came under similar scrutiny[150].

Contemporary scholar Lewis Darwen (b. unknown-d.–)[151] writes that people move during famine to escape starvation, disease and death. In 1847, these conditions led to what Ciaran O'Murchadha calls 'The Panicked Flood' with people from all social strata taking flight from Ireland. Continuing throughout that winter, Ireland's ports of embarkation mirrored the chaotic situation at Liverpool.

[150] *Hansard* discussion from 1854 referring to the 1851 Select Committee **https://hansard.parliament.uk/Commons/1854-03-02/debates/f5a38f43-4a74-4261-aea5-c38ae320c7ed/EmigrantShips?highlight=1851%20select%20committee%20passenger%20act#contribution-d2ab6e80-252c-4326-a7b8-3cae5c70792a** accessed 11 Mar 2025

[151] Lewis Darwen's ***Loughborough University*** biography **https://lboro.academia.edu/LewisDarwen** accessed 26 Feb 2025 and Ciaran O'Murchadha: *The Panicked Flood: Emigration and the Great Hunger* **https://www.rte.ie/history/post-famine/2020/0903/1163045-the-panicked-flood-emigration-and-the-great-famine** accessed 18 Jun 2025

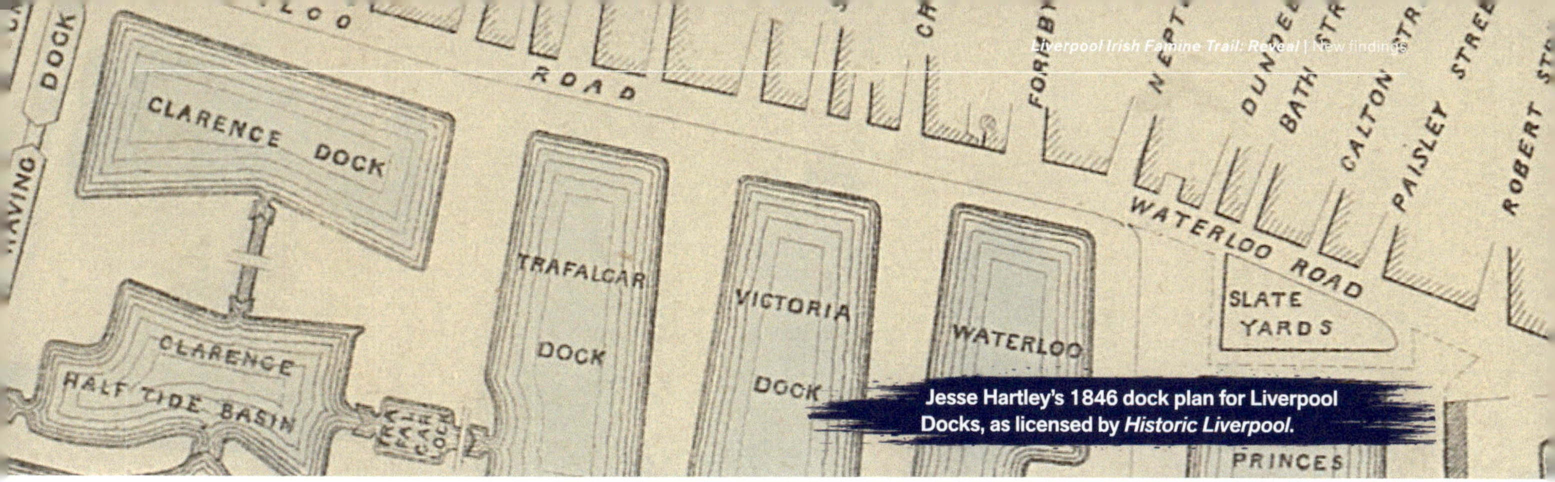

Jesse Hartley's 1846 dock plan for Liverpool Docks, as licensed by *Historic Liverpool*.

The exploitation of large numbers of Irish migrants was the result of what Sir James Stephen (b.1789-d.1859), permanent under-secretary at the Colonial Office, referred to as "lying and credulity". Many of the migrants were in a poor state of health and probably traumatised. It is highly unlikely that any of the travellers had ever been outside Ireland before and a high proportion, particularly from the western counties, did not speak English.

One device — used as part of 1835 *The Passenger Act* to provide greater order and regulation to the often-chaotic process of securing passage across the Atlantic — was to award migrants one shilling per day during a delayed embarkation. This procedure was difficult to enforce because the contract between passengers and shipping agents was legally difficult to define. In 1845, 20 shillings made up £1. In today's money a shilling is the equivalent of just over £5 based on inflation since 1845.

Passengers often knew little of their legal rights and were generally anxious to board as soon as possible. Delays in Liverpool during legal proceedings were simply unaffordable to most and people "just wanted to have done with preliminaries" and commence embarkation.

On his 1833 appointment as Emigration Officer Lieutenant Robert Low RN (b.-unknown-d. unknown) had immediately begun to grapple with "the cruel and complex system of deception" that characterised much of the pre-embarkation process at Liverpool[152].

Low's contact with the brokers ***J&W Robinson*** is described in other contributions later in this book, but echo the issues raised by the 1851 Select Committee. Low's team prosecuted another broker, ***PW Byrnes***, charged with assault of a migrant; he also prosecuted two of ***PW Byrnes***' runners for receiving money under false pretences from intending passengers. However, Low continued to encounter stern opposition from shipping brokers, agents and sometimes owners for years. Oliver MacDonagh is unsparing in his description of these individuals, referring to them as rough unscrupulous men. Embarkation procedures did not become fully regulated until 1855.

In summary, the pre-embarkation process at Liverpool was systemically and systematically corrupt, with individuals at all levels — and at all stages — attempting to defraud and steal from migrants awaiting sailing dates to North America. This caused intolerable hardship for a group that was already severely distressed and unable to comprehend the bewildering and deceitful proceedings that appeared to be the norm on arrival at the port.

Facts compiled by *History Research Group* researcher Kieran Daly.

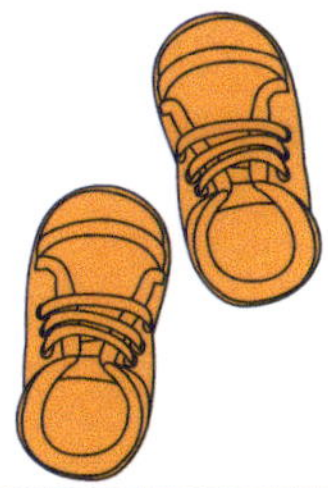

[152] Wainright, MD (1951) *Agencies for the Promotion or Facilitation of Emigration from England to the United States of America*, 1815-1861 **https://repository.royalholloway.ac.uk/file/6156f646-7c44-4521-97bd-5345af378b4c/1/10097845.pdf** accessed 26 Feb 2025

TIME AND TIDE WAITS FOR NO MAN

During the decade spanning 1845-55, it is estimated that over two-million people left Ireland to escape The Great Hunger. The social and economic status of people leaving the country prior to An Gorta Mór was varied, including seasonal workers, artisans, professionals, individuals and families from both the middle and lower social classes. However, by the late 1840s most people leaving were from the poorer rungs of society and included evicted tenants, assisted emigrants and paupers.

As varied as those who travelled, were the means by which travel was achieved. They included self-paid travel; tickets sent by friends or family who had previously emigrated; assisted migration by estate landlords and — in the case of some desperate people — committing crimes to be transported to the colonies.

Fares for travel to the United States of America ranged between £2-£5 (£197-£493 today) for steerage and £12-£15 (£1,185-£1,546) for cabin passengers. According to William Henry Ricketts Curtler (b.1862-d.1925) in *A Short History of English Agriculture*[153] an annual labourer's wage in England in 1850 was just £20. A tenant farmer would be on far less, meaning such costs would be a burden that could not be met.

The transatlantic voyage took about six to seven weeks. The cheapest fares tended to be for Canadian ships as Britain and Canada were intrinsically linked after 1763, following The Seven Years War and *Treaty of Paris* (see our timeline in chapter 2). Canadian ships were less regulated than their American counterparts, which were subjected to stricter regulation following the United States *Passenger Acts* of 1847[154]. If the duration of time at sea was extended, for example due to weather conditions or inept steering, the consequences could be catastrophic.

[153] ***Project Gutenberg*** (2005). *A Short History of English Agriculture by W. H. R. Curtler.* [online] Project Gutenberg. Available at: **https://www.gutenberg.org/ebooks/16594** accessed 26 Feb 2025 the book can also be found in the ***Wellcome Collection*** **https://wellcomecollection.org /works/g4qaep54/items?canvas=2** accessed 6 Mar 2025

[154] MacDonagh, O. (1961). *A Pattern of Government Growth: The Passenger Acts and their Enforcement.* MacGibbon and Kee

The Virginius, which sailed from Liverpool to Quebec in the summer of 1847, spent 63-days at sea after steering off course. This additional time at sea contributed to the deaths of 158 (34%) of its 467 passengers on the voyage[155].

During a voyage, British ships were only required to supply six pints of water per person per day. However, this was not always delivered, especially if supplies were low due to an extended crossing. Most passengers brought their own food for the journey. Assisted emigrants had their food supplied by their landlord. The types of food stuff that the passengers brought with them can be seen in the records from the Strokestown Estate (Roscommon, Ireland) which showed that assisted tenants were given the rations for their voyage of 6lb sugar, one dozen herrings, 10-ounces tea/coffee, 1.5-pounds of soap, 8-pounds of rice, 1 pint of vinegar, 14-pounds of oatmeal, pepper and salt.

In practice this means 28.6lbs (12.9kgs) per person for their onward journey. Even if a sailing only took four -weeks this is just a pound of low nutritional value food per day (plus half a herring); not enough to sustain good health. It is also a burden to carry when you are emaciated and thirsty. Imagine carrying 13-kilos of anything, after two years of hunger. At the Festival we imagine kilo sugar bags to help us imagine the prospect.

Ships undertaking transatlantic crossings during the period were not usually passenger ships. They were cargo ships (timber, cotton, sugar) that took passengers when space would allow or were repurposed for their return journey. However, during An Gorta Mór shipping companies — keen to cash in on the surge in migrant travel — began to redesign the ships to take greater numbers of passengers. Two distinct levels of accommodation — cabin or steerage — could be bought. Most travellers fleeing hunger would have been in steerage. Overcrowding was an issue on ships as demand for travel surged and agents and shipping companies took extra passengers to maximise their profits.

[155] The ***National Famine Way*** states *The Virginius* spent 63-days at sea **https://nationalfamineway.ie/did-you-know-20-interesting -facts-relating-to-the-national-famine-way** accessed 5 Mar 2025

This, teamed with the lack of hygiene on the ships, contributed to the spread of diseases among passengers. The most common diseases were typhus, smallpox, cholera and dysentery. Infants and the elderly were the most vulnerable to disease and it is within these groups that higher numbers of fatalities were recorded on the voyages. The health conditions on ships such as *The Virginius*, *The Naomi* and *Erin Queen* (boats that sailed Strokestown's 1,490 to Canada) were one of the key reasons why death numbers surged during the transatlantic crossings of 1847. Another determining factor in the outcomes of transatlantic travel was the port from which emigrants travelled. Cork and Liverpool were two of the busiest and most dangerous ports for to sail from during this period.

CONTEXTUALISING TRANSATLANTIC TRAVEL DURING THE 19TH CENTURY

Historian C. McMahon in his book *The Coffin Ship: Life and Death at Sea during the Great Irish Famine*[156], discusses how mortality rates were, in reality, lower than previously received numbers. His research shows that between 1845 and 1855, Irish emigrant mortality rates were on par with those of other European seafarers (between 1-2.5%). McMahon states that 'coffin ships' and the high rates of emigrant mortality during 1845-1855, refer to one route (Canada) in one year (1847). McMahon's re-examination of data and statistics does not detract from the horrific conditions and deaths suffered on ships, such as *The Virginius* and *Avon* (both of which lost over 50% of their passengers during their crossing that year), but it does contextualise these ships and their general conditions within shipping and sailing of the time. It should be noted that his research dates extend to 1855, after An Gorta Mór's heaviest casualties, which may lower the averages slightly.

Facts compiled by *History Research Group* researcher Catherine Leen.

[156] McMahon, C.T. (2023). *Revisiting the Coffin Ships: emigrant mortality during the Famine www.rte.ie* [online] Available at: **https://www.rte.ie/history/the-great-irish-famine/2023/1205/1420245-revisiting-the-coffin-ships-emigrant-mortality-during-the-famine** accessed 26 Feb 2025

SHIPPING AND STROKESTOWN

Having made deep connections with the ***National Famine Museum*** and ***National Famine Way*** at Strokestown in Ireland, we wanted to undertake additional research into the sailing connections between our locations. Where possible, we invite readers to read this section in conjunction with chapter 7.

THE PASSENGER ACTS

In his 1961 book, *A Pattern of Government Growth, 1800-1860: The Passenger Acts and Their Enforcement*, Professor Oliver McDonagh attempted to outline the effects of *The Passenger Acts* legislation in the nineteenth century.

Various acts, introduced from 1803 onwards, aimed to bring regulation — and what we would now refer to as health and safety processes — into the market for passengers on transatlantic voyages.

As part of the 1828 version of the act, Lieutenant Robert Low RN was appointed as Emigration Officer for Liverpool's port in 1833. This chapter attempts to outline Lieutenant Low's interaction with the ship brokering firm of ***J&W Robinson*** operated by brothers James and William Robinson. It will consider the activities of ***J&W Robinson*** in Liverpool and the firm's links with Ireland based in research undertaken in 2024. In particular, there is an examination of the brokers' role in arranging the passage to Quebec of assisted migrants from Strokestown, County Roscommon in 1847.

The first vessel Lieutenant Low became concerned about was *The General Brown*. The ship held forty-four passengers in a living space of 250 square feet, five-feet seven-inches (5'7" or 170cm) high. This space was full of luggage and sea stock with no partition to divide the passenger area and the cargo. *The General Brown* was allowed to sail despite Low's protestations.

The Walk of the Bronze Shoes **walkers arrive on *The Jeanie Johnston*, a replica coffin ship, docked at Customs House Quay in Dublin's docklands, 25 May 2024 (courtesy of Dave Redmond).**

Low's second concern was for the fitness of *The Cumberland*, which was grossly overloaded and unseaworthy. Because of these concerns he withheld a certificate of clearance to prevent the vessel from sailing. ***J&W Robinson*** refused to provide an alternative passage and ultimately Low was compelled to let *The Cumberland* sail, no doubt under duress from the passengers and crew. A fortnight later the ship returned having thrown all her cargo overboard because of its poor seaworthiness. ***J&W Robinson*** remained indifferent to the plight of *The Cumberland*'s passengers. There followed a public outcry. Under sufferance, ***J&W Robinson*** arranged another ship for the passengers of *The Cumberland* but this, in turn, foundered during the voyage and had to return to Liverpool. The Robinsons, MacDonagh notes, simply washed their hands of the affair.

In 1835 despite attempts by Lieutenant Low to prevent its departure, *The Henry* was dispatched in a state of disrepair, again by ***J&W Robinson*** from Liverpool. The ship, like *The Cumberland*, foundered and its passengers spent thirty-one days in open boats before being returned to Liverpool. Once more the Robinsons refused to accept any responsibility for these events.

Lieutenant Low's poor opinion of identifiable Liverpool shipping brokers led him to divide them into "the sheep and the goats". Among the goats were ***PW Byrnes & Co***, ***Beckett & Co***, ***Grimshaw***'s, ***Walkinshaws*** and ***J&W Robinson***.

JAMES AND WILLIAM ROBINSON

The brothers appear to have operated as brokers and agents in Liverpool for years. They traded under different guises including ***Robinson Brothers, James and William Robinson***, ***Messrs Robinson and Co*** and ***J&W Robinson***. They appear in ***Gore's*** trade directories[157] for Liverpool throughout the 1830s and 1840s, under slightly different names — including James and William Robinson, Robinson, James and William, Robinson J and W — and with different job titles ('Merchants and Ship Brokers', 'Ship Owners', 'Agents and Passengers', 'Merchants', 'general agents' and 'commission').

[157] ***British Online Archives*** reference to ***Gore's*** Liverpool Directory **https://britishonlinearchives.com/collections/8/volumes/5/gores-liverpool-directory** accessed 26 Feb 2025

Notably, their business address moves erratically through the trade directories trading from Baltic Buildings, 13 Redcross Street; Emigration Office, 1 Neptune Street; Great Howard Street; Cleveland Street, Birkenhead; 16 Goree Piazza; 46 and 48 Waterloo Road. This may have been a common business practice at the time or, more likely, a means to divert attention away from a poor professional reputation.

The Neptune Street address reoccurs in other sources; in the first census of 1841 the brothers are reported as living there. It remains as their address on the electoral roll in 1845, where the property is noted as a 'counting house and house', indicating that it was a business and home (or 'live-work space' as we'd call it now). It is not known if this was an official Emigration Office, as recorded in ***Gore's***. Located in the north of the city close to Clarence and Waterloo docks, it would have been close to embarkation points for Irish migrants.

Liverpool also had a growing market in domestic steam passages to north Wales. The brothers were not agents for this type of conveyance, perhaps preferring the more lucrative international market. Despite their interactions with staff from the Port of Liverpool, the Robinson brothers may have been viewed very differently in Ireland.

In ***The Belfast Commercial Chronicle*** dated 13 March 1833 (accessed via ***Documenting Ireland: Parliament, People and Migration*** also known as ***DIPPAM***) there was a 'notice to emigrants' pointing out that the United States British and British American Shipping companies were "... aware of passengers being conned by bogus shipping agents, so the company will appoint named agents in each province in Ireland and will continue to work with Messrs Robinsons Brothers", suggesting they were trusted domestically.

In ***The Enniskillen Chronicle*** dated 27 February 1834, under 'Shipping Advertisements' is a listing for the Robinson brothers. They are based in Goree Piazza and are listed as agents, inviting people to contact them regarding terms of passage, with ships regularly sailing to New York, Philadelphia, Baltimore, New Orleans, Quebec and Montreal (again, accessed via ***DIPPAM***).

ARRANGEMENTS WITH STROKESTOWN

The firm of ***J&W Robinson*** were engaged as passenger agents by Major Denis Mahon, landlord of the Strokestown, by his land agent John Ross Mahon (b.1818-d.1877, Denis's cousin)[158] who negotiated and facilitated the passage of the 1,490 migrants from Liverpool to Quebec in May-June 1847. Correspondence between the estate and ***J&W Robinson*** investigated the following: the means of emigration; the best port to use; whether cheapest passage was from Liverpool or an Irish port and the mode to use (either charter or transit ship).

Peter Duffy (b.1969-d.—)[159] states that it is not clear if Major Mahon knew of ***J&W Robinsons***' reputation. He pointedly explains that certain Liverpool shipping agents were seen as swindlers at the time. ***J&W Robinson***, Duffy further notes, "offered the lowest fares to the cheapest destination, Quebec in British North America".

Ciarán Reilly (b.1988-d.—) writes that Mahon travelled to Liverpool to discuss "...our plan for emigration"[160]. A Memorandum of Agreement was signed on 7 May for emigration and a fixed salary to agents J[ohn] and W[illiam] Robinson. Days later money was lodged with the Robinsons' bankers. Letters continue between the parties, discussing numbers and costs at each stage of the journey, including stores and provisions.

Arrangements were made for the passage of 800 'statute adults' at £3.12 per person with children under fourteen travelling at half price. Converted into total values, the figures are substantial (see next page).

[158] ***National Library of Ireland*** listing for John Ross Mahon **https://catalogue.nli.ie/Record/tls000841471** accessed 11 Mar 2025

[159] Duffy, P. (2008). *The Killing of Major Denis Mahon: A Mystery of old Ireland.* New York, USA: ***Harper***, p.111

[160] Reilly, C. (2014). *Strokestown and the Great Irish Famine.* ***Four Courts Press***, p.67

The mast of the ***The Jeanie Johnston***, a replica coffin ship, docked at Customs House Quay in Dublin's docklands, May 2024 (courtesy of Dave Redmond).

Strokestown transfer fees	**People**	**d per person (240d per £)**	**Total in £s (1847)**	***BoE**** **inflation calculator value - 1847 to Jan 2025**
				* *Bank of England*
Adults	800	732	£2,440	£214,529
Children	690	366	£1,052	£92,494
£ for assisted passage	**1490**		**£3,492**	**£307,023**

PREPARATIONS FOR TRAVEL

America's 1819 *The Manifest of Immigrants* or *Steerage Act*[161] decreed that passengers — like the Strokestown migrants — be supplied with bread, flour, oatmeal along with water and cooking fuel. According to John Ross Mahon, Major Mahon's land agent, the Strokestown cohort should also have received a supply of sugar, tea and coffee in addition to their other rations.

There remains scepticism that these provisions were supplied. An investigation by the US senate found that some shipping agents displayed a loaf of bread in their offices to delude the poor that they would be fed at sea (Reilly). Oliver McDonagh found that agents very often supplied foul inedible bread (MacDonagh, page 99).

Prior to embarkation, the Strokestown migrants were housed in dockside lodging houses arranged by ***J&W Robinson***. These lodgings were usually of inadequate quality, with masses of people required to stay in overcrowded accommodation.

Typhus — a disease spread by person-to-person contact — was rife in Liverpool at this time. The overcrowded conditions in which people were housed left an already vulnerable group extremely susceptible to a disease, which was highly infectious and for which they had ill-prepared resilience for. A proportion of the Mahon tenants had contracted typhus before they left Liverpool. Contemporaneous reports suggest that dead passengers were thrown overboard in the Mersey estuary as ships set sail from Liverpool (Reilly, 2014).

[161] America's 1819 *The Manifest of Immigrants Act* **https://maint.loc.gov/law/help/statutes-at-large/15th-congress/session-2/c15s2ch46.pdf** accessed 5 Mar 2025

THE LIVERPOOL-QUEBEC ROUTE

During An Gorta Mór, particularly 1847, the Liverpool-Quebec route was the most lethal passage, with death rates of up to 20% on voyages([162], page 5). These catastrophic outcomes were due to a combination of factors:

- microbial regimes (disease) in port cities like Liverpool
- general poor mental- and physical- health of migrants and their increased susceptibility to diseases like typhus in ports
- poor conditions at sea. Most vessels sailing the Liverpool-Quebec route were repurposed cargo ships, which mainly carried timber from the Canadian forests. Shipowners focused on getting the greatest possible numbers of passengers on board to maximise profit. This meant that the cramped disease-ridden environment in Liverpool lodging houses was replicated on board ship with terrible consequences
- the seaworthiness and preparedness of ships. With ***J&W Robinson***'s record of routinely flouting regulations and requirements it is difficult to have confidence — in this case — in their willingness to provide ships that were properly equipped and maintained to withstand the rigours of a five-week voyage to Canada.

On 22 May, *The Virginius* left Liverpool with 476 passengers. It was recorded that 158 passengers died during the voyage[163] with a further 19 passing whilst at anchor, with another 90 dying on their arrival at Grosse Île. This was followed by *Erin's Queen* which departed on 1 June with a smaller number, around 30 to 40.

Mahon sought competitive terms from other agents. However, further arrangements were later made with the Robinsons, who were paid £729 13 shillings and 4d for passage on *The Naomi* and *The John Munn*. Using the ***Bank of England***'s inflation calculator, this would be a cost of £75,122 in January 2025. On 15 June 334 Strokestown migrants boarded *The Naomi.* During the voyage 196 of the total 421 passengers died. *The John Munn* departed on 16 June with a smaller group. According to Reilly, ***J&W Robinson*** were required to refund Major Mahon for overcharging for passengers on *The John Munn* and *The Virginius* (Reilly, page 67).

Facts compiled by *History Research Group* researchers Vicki Caren and Kieran Daly.

[162] McMahon, C.T. (2023). *Revisiting the Coffin Ships: emigrant mortality during the Famine. www.rte.ie.* [online] Available at: **https://www.rte.ie/history/the-great-irish-famine/2023/1205/1420245-revisiting-the-coffin-ships-emigrant-mortality-during-the-famine** accessed 26 Feb 2025

[163] ***National Famine Way*** figures for deaths on *The Virginius* and *The Naomi* **https://nationalfamineway.ie/about-the-1490/the-story-of-the-1490** accessed 26 Feb 2025

NAMES AND NUMBERS

Not everyone who made it to Liverpool from Ireland made 'it'. Tens of thousands of people died within the seven-years of An Gorta Mór and more suffered ill health or trauma for the rest of their lives. How Liverpool dealt with this in real terms was practical, though often unceremonious. Record keeping takes resources, will and maintenance. Managing the high volume of dead people often involved pit graves. Sometimes those mass burials were not recorded, or their records have been lost through the annals of complex histories. Returning names to every person who died may not be possible, but we will continue to identify all we can. The following section aims to look at how Liverpool managed this complicated and — no doubt — traumatic time.

In 1847 there were 7,219 burials across two sites[164]. These individuals were placed in ***St Mary's Cemetery*** and ***St Martin-in-the-Fields Church***. The figure includes paupers and non-paupers; An Gorta Mór deaths and all others. The highest death rates associated with The Great Hunger were in the wards of Vauxhall (where Lace Street is located), Scotland Road and Exchange. 3,176 of the 7,219 were buried between mid-March and mid-July 1847.

In the 1990s, the ***Liverpool Great Hunger Commemoration Committee*** was aware of 2,600 pauper burials at ***St Mary's Cemetery***, situated near Mulberry Street (Liverpool) and the marked it accordingly with a plaque. Until 2024, it had been assumed that the identity of the individuals interred at ***St Mary's*** was not available.

A discovery by the *Liverpool Irish Famine Trail*'s *History Research Group* revealed that the burial records for ***St Mary's Cemetery*** were on microfilm at *Liverpool Central Library* where they had been deposited by Liverpool's then Rector in March 2000. They had previously been in the custody of the ***Liverpool Parish Church: Our Lady and St Nicholas*** (The Old Churchyard, Liverpool L2 8TZ)[165].

Because of the magnitude of the record, our researchers decided to aim for an initial snapshot review. A reel of microfilm covering the period 17 March to 15 July 1847 was chosen. It gradually became evident that a list of all the paupers who were buried at ***St Mary's Cemetery*** were accounted for in a printed booklet used during The Great Hunger Commemoration Service at ***St Anthony's Roman Catholic Church*** (Scotland Road, Liverpool L5 5BD)[166] held on Friday 3 October 1997. This ceremony had been undertaken in commemoration of the sesquicentennial (150th) anniversary of An Gorta Mór and a pamphlet was produced. This pamphlet was reprinted by ***Newsham Press*** in 2004-5.

ST MARY'S CEMETERY

St Mary's Cemetery was opened in 1806 and final burial records end on 3 October 1848. The cemetery was laid out as a public garden in 1882 and in 1949 all bodies previously buried there were disinterred to make room for a new wing of the ***Myrtle Street Children's Hospital***. The remains of those buried in ***St Mary's Cemetery*** were moved and reinterred at ***Walton Park Cemetery*** (27 Highfield Road, Walton, Liverpool L9 1AS). To date we have not located any official record as to the whereabouts of those who were reinterred in ***Walton Park Cemetery***. Whilst all of those buried at ***St Mary's Cemetery*** are assumed to be British subjects (being pre-Irish independence), we do not *know* their ethnicity (e.g., white-English, white-Irish, Black-Irish) from the burial record.

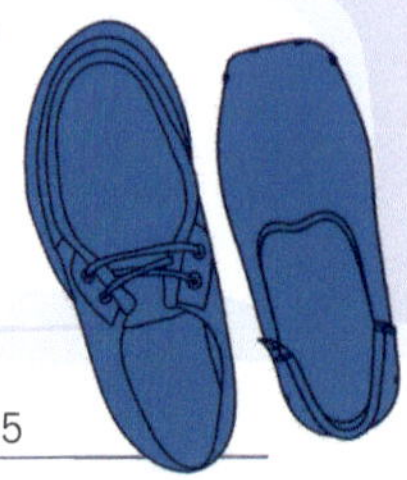

[164] As referenced in the list of names cited in Williams, T.A. and Neal, F. (2004). *Great Hunger Commemoration Service:* ***St Anthony's Church*** *Liverpool, 3 October 1997.* ***Newsham Press Ltd***

[165] ***Liverpool Parish Church: Our Lady and St Nicolas*** website **https://livpc.co.uk** accessed 25 Feb 2025

[166] ***St Anthony's Roman Catholic Church*** website **https://stanthonyscotlandroad.wordpress.com** accessed 25 Feb 2025

Today, we would regard an all-white assumption as an oversimplification of genetics and ethnographies. Understanding Ireland's 1840s racial and ethnic composition means people of non-white ethnic backgrounds will have come to or through Liverpool, though as the percentage of Ireland's population would have been low, we can assume the individual figure would be low. Without better evidence it is impossible to put an actual figure on.

Of the total of 7,219 burials in 1847 5,237 – or 73% – were Catholic, but this is not isolated from the idea of pauperism. The 1997 commemoration booklet advises that those defined as Catholic be interpreted as Irish, too. As with assuming white-Britishness above, this would be inadvisable for today's populations, being an over-generalisation. Nevertheless, our desire is to look at mortality numbers rather than faith accounting, and therefore we are presenting the information as it is provided.

LACE STREET

Although typhus was present in Liverpool prior to Ireland's mass migrations, the incoming Irish were blamed for the scale and intensity of the problem. Greg Quiery explains the endemic problems in Lace Street by quoting Professor Frank Neal who noted that "the area was almost entirely Irish and contained many cheap lodging houses, prime breeding grounds for disease". Quiery writes that the legacy of An Gorta Mór in Liverpool was poverty and deprivation with accompanying poor housing and sanitation. These multiple problems created great hardship, and it was many years before they were resolved.

During initial examinations, it became apparent that clusters of deaths were being recorded for the Lace Street area of Vauxhall (an inner-city district, north of Liverpool's city centre), known to have homed many Irish people in the 1840s. Tony Birtill (b.1954-d.2021)[167] writes that in 1847 Lace Street was home to 89 families. Leading off the street were 25 courts, which housed another 90 families.

The total population of the street and its adjoining courts was 1,110. Incidentally, Birtill's work suggests that 85% of people in Lace Street were Irish speaking, which supports the view that those buried from Lace Street were overwhelmingly Irish people.

The following table outlines the number of deaths at Lace Street and the number of burials at ***St Mary's Cemetery*** between 17 March and 15 July 1847, as identified from the test microfilm.

	Dates	**Lace St**	**St Mary's**
1847	17-31 March	14	251
	April	67	499
	May	54	1,064
	June	30	955
	1-15 July	13	407
=	**120 days**	**178**	**3,176**

The death rates in Lace Street are shocking by today's standards. 178 of 1,110 represents a death rate of 16% over an area less than 100-metres long. Over 120 days (the duration between 17 March and 15 July 1847) this tiny community lost one of its members every 16-hours.

The availability of a microfilm record of those buried at ***St Mary's Cemetery*** is an opportunity to improve our knowledge of The Great Famine in Liverpool. Such a valuable primary source will be of great assistance to professional and amateur historians. Importantly this new resource will allow researchers to engage with the number of deaths *and* the identities of those who suffered most grievously in 1847. It may also allow us to reappraise our understanding of the Mulberry Street plaque, which states "Near this place in 1847, some 2,600 destitute Irish Famine migrants were buried in unmarked pauper graves", giving names to each of them.

Facts compiled by *History Research Group* researcher Kieran Daly.

[167] Tony Birtill obituary in ***The Guardian*** **https://www.theguardian.com/education/2022/jan/18/tony-birtill-obituary** accessed 25 Feb 2025

9/ SHARED STORIES: A SOLEMN AND INTERLOCKING HISTORY

In previous sections, readers will have seen described how Irish landlord Major Denis Mahon arranged the assisted emigration of 1,490 tenants from his Strokestown estate (County Roscommon, Ireland). These tenants walked to Dublin, sailed to Liverpool, and continued by ship to Canada. Had Mahon's agents directed them to Sligo, just 70km/44miles north, their fates might have been entirely different. While we cannot know these alternate outcomes, understanding the actual historical events remains crucial. The decisions made in 1847 created lasting connections between these three locations — Strokestown, Liverpool, and Canada— and laid the foundation for countless Irish diaspora family histories that continue to this day.

The timeline of these actions, interlocked with the wider story of the mass migrations, politics and policies that informed the era is provided in chapter 2 of this book. This chapter identifies how links between our locations have been connected to become the foundation of the ***Global Irish Famine Way***.

THE NATIONAL FAMINE WAY'S BEGINNINGS

The Palladian style house at Strokestown — the heart of the Strokestown Estate — was originally built in the 1740s. At its height, had roughly 27,000 acres to its name. The remaining estate of 300 acres was purchased by ***Westward Garage Group*** [168] in 1979, which sought additional grounds for its logistics business. Under the custodianship of Jim Callery (b.1934-d.—, ***Westward***'s owner), and his daughter Caroilin (b. unknown-d.—), Strokestown Estate has become what is today after Callery also purchased the entire contents of the house containing 300-years of family history. ***The National Irish Famine Museum*** was opened in 1994 in the stable wing of Strokestown Park House, where an archive comprising of 55,000+ documents has become renowned as one of the most important An Gorta Mór archives in existence.

[168] Jim Callery's ***Westward Scania Group*** obtained Strokestown Park in 1979 **https://www.westwardscania.ie/who-we-are** accessed 26 Feb 2025

The archive is unique in both its completeness, but also in its existence at all. As The Great Hunger's trials and tribulations became more deeply understood, large amounts of associated personal archives were destroyed to protect peoples' reputations. As Frank Harte (b.1933-d.2005) said "those in power write the history, those who suffer write the songs. Given our history, we have an awful lot of songs"[169]. Not only this, but the 1922 ***Four Courts*** fire means Ireland's archives are themselves incomplete (though much has been done to restore these in recent years).

In 2014, assisted emigration ship lists were found within a batch of Major Denis Mahon's documents allowing the Strokestown team to reclaim the names of the majority of 1,490 souls from the depths of time. This returned family names to diaspora communities and offered a little dignity to those that had perished and been erased by time.

In 2015, a group of five Strokestown natives decided to follow in the footsteps of the 1,490's long trek from Strokestown to Dublin's docks, garnering local, national and international attention, including coverage on the Irish television's national news and in US publications.

On the second day of the 2015 walk, news reached the group of a shipwreck off the Italian Coast, with an estimated loss of hundreds of lives. The tragedy resulted in over 700 migrants killed in the disaster[170]. Knowing that many of Strokestown's tenants had met a similar watery grave and that the 1,490's past was someone else's present was sobering.

[169] ***An Phoblacht*** obituary for Frank Harte **https://www.anphoblacht.com/contents/13805** accessed 11 Mar 2025

[170] ***The Guardian*** report of a modern shipping disaster **https://www.theguardian.com/world/2015/apr/20/italy-pm-matteo-renzi-migrant-shipwreck-crisis-srebrenica-massacre** and ***BBC*** report of the wreck being raised **https://www.bbc.co.uk/news/world-europe-36278529**, both accessed on 26 Feb 2025

After the 2015 walk Strokestown Estate's owners were contacted by communities and official bodies about developing a permanent trail.

Reminiscent of America's ***National Park Service***'s *Trail of Tears* – commemorating the displacement of the First Nations communities[171] – or the ***Camino de Santigo*** (***Way of St James***)[172], the idea of the ***National Famine Way*** was born.

2017 saw a second re-enactment of the walk with a larger group including several international experts on An Gorta Mór.

Improved pathways and signage were completed and on 30 May 2019 the ***National Famine Way***, as we know it today, was launched. It had become a 165km long-distance accredited trail. A series of 30+ pairs of bronze shoes, cast from originals found on the Strokestown Estate, were used as trail markers for Ireland's ***National Famine Way***.

A 2019 re-enactment walk was delivered, involving a group from ***New Horizons***[173], a voluntary organisation collaborating with migrant communities in the locale. The party engaged deeply with community groups and schools as they walked. Over 1,000 people joined in across the six days, with daily videos reaching up to 10,000 views.

Today, people can 'apply for a passport', checking off all the sites on the ***National Famine Way***, travelling in the name of one of the 1,490's identified families, receiving completion stamps along the way. It can be undertaken in full or in parts, officially or informally. A Strokestown-led walk is organised as demand, anniversaries and resources permit. The next anticipated walk will be held in conjunction with their *Famine Summer School* in 2027.

The Strokestown Estate mansion house, from which Major Mahon ran his operations. The connected Museum marks the beginning of the ***National Famine Way***.

[171] USA's ***National Park Service***'s *Trail of Tears* information pages **https://www.nps.gov/trte/index.htm** accessed 26 Feb 2025

[172] ***Follow the Camino*** website, with routes and information on its history **https://followthecamino.com/en/camino-de-santiago-routes/?utm_source=google&utm_medium=organic&utm_campaign=undefined** accessed 26 Feb 2025

[173] ***New Horizons Athlone*** website **https://newhorizonathlone.org** accessed 26 Feb 2025

THE WALK OF THE BRONZE SHOES AND THE START OF THE GLOBAL IRISH FAMINE WAY

At the end of 2023, the Festival had a plan of the Trail works we wanted to undertake in 2024, underwritten by a successful ***National Lottery Heritage Fund*** bid. This included creative projects (artworks, digital asset creation, a song commission, research for this book), authoring this book and developing a Trail app. Then, new things happened...

Shortly after returning from the 2023 Christmas break, our Festival team received news from colleagues in Strokestown—particularly Caroilin Callery, who had hosted us during our May 2023 research trip that Dr. Eamonn McKee (b. unknown-d.—), the Irish Ambassador to Canada, was eager to establish connections between Strokestown, Liverpool, and Canada. In subsequent discussions, we learned that Dr. McKee planned to complete the 165km ***National Famine Way*** walk and had commissioned a couple of pairs of replica bronze shoe markers to be placed in Canada and North America. Our team recognised the importance of ensuring Liverpool's inclusion in this international commemoration.

Sometimes work connections come from peculiar places. Sat in a yurt, for a ***Creative Organisations of Liverpool*** Christmas party in December 2022, our Director Emma Smith (b.1978-d.—) met filmmaker Ailsa McQueen (b.1990-d.—). Such is Liverpool's network that this chance meeting led to many more meetings and introductions. Roll-on ***Fréa***'s *Women in Heritage* event in 2024. Emma invited Ailsa, making an introduction to the General Consul, Sarah Mangan. On that same night, all three discuss *The Walk of the Bronze Shoes* and Ailsa says to Emma: "You could make a documentary about that...".

Within a month a comprehensive plan took shape that involved international film-crews, cross-country data-sharing arrangements, campaign plans, ambassador interviews, ***Waterways Ireland*** access and even details like anti-blister socks; a seemingly random collection of activities!

Supported by ***Government of Ireland*** *Strategic Diaspora Funds*, the documentary discussed that night is set for release in 2025. Shot by ***Overshoot Productions***, Ailsa's Liverpool-based company, it will be submitted into international documentary festivals, taking forward the ***Global Irish Famine Way*** message and that of our city's history with An Gorta Mór. It will also (when licensing allows) grace our website and share the impressive work and relationships forged in 2024.

LIVERPOOL, STROKESTOWN AND CANADA: A TRI-PARTISAN STORY AND MEMORIAL

By the end of May, two of our team (Emma Smith and John Maguire (b.1977-d.—)) had completed *The Walk of the Bronze Shoes*, clocking up over a thousand kilometres of training between them. Supported by Greg Quiery (founder of the ***Liverpool Great Hunger Commemoration Committee***) and a 10-15+ strong group of daily walkers, they completed the ***National Famine Way*** carrying a 3kg pair of the bronze shoes between them. Again, with schools, community groups and individuals joining them along the way, over a 1,000 people had walked — in stages — to Dublin.

On reaching the docks, after the Royal Canal meets the River Liffey, the walkers headed past Spencer Dock to Custom House Quay to board ***The Jeanie Johnstone Tall Ship***[174], a replica coffin ship. Looking back to the dock wall, from within the ropes and masts of the ship, was incredibly moving. What would those of the 1,490 that had made it to Dublin have seen? Almost all the people they knew in the world would have been with them, be back at Strokestown or perished on route. There was no one to wave them goodbye. After this tearful and poignant moment of reflection, the group moved to ***EPIC***[175] (Ireland's migration official museum). There were speeches from the lead parties, including the Strokestown and Festival teams, ***Irish Heritage Trust***, Professor Christine Kinealy (b.1956-d.—) of ***Quinnipiac University*** and dignitaries, including Dr Eamonn McKee.

[174] ***The Jeanie Johnston Tall Ship*** website **https://jeaniejohnston.ie** accessed 26 Feb 2025

[175] ***EPIC***'s website **https://epicchq.com** accessed 26 Feb 2025

During the ceremony, the Festival presented the ***Strokestown Estate*** team with a porcelain court-house, representative of the sort of dwelling the 1,490 may have stayed in during their time in 1840s Liverpool. From the offset, the Festival did not want to leave Strokestown without providing a gift, believing enough had been removed from there. Correspondingly, they commissioned local artist Pam Sullivan to create the artwork, a delicate rendering of an ugly building. Pure white — reflecting innocence — porcelain is delicate yet resilient. Pam joined the team on the stage at ***EPIC*** to present the work, which now resides in the reflection room at the ***National Famine Museum***. This presence creates an exchange between locations, rather than a mere absence, just as the shoes will when they are permanently sited. Speaking of exchange — after speeches in Dublin — Caroilin, Eamonn and Emma were sped to Dublin's portal to create an exchange of the shoes with friends in New York City, passing them through a live-virtual portal to Vice-Consul General Gareth Hargadon and Elizabeth Stack, Executive Director of the ***American Irish Historical Society***[176].

After Dublin, the Liverpool team began their journey back with the bronze shoes. Historically, the 1,490 emigrants would have sailed directly from Dublin to Liverpool's ***Mersey Ports***, arriving at Clarence Dock. However, passenger sailing between Dublin and Liverpool was not possible in 2024. The team had to find alternative routes to ensure the shoes followed a path close to that of the original migrants' journey.

As a brief aside to this story: ***The Robinson Brothers*** were the shipping contractors who organised the vessels for the 1,490, working in coordination with Major Mahon's land agent. Part of the compromise the Liverpool team had to make was to sail out of and into Holyhead. In a moment of synchronicity, it was realised that the driver — arranged to transport the team from Liverpool to Holyhead's ferry terminal — was none other than Liverpool born and bred Paul *Robinson* (b.1972-d.—), though it would take further research to uncover any familial line to the original pair of unscrupulous operators.

[176] Dr McKee's recollection of the walk and portal **https://eamonncmckee.com/2024/05** accessed 11 Mar 2025

Meeting at ***Woodside Ferry Terminal***, the team regrouped — with Caroilin Callery and a handful of new day walkers — to bring the shoes to Liverpool via ***Mersey Ports***, just south of Clarence Dock. The group walked the shoes up to the Clarence Dock gates, where words of gratitude were uttered, before setting off to the Liverpool Irish Great Hunger commemoration memorial, almost due south, where more onlookers gathered for a small remembrance tribute.

The team had walked with Ireland's Ambassador to Canada Dr Eamonn McKee, Canada's Ambassador to Ireland Nancy Smyth, members of the ***Strokestown Estate*** and ***National Famine Museum*** and ***Irish Heritage Trust***, schools, politicians, press, a founder of the original ***Liverpool Great Hunger Commemoration Committee***, members of our *History Research Group* and many more. In doing so, they were part of a group of less than 60-people who have undertaken that walk by choice! Furthermore, 15-pairs of shoes made their way to Canadian sites in Grosse Île, St John's Newfoundland, Quebec City, Montreal, Ottawa. Toronto, Niagara, Saint John Partridge Island, Hamilton with other pairs yet to find their final destinations. Collectively, these actions heralded the beginning of the ***Global Irish Famine Way***.

During the ***Liverpool Irish Festival*** that followed, the Festival held a Liverpool Irish Famine memorial event, at ***St Luke's 'Bombed Out' Church*** (site of the Liverpool Irish Great Hunger commemoration memorial sculpture) on 27 October 2024. 85-people took part in a vigil, repeating the Clarence Dock to ***St Luke's*** walk, arriving to 50 singers from the ***Roscommon Solstice Choir***[177] performing.

With over 300 attendees, speeches we offered by Ireland's Ambassador to the UK Martin Faser, Consul General Sarah Mangan, Tomás Ryan (Chair of ***Conradh Na Gaeilge Learpholl***) and Greg Quiery, before the Festival unveiled a new song, dedicated to all people affected by displacement and hunger, *The Ullaloo* (see chapter 11).

[177] ***Roscommon Solstice Choir*** website **https://rsc2013.wixsite.com/solsticechoir13** accessed 26 Feb 2025

Here we reminded people of the ***Global Irish Famine Way,*** reshared the deep-rooted international links between our homes and paid tribute with a minute's silence. The Festival is committed to marking this every year with a memorial event.

Work in Liverpool is ongoing to find the shoes a permanent home. In the meantime, like their An Gorta Mór counterparts, they will find temporary accommodation in the region.

We owe considerable thanks to ***National Lottery Heritage Fund*** and the Consul General, Sarah Mangan, of the *Department of Foreign Affairs and Trade* within ***The Government of Ireland*** for their financial assistance with the above.

STROKESTOWN TODAY

Being almost as wide as Dublin's famous O'Connell Street, Church Street — leading to Strokestown's gothic gates (built by Maurice Mahon, First Baron Hartland (b.1738-d.1819) in the early 1800s) — is 44.5-metres wide, being designed to highlight the Estate's scale and influence. It is the second widest road in the country.

Today, Strokestown has Heritage Town status within Ireland, being one of only 27 carrying the same title. The town sits northwest of Dublin by 143km/89miles, as the crow flies. In the early 1840s Strokestown's population was over 11,000. Today, Strokestown's population is roughly 825. This is primarily to do with the impact of the estate clearances that saw most of the population evicted.

A pretty place to visit there are pleasant pubs and restaurants, hotels and guesthouses. As well as the Estate House, Museum and memorial to the 1,490, the Strokestown Estate has operational gardens and grounds that can be walked around and nearby visitors can enjoy fishing, mountain walks and a ***Heritage and Genealogy Centre***[178], in which you can unearth family histories.

[178] ***Roscommon Heritage and Genealogy Centre*** website **https://www.roscommonroots.com** accessed 26 Feb 2025

A WALKER'S REFLECTION: JOHN MAGUIRE

Thought provoking, poignant and life changing. A rare opportunity — in a speedy modern world — to take a journey in sync with nature's rhythms and to reflect, respect and remember the 1,490 of Strokestown. A chance to honour all those who suffered and passed during An Gorta Mór and highlight the resilience and tenacity of the Irish people and their rich contribution to the Global community.

The stone pillars that flank the entrance to the drive are intimidating. Huge granite sentries inspecting all those who pass. A portal to another world, back in 1847 this would have been the case for this way led to plenty, out of bounds to the locals. This was a place where food was not in short supply and the inhabitants had luxuries far beyond the basic living standards of those who had to bed down on the earth in their turf cottages.

The Strokestown Mansion — the 'Big House' — imposes on first sight.

Now the grounds are a haven for wildlife. The lawn has been left to run wild. Wildflowers have taken over and replaced the once neatly trimmed and precise acres of grass. Nature always finds a way to fight back.

The night before our departure we take the famine soup. It tasted a little like the barley recipe my Irish Nan used to make; cheap ingredients, but filling. The poitín was like a strong mouthwash, one that should be gargled, spat out and not swallowed.

Rest before the beginning of the journey. A stillness invades Strokestown to this day. At night, a blanket of quiet suffocates the town until the sound of heavy goods vehicles start to bomb through the oversized roads in the early hours of the morning.

And so we begin. In An Gorta Mór tenant costume, with my fellow walkers, we were harangued by an overzealous bailiff (a local who has dressed up for this part for several years). He has a look of Charles Dance. The man roars and berates a crowd of people in rags, safe in the knowledge that this is just re-enactment, not real.

A horse and cart are on hand to emphasise the period. The horse, wearing blinkers, takes the opportunity to munch on a nearby oak tree branch and digest all the leaves. His owner stands next to him with a beard that is overgrown and haphazard. I joke that perhaps the mare has helped itself to his hairy features, too. He agrees with good humour tickled by my raw honest comment.

Locals and school children gather to look on at this very unusual Monday morning spectacle. The names of all the 1,490 are read out aloud and each is like a painful pinch down the spine. A number dehumanises but an actual name really hits home the reality. The 'surplus population' were actual real people. Everyone agrees how sad this is, yet people are being forced off the land now in our contemporary times and history repeats itself continually.

The heat today is at 24°C and in the costume it is itchy, uncomfortable and draining. We only have to wear it for thirty minutes or so on the walk out of the town, before being allowed to rip it off, continue, hydrated and with sun cream plastered on any skin to avoid burning.

The old Dublin Road is littered with ghost houses. Cottages and buildings from previous eras left to the elements; roofs caved in, choked to death with ivy. New builds spring up like dolls houses, a picture of what a spacious dream home should look like, yet they look alien in the desolate landscapes.

The burning sun, unusual for Ireland, is so hot the tar is coming off the road as I stamp my foot down, on a winding road through green fields and over trickling streams. The absolute silence is strange to my city ears.

At one point we are forced to stop because a flock of cows have escaped their field and play havoc in a sculpted garden, leaping over the wall, like horses on a steeple chase.

Once the walkers reach the canal, it becomes the one constant that stays with us over the next few days. The backdrop changes from woodland to marsh, fields of ferns, soggy bogs and carved stone hills. The wildlife makes an appearance with swifts, ravens, a woodpecker and a regular visitor we call 'Harry the Heron'. He partakes in a ballad with me, landing in the distance. As I get closer, he flies with grace and elegance into the cotton wool clouds, loops and circles around. A private performance for my eyes before he lands 300-metres ahead. I walk onwards and the gesture is repeated, like he is leading me along the way.

Time dissolves and is broken down into manageable chunks. Walk till a break at 11, or plough on to stop for lunch, away again till the next break. Small drops make the Royal Canal.

Stopping at a cottage (that could have fallen straight off the pages of a 'Rural Ireland' calendar), I take hospitality in the shape of scones, sausage rolls with figs and delicious sandwiches. All with a secret ingredient, layered in care. Two donkeys look on at the strangers. A local lady tells me how her ancestors actually fed the 1,490 at this very spot. I feel like an impostor as I trek in honour of those people. The walking crowd I am with have the modern conveniences of beds, hot water and food at our disposal. They may have experienced snatches of hospitality along the way, but each night would need to fall asleep, camped at the canal side.

Days into the walk, the green landscape and solitude starts to make way for urban build up. Mankind seems to be a stain on the very canvas nature has created. Civilisation makes its mark on the landscape. Its housing infrastructure and branded supermarkets feel like intrusive strangers that are out of place with what we are doing. I want to shout at them to go away and give me back the curtain of foliage, but I guess that would make me look like many other poor souls who haunt the canal pathways in towns and cities, wearing a coat of addiction and all the fall out that comes with it.

The gates at Strokestown.

On the final day, the collective head towards Lock Six, the bordering wall near Custom Quay, through the industrial heartlands of Dublin's docks. The sight of copious amounts of tents littering the canal banks like weeds that have sprung up almost overnight, saddens. People fleeing, taking flight and landing here on the Emerald Isle hoping that the new land – and tomorrow – will herald a better future. History is repetition. The contemporary reality jars and it's as if the tent poles pierce my heart and deflate the beating organism. I suddenly feel out of sorts, walking these six days in honour of the 1,490, yet still today there are people like the 1,490 forced to flee.

John Maguire, Director of ***ArtsGroupie CIC*** and leader of the *Liverpool Irish Famine Trail*'s *History Research Group*

WITH THANKS

We hope readers will not mind the Festival taking a moment to mention our thanks to Mr Maguire. The Festival is indebted to John, who – unflinchingly – agreed to undertake this pilgrimage, brought good spirit to every day and has led our *History Research Group* with humour, kindness and generosity. A person of action and deed, John is a powerhouse philanthrope and friend. His commitment of time, energy and hard-earned funds have not gone unnoticed or unappreciated, whilst his care, skills and talents have been used ceaselessly across these projects. The world needs more people like you, John. Thank you from the Festival and Papi (a little in-joke from our time in Dublin in 2023).

WHAT WILL HAPPEN NEXT IN LIVERPOOL?

As John Maguire's reflections above show, members of the Festival teams have undertaken intense work and experiences that have revealed considerable parity between issues in the 1840s and today. We must continue to tell people that famine is not inevitable and raise messages from history that might prevent recurrence.

As committed previously, the Festival will continue to host a memorial every October. The two exhibitions we generated in 2024 – *Postcards from a Pilgrimage* and *Revealing Trails* – are available for hire/export and our work developing the plaques, refreshing the memorial site, creating an education programme and updating the app continue.

It is critical for us to find ways to communicate the Liverpool Irish story to our friends in Strokestown (and across Ireland) and in Canada and North America, triangulating learning. Ensuring our research is in good order means we should be able to answer new questions on the impact and legacy of An Gorta Mór, so we continue to challenge ourselves on this front.

We are doing our utmost to ensure that research is quality checked, verified and shared as well as developing experiences people can take part in to help embed and engage learning. Bitesize and two-hour guided headset tours keep us in direct contact with audiences, whilst consistently updating the app and website help to reveal what we learn and provide access to forgotten histories.

Emma and John headed to Strokestown's 2025 *Famine Summer School*, and presented on *Humanitarianism and Hunger*, the theme of the conference. Plans are already afoot to join the pilgrimage in 2027, which will be linked with that year's summer school. Creating solid links with the ***Global Irish Famine Way*** is a long-term pursuit, ensuring international links and support.

RESOURCE LIST

A vast collection of resources is available about the ***Liverpool Irish Festival***'s *Irish Famine Trail* work, Strokestown's research and archive and the ***Global Irish Famine Way***. We recommend readers reference the extensive bibliography for this book, but for direct connection with the work visit

- **liverpoolirishfaminetrail.com**
- **nationalfamineway.ie**
- **strokestownpark.ie**
- **ireland.ie/en/canada/global-irish-famine-way-the-longest-heritage-trail-in-the-world/**

'Harry the Heron' danced with the walkers as they progressed along the ***National Famine Way***.

The bronze shoes cross the Mersey on *The Snowdrop*, looking out at Liverpool's waterfront and up to the ***Anglican Cathedral***.

10/ OTHER GREAT HUNGER MEMORIALS AND MARKERS OF IRISH INFLUENCE IN LIVERPOOL CITY REGION

In the process of undertaking our Trail research, we have uncovered an extensive list of other Irish connected memorials or markers that highlight either a link with An Gorta Mór, acknowledgement of Irish allies in a peace, reconciliation or war memorial settings or people, concepts or occasions that have an Irish link. By reviewing the related objects through these themes, we can see how Ireland is woven through the fabric of Merseyside's collective memory and its official markers. What we are attempting to show is a new interpretive framework for understanding these scattered monuments as part of a cohesive narrative about Irish-Liverpudlian relations. Whilst some of the features of this listing may not seem to be 'memorials', they each commemorate something that pertains to intangible cultural histories.

Though these are not 'official' Trail sites, we feel it is important to let readers and visitors know that these are also available. Collectively, the memorials reveal layers of historical relationships, including colonial experiences, migration, reconciliation and cultural memory. The statues and commemorations create a profound narrative about global connections through painful histories, locating Liverpool — and its Irish counterparts — within an international story.

We only intend to provide minimal information on each, being an indicator that Liverpool — and the region — is a location that recognises its Irish connection. It is not an exhaustive list and should not be assessed as such.

Below: Close up of plaque on the bench outside the ***Liverpool Records Office***. **Above right:** the same bench, in situ on William Brown Street.

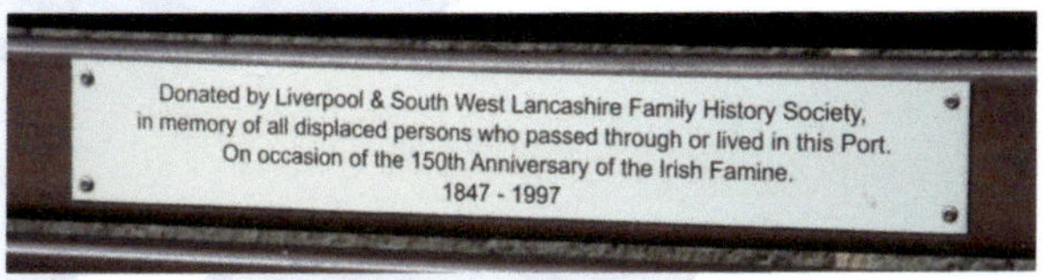

...TO AN GORTA MÓR

Anglo-Irish Family History Society* (*FHS*) commemorative bench (outside) *Liverpool Records Office*, William Brown Street, Liverpool**[179]. In 1997, the *Anglo-Irish FHS* — a subgroup belonging to ***Liverpool FHS — installed a commemorative bench outside the ***Liverpool Records Office*** to mark 150-years since 'Black '47', 1847 being the year that saw the highest fatalities during An Gorta Mór. It is dedicated to all the peoples that passed through Liverpool in that period, most of whom were Irish (pictured above, with a detail inset below left).

A New Life in the new World (plaque), ***Mersey Ferries*, Pier Head**[180]. Unveiled on 30 March 2001, the plaque commemorates "the millions who landed in Liverpool from Dublin on their passage to New York".

The Crossing/Legacy (statue), ***Piermaster's House*, Albert Dock, Liverpool (artist Mark DeGraffenried)**[181]. Unveiled at Albert Dock in 2001, this sculpture of a family commemorates all those from Europe crossing the seas to America.

[179] A link to the current ***Liverpool and SW Lancashire FHS*** website **https://www.lswlfhs.org.uk/index.php/Liverpool** accessed 5 Mar 2025

[180] ***Open Plaques*** reference to the plaque described **https://openplaques.org/plaques/39893** accessed 4 Mar 2025

[181] Limited information from ***National Museums Liverpool*** about the statue by the Piermaster's House on Albert Dock (Liverpool) **https://www.liverpoolmuseums.org.uk/artifact/legacy-statue** accessed 19 Mar 2025

A gift from the Church of Latter-Day Saints to the people of Liverpool, there is very little information to be found on either the sculpture or its true intended meaning (e.g., dates, specific cultures or communities it commemorates).

Dr Duncan's*, St John's Lane, Liverpool (building)**[182]. A stone's throw from *St James' Garden's* (which hosts several Irish connected memorials and sites), ***Dr Duncan's is a 1901 built public house dedicated to Liverpool's First Chief Medical Officer, whose work deeply affected Liverpool's relationship with An Gorta Mór and how it was handled. You will see his work in our timeline (chapter 2).

Memorial to the Tragedy of the Famine* (relief stone), crypt of *St Anthony's Church*, Scotland Road**[183]. We cannot find a lot of information on the creation, artist or date of the relief stone, shown on a wall of the crypt here. Visitors should seek permission to enter the crypt in advance of a visit. The stone reads: "A memorial to those originally buried in the grounds of ***St Anthony's Church who were later reinterred in this crypt. Many of whom fled Ireland because of famine only to die of typhus in Liverpool. May they rest in peace". Those making the visit should be sure to find the 'Dandy Pat' relic in the gardens of the churchyard (site 13 of our Trail).

***The Wavertree Society* Lock-Up, Village Green (bordered by Lake Road, Mill Lane and Childwall Road), Liverpool (building)**[184]. Built in 1796 as a miniature bridewell (overnight gaol) this building is known to have housed out-of-town An Gorta Mór victims as well as those suffering with cholera. A pretty suburban location, it is close to the blue plaque for George Harrison's birthplace at 12 Arnold Grove.

...TO PEACE AND RECONCILIATION

Bootle War Memorial, Stanley (or King's) Gardens, Stanley Road, Bootle, Sefton, Merseyside[185]. At the unveiling of this war memorial in 1922 the Seventh Battalion of *The King's Liverpool Regiment* formed a guard of honour. In April 1860 Liverpool's large Irish community had formed *The 64th Lancashire Rifle Volunteer Corps* becoming one of many volunteer corps raised in Lancashire in response to heightened tension with France. *The Liverpool Irish* became a volunteer (later Territorial Force) battalion of *The King's (Liverpool Regiment)* in July 1881, with many going on to fight in the Boer War and World War I. This is an impressive memorial, in the north of the city. For people wanting more information on the Liverpool Irish we recommend ***History Press*** and Colin Cousins's book *Cinderella Soldiers*[186].

Memorial to Captain Noel Chavasse (b.1881-d.1917) Abercromby Square, Liverpool (bronze memorial)[187]. Commissioned by the ***Noel Chavasse VC Memorial Association*** in 2008 – and made by local sculptor Tom Murphy (b.1949-d.–) – the memorial honours the two-time Victoria Cross holder Captain Noel Chavasse, one of only three people to hold two crosses. Located close to his family home (19 Abercromby Square), Chavasse was a member of the *Liverpool King's Regiment*, a regiment highly populated by Irish soldiers.

[182] ***Dr Duncan's*** official website **https://www.doctorduncansliverpool.com/** and ***Pub Gallery*** **https://pubgallery.co.uk/pubs/doctor-duncans-liverpool** both accessed 5 Mar 2025

[183] ***Royal Liver Friendly Society*** information on the ***St Anthony's*** memorial **https://royalliverhistory.co.uk/2020/10/04/dignity-in-poverty/kevind** and ***Liverpool Echo*** article about the crypt **https://www.liverpoolecho.co.uk/news/liverpool-news/secret-tunnel-runs-beneath-famous-30748328** both accessed 5 Mar 2025

[184] ***The Wavertree Society*** Lock-Up description **https://thewavertreesociety.uk/wavsoc/dhw/page50.html**; ***Prison History*** building description **https://www.prisonhistory.org/lockup/wavertree-lock-up-house** and a George Harrison blue plaque article **https://www.georgeharrison.com/blue-plaque-unveiled** all accessed 5 Mar 2025

[185] ***Sefton War Memorials*** information on the Bootle War Memorial from **https://seftonwarmemorials.org/bootle_war_memorial** accessed 5 Mar 2025

[186] Cousins, C. (2019). *Cinderella Soldiers: The Irish in Liverpool in the Great War.* Stroud: ***The History Press***.

[187] ***University of Liverpool*** article on the Noel Chavasse memorial **https://news.liverpool.ac.uk/2012/01/13/chavasse-statue-finds-permanent-home-on-university-campus** accessed 6 Mar 2025

Frongoch 1916 Easter Rising memorial, A4212 (near Bala), Wales (marker stone and plaques)[188]. Slightly outside of Merseyside, but championed by an enthusiastic Scouser, the former prisoner of war camp at Frongoch was used to intern 1,863 Irish republicans, including Michael Collins[189], following the 1916 Easter Rising in Dublin. Tony Birtill, Liverpool Irish Gaeilge stalwart, was a leader in having the plaques installed.

Irish Guards memorial stone, St John's Gardens, Liverpool[190]. Remembered with their regimental badge, this polished granite tablet is one of 20-conflict related memorials flanking a statue of Prime Minister Gladstone in the gardens of St George's Hall. It simply states "In memory of fallen comrades. The Irish Guards. Quis separabit (Who shall separate us?)".

***Reconciliation* (statue), Bold Street, Liverpool (artist Stephen Broadbent, *Broadbent Studio*)**[191]. Installed in 1990, with project expansions in 2005 and 2009. Originally there were three statues co-located in Liverpool, Glasgow and Belfast (all UK) to consider the reconciling of faiths. Later these were added to with matching (though updated) statues added in Cotonou, Benin (West Africa) and Richmond, Virginia (USA) marking significant points in the trading of enslaved peoples. Featuring two androgynous figures in an embrace, the sculpture crosses time, age, gender, faith, race, class to produce a calm, caring and compassionate figurative sculpture.

[188] ***The Irish Place*** article on the Frongoch centenary and memorials **https://www.theirishplace.com/heritage/854** and information on the memorial on ***The Free Library*** **https://www.thefreelibrary.com/Irish+camp+remembered.-a088101898** accessed 5 Mar 2025

[189] History overview of the internment at Frongoch by ***Never Such Innocence*** **https://www.neversuchinnocence.com/migration-irish-war-of-independence** accessed 6 Mar 2025

[190] ***Imperial War Museum*** *War Memorial Register* for an Irish Guard tablet, Liverpool **https://www.iwm.org.uk/memorials/item/memorial/101601** plus additional information on Gladstone's relationship with Ireland **https://www.historylearningsite.co.uk/ireland-1845-to-1922/gladstone-and-ireland** accessed 5 Mar 2025

[191] Information on the *Reconciliation* project **https://broadbent.studio/reconciliation-triangle-casestudy** accessed 4 Mar 2025

River of Life* (sculpture), Bridge Street, Warrington (artist Stephen Broadbent, *Broadbent Studio*)**[192]. Installed in 1996, this is a memorial to those killed and injured in the attacks on Warrington in 1993 by the ***Provisional Irish Republican Army (see timeline listing for the same year in chapter 2). Featuring a large water flume, elements of nature, handprints and a pavement mosaic, this mixed media sculpture creates a space for reflection, memory and connection with the community who helped to make it.

(St) Brigid's (Chalybeate) Well, *St James's Gardens*, *Anglican Cathedral*, Hope Street, Liverpool (natural well emerging from outer garden wall)[193]. This natural well flows out of the wall and – if aided by a rolled leaf – can produce a beautiful arc of water before travelling to the square pool in front. Known for its pure quality, many people come here to heal themselves with the water. A place of tranquility and reflection, Brigid (b.451-d.525) is remembered here. Brigid (also known as Brigid of Kildare) is honoured in Ireland with her own bank holiday and represents many things, including female empowerment.

...WITH AN IRISH LINK

The Beatles statue*, Pier Head, Liverpool (bronze 7-foot-six/2.3m statue)**[194]. Liverpool is littered with ***Beatle ephemera, statues and plaques, but this sculpture really encapsulates the Fab Four and draws considerable tourist attention. Weighing in at 1.2 tonnes, Andrew Edwards's (b.1946-d.–) statue commemorates 'our lads', three of whom had Irish grandparents (Ringo being the one without known Irish connections).

[192] Information on the *River of Life* sculpture project **https://broadbent.studio/river-of-life** accessed 4 Mar 2025

[193] An article on the well in *St James's Gardens* **https://theguideliverpool.com/the-history-of-liverpools-chalybeate-spring-at-st-james-gardens** accessed 6 Mar 2025

[194] ***Bare Wall*** history description of ***The Beatles*** sculpture **https://www.barewall.co.uk/collections/andy-edwards/products/the-beatles-statue-2015-maquette-sculpture-by-andy-edwards** accessed 6 Mar 2025

Above: ***The Beatles***' statue at Pier Head, Liverpool UK, 2022.

Visitors to this site might also be interested in going to see the gates at Strawberry Fields; visiting the ***National Trust***'s Mendips and 20 Forthlin Road properties and ***The Beatles Story*** (Albert Dock); going to Penny Lane, Mathew Street (***The Cavern***) or Woolton Quarry; hopping on ***The Magical Mystery Tour*** bus or popping over to see Brian Epstein b.1934-d.1967) on Whitechapel and Eleanor Rigby (b.1895-d.1939) on Stanley Street.

William Brown plaque, William Brown Street, Liverpool (plaque)[195]. Sir William Brown (1784-1864), a British merchant, banker and *Corn Law* abolitionist, was a Ballymena man. He opened his first business in Liverpool in 1809. Remembered for his munificence with the *Derby Museum* (now known as the *World Museum*, opened in 1860) and the public library (*Central Library*), the street in front of them – facing on to *St John's Gardens* (where the Father Nugent, Irish Guards and William Gladstone memorials are) – bears his name, as does an ***Eric Scott Lynch Slavery History*** plaque (installed on the street in April 2022), declaring Brown's links with the slave trade via his ownership of slaves in America.

[195] ***History Reclaimed*** information on the unveiling of the William Brown Street plaque and history that led to it **https://historyreclaimed.co.uk/remembering-slavery-the-city-of-liverpool-gets-it-right** accessed 5 Mar 2025

The Calderstones, *The Reader*, Mansion House, Calderstones Park, Liverpool (six sandstone stones with carvings)[196]. Thought to be 5,000+ years old, these stones bear marks found across our region, Wales and Ireland. Carved before Ireland receded from the mainland, opening the Irish Sea, they are believed to have been touched by (St) Brigid. These are a must see for any fans of the neolithic age, though the stones have been moved from their original configuration and the tomb they were once a part of is no more.

Frederick Douglass plaque, *Liverpool Everyman*, Hope Street, Liverpool (plaque)[197]. Turning 180-degrees from the enslavement of others, famed African American abolitionist and social reformer Frederick Douglass (b.1818-d.1895) sailed to Ireland from Liverpool in 1845, witnessing at first hand the suffering caused by the Irish Famine. It is understood two Irishmen[198] inspired Douglass to escape his enforced slavery in America, which remains celebrated in a mural on the Falls Road, Belfast. Before sailing to Ireland, it is understood that Frederick stayed in a temperance house in Liverpool, later speaking at Hope Place (where now stands the ***Liverpool Everyman***, where the plaque is located).

Percy French grave, *St Luke's Church*, Formby (grave and memorial)[199]. Percy French's (b.1851-d.1920) grave is significant within the bucolic church grounds, consisting of a large cross, mounted on a triple stone base. From County Roscommon, French is best remembered for his famous song *The Mountains of Mourne*, though his poetry, paintings and writings also live on. On a trip through Britain, he fell ill with pneumonia in Formby whilst staying with Canon Richardson of Green Lea (his cousin).

[196] ***Historic Liverpool*** entry on the Calderstones **https://historic-liverpool.co.uk/calder-stones-a-new-more-accessible-home** accessed 6 Mar 2025

[197] ***Liverpool Black History Research Group*** announce ***Liverpool Everyman*** plaque installation in 2024 **https://lbhrg.com/frederick-douglass** accessed 5 Mar 2025

[198] ***Frederick Douglass Ireland Project*** quotes Christine Kinealy on Douglass's Irish inspiration **https://www.douglassireland.org/douglass-in-ireland** accessed 6 Mar 2025

[199] ***St Luke's Church*** (Formby) website page about the Percy French grave **https://www.stlukesformby.org.uk/french.html** accessed 5 Mar 2025

Above: William Percy French's grave at Formby, UK (2022).

In recent years, ***The Irish Post***'s Gerry Molumby and the ***Roscommon Solstice Choir*** have renewed interest in his story. Please note, this is ***St Luke's Church*** in Formby, not Liverpool city centre.

William Ewart Gladstone memorials, *St John's Gardens*, Liverpool and *Lady Lever Gallery*, Port Sunlight, Wirral (bronze statue and marble bust)[200]. A 1904 memorial designed by Sir Thomas Brock (b.1847-d.1922) commemorates WE Gladstone – British Prime Minister on four occasions – who was born on Rodney Street (Liverpool) stands in ***St John's Gardens***. Famed for his pro-Irish stance, his statue is flanked at its base by the physical embodiments of justice and truth. A marble bust is on display at the ***Lady Lever Gallery***. Whilst seen as quite a benevolent figure for some time, WE Gladstone is coming under greater critique today as a benefactor of his father's great wealth, achieved through enslaving thousands of people in British Guiana (known today as Guyana or the Cooperative Republic of Guyana)[201].

[200] ***St John's Gardens*** WE Gladstone statute information **https://victorianweb.org/sculpture/brock/30.html** and ***NML*** listing for ***Lady Lever*** marble bust **https://www.liverpoolmuseums.org.uk/artifact/william-ewart-gladstone-0** both accessed 5 Mar 2025

[201] ***The Observer*** on *How William Gladstone defended his father's role in slavery* **https://www.theguardian.com/world/2023/aug/19/how-william-gladstone-defended-his-fathers-role-in-slavery** accessed 11 Mar 2025

Halsall Navvy statue, Summerwood Lane, Ormskirk (millstone grit sculpture)[202].
A sculpture commemorating the navvies[203] that built the Leeds and Liverpool Canal, it is sited close to where the first piece of earth was dug commencing the project. Created by Thompson Dagnall (b.1956-d.–) it features the head and torso of a man, looking to the sky, surrounded by rocks. Begun in 1770 the canal was not completed until 1816. It is understood many of the navvies that built this, and other canals, were of Irish origin.

John McKenna's grave and memorial, *Toxteth Park* Cemetery (Smithdown Road)[204]. A founder member of ***Liverpool Football Club*** and long-time Chairman of the ***Football League***, County Monaghan's "Honest" John McKenna (b.1855-d.1936) is interred in Section E Left, Grave 149, Consecrated Section.

***Memorial to the Heroes of the Marine Engine Room*, St Nicholas Place, Liverpool (48-foot/14.6m tall granite statue)**[205]. Built in 1916 by Sir William Goscombe John RA (b.1860-d.1952), the memorial cost £4,500 (£331,736 in today's money). It was originally intended to honour the 35-engine room stokers that died ensuring the lifeboats could be lowered and that the lights and wireless remain operational whilst *The Titanic* sank, ensuring many lives were saved. During the memorial's construction further boat tragedies, brought about by war, saw the memorial revised to honour all marine engineers. The pedestal is flanked by figures representing the four elements – earth, water, air and fire – and bears two emotive inscriptions including "The brave do not die. Their deeds live forever and call upon us to emulate their courage and devotion to duty".

[202] *Halsall Navvy* sculpture overview on ***Lancashire Past*** **https://lancashirepast.com/2020/08/16/halsall-navvy-sculpture-leeds-liverpool-canal** accessed 6 Mar 2025

[203] Who were the navvies? Article form the ***Railway Museum*** **https://www.railwaymuseum.org.uk/objects-and-stories/navvies-workers-who-built-railways** accessed 6 Mar 2025

[204] Biography of "Honest" John McKenna **https://www.liverpoolirishfestival.com/liverpools-football-transformed-by-irishman** and information on his grave location **https://toxtethparkcemetery.co.uk/notable-people** accessed 19 Mar 2025

[205] ***Titanic Memorials*** listing for the Memorial **https://www.titanic.memorial/post/memorial/engineers+memorial+liverpool** accessed 6 Mar 2025

National Museums Liverpool*'s *Irish Heritage Trail, Museum of Liverpool*, Pier Head, Liverpool (self-guided trail)**[206]. The ***Museum of Liverpool holds 10 Irish artefacts in its public exhibitions and provides paper copies of a leaflet to undertake a self-guided Trail. The ***Liverpool Irish Festival***'s *History Research Group* offer occasional guided tours, so if you are interested in this, keep an eye on the Festival's event pages online.

Robert Noonan (better known as Robert Tressell, b.1870-d.1911) blue plaque, 70 Pembroke Place, Liverpool (plaque)[207]. Author of *The Ragged Trousered Philanthropists*, Tressell's text is internationally lauded as a seminal text for socialists. He died on (or very close to) the *Brownlow Hill Workhouse* site, in the Infirmary. His book was published posthumously by his daughter. Tressell (b. Dublin-d. Liverpool), also known as Robert Croker and occasionally by his mother's family name Noonan, had various professions and aspirations but history remembers him as a radical emigre. He was buried in a paupers' grave in ***Walton Park Cemetery***. In 1977 a headstone was created for him, which can still be viewed there.

***Our Lady and St Nicholas Church* also known as *Liverpool Parish Church*, Old Churchyard accessible from George's Dock Quay (church and gardens)**[208]. Built after the second world war but on its thirteenth century site, this is the philosophical home of the *Liverpool Select Vestry* as operated during An Gorta Mór. Not yet a *Liverpool Irish Famine Trail* site, it is nevertheless important to the Liverpool Irish Famine experience. In its care are several memorials that would be important to people interested in docker, maritime and war histories as well as those interested in the *Homeless Jesus* sculpture, by Canadian Timothy Schmaltz (b.1969-d.–).

[206] Self-guided ***Museum of Liverpool*** tour of Irish objects **https://images.liverpoolmuseums.org.uk/2020-01/Liverpool-Irish-community-trail.pdf** accessed 5 Mar 2025

[207] ***Liverpool Echo*** reports on the unveiling of the blue plaque at Pembroke Place and headstone at ***Walton Park Cemetery*** **https://www.liverpoolecho.co.uk/whats-on/how-working-class-writer-robert-15276215** and gives a biographical account of his life here **https://www.liverpoolecho.co.uk/news/liverpool-news/remembering-ragged-trousered-philanthropists-author-3386148** both accessed 5 Mar 2025

[208] ***Liverpool Parish Church***'s gardens page, which includes references to the memorials there **https://livpc.co.uk/garden** accessed 5 Mar 2025

Above: St Patrick's Cross near Lace Street, Liverpool, UK.

St Patrick's Cross, Standish Street near Lace Street, Liverpool (plaque)[209]. Mounted to gates, ***Merseyside County Council***'s plaque to St Patrick (b. fifth century-d. fifth century, exact dates unknown) sits in front of a corner plot holding an array of relics. Believed to mark the site of St Patrick's final sermon before going to Ireland (AD 432). This site was very close to the Lace Street *Liverpool Irish Famine Trail* plaque, which has since been removed due to building developments.

Travellers' rest stones[210] **at Redbank and Stag Inn (low level stones with text engraving)**. Rediscovered in 2023 were 12 stones used to line the roads between Liverpool and Manchester in the 1860s. Thought to be from a collection of over 30 laid to assist itinerant works on their route through the north-west, the stones were built to be tall enough for a man to sit on, with a raised section to keep bags from resting on muddy or wet floors. Each had a domed top to prevent water pooling.

[209] ***Discover Liverpool*** and Ken Pye article on *St Patrick's Cross – Over 1,000 Years of Pilgrimage* **https://www.discover-liverpool.com/local-history-stories-to-read/st-patricks-cross-over-1-000-years-of-pilgrimage** accessed 5 Mar 2025

[210] ***Historic England*** information about the discovery and listing of the stones **https://historicengland.org.uk/whats-new/news/rare-travellers-rest-stones-in-north-of-england-listed** accessed 24 Mar 2025

Arthur Wellesley, The First Duke of Wellington (b.1769-d.1852) memorial, St George's Plateau, Liverpool (132-foot/40.2m statue and column)[211]. The Irish born one-time British Prime Minister's military victories – including Assay, Talavera and Waterloo – are honoured in this huge statue. Erected between 1861 and 1865, it is allegedly made of smelted canons taken from The Battle of Waterloo. Interestingly, Sir William Brown, also mentioned in this list, attended the statue's inauguration ceremony.

Waterloo Dock, Liverpool. Three docks south of Clarence Dock is Waterloo Dock, situated between Victoria Dock and Princes Basin. We have more research to do on this, but it is our current understanding that most ships sailing to the Americas in the 1840s left from this dock. Consequently, the Irish poor that did not stay in Liverpool, having come through Clarence Dock, may well have left through here, making it an important stop for those undertaking any kind of pilgrimage. A plan of the docks in 1846 shows that to get out to sea from Waterloo Dock, ships must pass through Princes Basin to join the Mersey[212].

The Wellington Rooms*, Brownlow Hill, Liverpool (building)**[213]. Built by Edmund Aikin (b.1780-d.1820) in the Regency period and in neo-classical style, *The Wellington Rooms* were completed in 1816 for ***The Wellington Club, who left in 1922 after which it became an Embassy Club until bomb damage occurred in 1941. It reopened in 1965 as an Irish Centre, which it stayed as for 27-years, before the organisation closed and moved to St Michaels. It has remained empty since then. Remembered for its great parties, classes and 'hatches, matches, dispatches' it was the natural home of the Irish community in Liverpool for that period.

Above: *The Wellington Rooms*, Liverpool, UK (c) AB, 2022.

The Wellington Rooms now represent a microcosm of cultural transformation; a building once famed for its grandeur belies its current dereliction, but demonstrates a move towards buildings with outdoor space, specific interests and an array of services. This three-roomed showpiece no longer 'fits the bill'. We wonder what its future holds now.

Kitty Wilkinson statue and window, *St George's Hall*, Liverpool (marble statue)[214] **and *Anglican Cathedral***. For details of Kitty's life and biography do look at the Trail's information, linked with her gravestone in *St James's Gardens* (Trail site 6). In 2012, ***St George's Hall*** installed Simon Smith's (b.1982-d.–) marble statue of Kitty, in their main hall, becoming the first statue to represent a named woman and the first addition to the space in over a century. There is also a small window in the Lady Chapel of the ***Anglican Cathedral***, for anyone who would like to follow Kitty more.

[211] ***National Army Museum*** biography **https://www.nam.ac.uk/explore/duke-wellington** and *Embassy of Ireland Ottawa* case for Wellesley being considered a father of modern Canada **https://www.ireland.ie/en/canada/ottawa/news-and-events/news-archive/wellington-and-the-birth-of-modern-canada** both accessed 5 Mar 2025

[212] ***Historic Liverpool*** map of Jesse Hartley's docks in 1846 **https://historic-liverpool.co.uk/old-maps-of-liverpool/1846-plan-liverpool-docks-jesse-hartley-dock-surveyor/#4/61.82/-54.14** accessed 6 Mar 2025

[213] ***Liverpool 1207*** article on *The Wellington Rooms* **https://liverpool1207blog.wordpress.com/buildings/the-wellington-rooms** accessed 5 Mar 2025

[214] ***Simon Smith Stone Carving*** information about Kitty project **https://simonsmithstonecarving.com/portfolio/kitty-wilkinson-statue** accessed 5 Mar 2025

Tadhg Devlin's group worked with cyanotypes in many locations, including inside ***St Anthony's Church*** (c) Tadhg Devlin, 2024 (detail only).

11/ CREATIVE RESPONSES TO EXISTING TRAIL SITES

The ***Liverpool Irish Festival*** believes telling stories in new and creative ways enables more people to access complex information. Involving people in telling these stories — including those with first-hand or lived-experience — is important to ensuring there is a good range of voices available. It means that critical objectivity can be shared and maintained, whilst people are offered ownership of their own narratives. In contested historical spaces this is extremely important because this provides an environment for unpacking complexities, making compromise and arriving at reconciliation. The *History Research Group* has been critical to this.

There is no single way to do this. During the project planning the Festival selected multiple pathways to locate, create and express the heritage the project has uncovered, both in reference to facts and history, but also story and creative response. In this chapter, these methodologies and formats are outlined.

This hasn't been a scattergun approach. Utilising different formats and methodologies allows the Festival to speak with different people and reach and connect with different audiences. Sometimes the practices can be creative and uplifting; sometimes they are – by necessity – technical and complicated. More often there is an overlap between the two. For instance, when the Festival embarked on creating an app to help communicate the research and history of the Trail to everyone, it became critical to involve creative thinkers as well as technicians. Technological assistance was required to create the software to deliver specific tasks *and* the app needed the narrative power of creatives to communicate the stories and intangible cultural heritage.

These creative expressions help to breathe life into history. By using these complimentary skill sets the artists translated multiple stories and the accompanying 'intangible cultural heritage' into something understandable if not touchable. So, what is intangible cultural heritage and why does it matter?

Folklore, customs, songs, beliefs and inherited histories are all forms of intangible cultural heritage. It doesn't have to be historic; it can be the active transmission of a living custom or practice. It is a thing that can be felt but not touched. These are not physical items, yet they can hold (intellectual and emotional) space. It is that memory of an event on a place; the feeling left in the wake of a big event.

This matters because intangible cultural heritage immortalises the internal, connecting us deeply with times, people, locations or events that matter to our understanding of the society at large and the lives people are inhabiting. Therefore, finding ways to communicate such heritage in creative ways — to make tangible something which has not been — for an historically overlooked community felt important.

Built into the Festival's ***National Lottery Heritage Fund*** application was the development of eight creative responses, to our plaque and memorial sites, telling the history of each site. Led by a selected artist they would co-author an expressive output with a nominated community group. This work would have to be something they could transform into a digital product to be shared on a new *Liverpool Irish Famine Trail* app. The citizen research groups brought personal stories and insight to the history of each site, bringing expressive interpretations to the established histories. Alongside these, the Festival stated it would...

- generate additional research in response to specific outstanding questions
- maintain the *History Research Group,* which the Festival would train to produce their own recordings, talks and tours
- use any artworks created to help communicate the story of An Gorta Mór in as many ways as it could
- lead a series of headset-led walking tours. The headsets work via a guide's microphone transmitter, reducing background noise and creating an intimate space in which to hear the stories over the high winds known at Liverpool's docks
- a television-style feature documentary to export the Liverpool Irish Great Hunger story to a larger and different demographic.

In the rest of this chapter, readers will benefit from a detailed breakdown of the creative responses made since *Revive* that are collectively helping us to tell the Liverpool Irish Great Hunger story.

THE HISTORY RESEARCH GROUP

When the Festival was awarded its first ***National Lottery Heritage Fund*** grant in 2021, it set up a *History Research Group*. Its members have contributed to the research of many of these chapters and much of what you will find on our website and app. Consisting of local history enthusiasts, these intrepid volunteers helped us to write our first book, *Revive*, and research all the original sites of our 1990s Trail.

Since then, they have trained in podcast making, taken the public on tours of the ***Museum of Liverpool***'s Irish objects collection, functioned as advisors to artists commissioned to work on the Trail project (more later) and further developed our digital archive. They have contributed 1600-hours+ of volunteer time, providing us with a wealth of knowledge for our archives and adding much to the new book.

You can hear the voices of the *History Research Group* throughout our app and members often appear in and speak at our events. Their research and outputs are primarily directed by the needs of the project, being task-led, though individuals can and do opt to undertake research in their specialist field of interest.

It is not easy to spend long periods in the archives and histories related to An Gorta Mór. The friendship the group have forged is not only a substantial support in keeping them going through difficult research but provides great critical friendship. They continue to sharpen and share their skills and maintain their determination to locate missing information. They are an inspiration.

They are a huge asset to the Festival and a brilliant focus group for consultation on Trail directions. The *History Research Group* remains an open one and new members are welcomed. Anyone interested in this kind of volunteering should visit: **liverpoolirishfestival.com/engage/volunteer**

CITIZEN RESEARCH GROUPS

The National Lottery Heritage Fund's vision "is for heritage to be valued, cared for and sustained for everyone, now and in the future". Thus, it was the Festival's responsibility – as recipients of an award – to involve people deeply in heritage. This meant ensuring more people were in touch with heritage; that they were helped to link with their identity, health and wellbeing as well as contributing to placemaking, civic pride and social cohesion.

The Festival commissioned four artists – Tadhg Devlin (b.1971-d.–), Nicola McGovern (b. unknown-d.–), Lydia O'Hara (b.1989-d.–) and Pamela Sullivan (b. unknown-d.–) – to work with four pre-selected community groups:

- *Birkenhead Library*
- *Liverpool Central Library*
- ***Powerfull Beyond All Measure***
- ***Spider Project***.

The members of these groups revealed new (and sometime personally related) stories, bringing local and varied voices into the Trail's storytelling, simultaneously forming a pool of consultants and advocates to work with on further Trail developments.

Directed to produce digital materials that could be used on the app, the groups developed films, cyanotypes, aprons, embroideries, banners, long-form histories, ceramics and more besides. On the basis that the book cannot incorporate everything, some of these works and descriptions are presented here, but readers are encouraged – wholeheartedly – to visit the app and see the incredible artworks on display there as they were intended. The app and its contents are completely free to access, with each artwork listed under its relevant sites. Visit **liverpoolirishfaminetrail.com** to access the app.

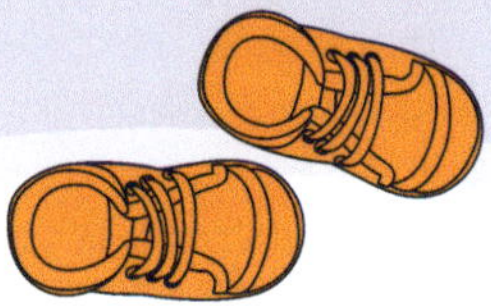

Tadhg Devlin, *Liverpool Central Library*
***The 16 Canvasses: Personal Stories and Collective Memory*; Liverpool Irish Great Hunger Memorial, (officially untitled) the artwork comprises 16 mixed media A4 canvasses**.

This collection of artworks is a collaboration between the group members in Tadhg's group, who responded to the Liverpool Irish Great Hunger commemoration memorial. Based at ***St Luke's 'Bombed Out' Church***, the grounds are now a symbol for peace, having been seriously damaged by bombing in World War II. Tadhg's group found personal stories to connect with the site and means of displaying them together, to help share collective stories of their connections with An Gorta Mór. The 16 panels including poetry and writing, through to conceptual collage pieces, as chosen and created by the participant. The work aims to peel back 'today' to reveal the layered histories beneath, from the personal to the political, and beyond.

The collaborative artwork consists of 16 canvasses arranged in a grid, each telling a unique story of connection to An Gorta Mór. To help present them here, the Festival has provided nominal titles for the works, but the group presented them as a collective piece. Reading from left to right, row by row, the collection reveals:

Row 1

1. *Paul White's War Memorial*: A collage inspired by a family photo of his great uncles in the *Liverpool Convalescent Hospital* (1917), reflecting on the thousands of Irish people who contributed to both World Wars

2. *Lesley Woolvine's Migration Paths*: A combination of cyanotype and stitching showing the routes of migrants to Dublin and onward to different lands

3. *A Place of Hope*: A poem created by Paul White, inspired by discussions and meetings throughout the project

4. *Isabella's Story:* Richard Orritt's tribute to his aunt (born 1902), named after her grandmother, who arrived in Liverpool around 1850 with her father and brother

Row 2

5. *Letters of Faith*: Richard Orritt's piece featuring letters that reflect contrasting views on life and death, capturing the testing of faith experienced by Irish settlers in Liverpool

6. *The Direction of Travel*: Lesley Woolvine's artwork inspired by Jean Maskell's poem of the same name

7. *Then and Now*: Paul White's reflection on historical portrayals of Irish people, juxtaposed with contemporary migration stories in Ireland

8. *Family Map*: Juliet Shreeve's work featuring a photograph of her mother Ann and aunt Stella (née O'Brien) at a 1963 Liverpool wedding, displayed on a map of Doncaster Street where they grew up. The piece includes mushroom spore prints[215] and blackberry fingerprints, reflecting her mother's childhood experiences gathering food with her grandfather in Wexford

Row 3

9. *Liverpool's Irish Names*: Lesley Woolvine's linocut overlays the countless Irish surnames that remain popular in Liverpool today

10. *The Final Letter Home*: Paul White's tribute to his Irish relatives killed by a U-boat in 1942, featuring the final letter they sent home

11. *Kate's Memory Tin*: Paul White's representation of his grandmother Kate Harte from Galway, who met John O'Neil from Armagh, displayed with treasured items the family preserved from her life

12. *Whose Is It?*: Juliet Shreeve's exploration of land ownership using mushroom spore prints and blackberry juice fingerprints, interwoven with Irish phrases her mother brought from Wexford to Liverpool

Row 4

13. *The Journey*: Richard Orritt's poem imagining the emotions of those fleeing hunger as they faced the perilous journey from Ireland to Liverpool

14. *The London Window*: Lesley Woolvine's mixed-media piece inspired by the notorious "No Irish" signs seen in 1960s London windows [216]

15. *Trevelyan's Legacy*: A collaborative piece inspired by Charles Trevelyan's infamous quotes during The Great Hunger*

16. *Beyond the Blight*: Juliet Shreeve's examination of the historical causes of The Great Hunger beyond potato blight, framed by contemporary quotes from the period.

*Charles Trevelyan, Assistant Secretary to the Treasury for 19-years, infamously stated: "If the Irish [learn] they can get free government grants, we shall have a system of mendicancy [begging] such as the world never knew," after a million had already starved to death. He added: "The great evil with which we have to contend is not the physical evil of the famine, but the moral evil of the selfish, perverse and turbulent character of the people". The Festival would remind readers: famine is never inevitable. It can be avoided.

This project — and many of the cyanotype images the group prepared — are included in Tadhg's fascinating films about the memorial and Clarence Dock, all available through the app.

A photograph of the group's image collection follows on the next page.

[215] ***First Nature*** describes how to create your own mushroom spore print **https://www.first-nature.com/fungi/~sporeprint.php** accessed 12 Mar 2025

[216] ***The Irish Times*** share reflections on variants of the 'No Blacks. No Dogs. No Irish signs' **https://www.irishtimes.com/ireland/social-affairs/2024/05/06/no-irish-no-blacks-no-dogs-irish-times-readers-recall-encountering-notorious-signs-in-britain** accessed 12 Mar 2025

Left:
The 16 canvasses: Personal Stories and Collective Memory (c) Tadhg Devlin, 2024.

Above: Still from *An Naprún/The Apron* (c) Nicola McGovern, 2024.
Below: A close up detail of the apron made by Nicola's group in 2024.

Nicola McGovern, *Powerfull Beyond All Measure* *An Naprún/The Apron*, representing *The Brownlow Hill Workhouse* and Paupers' Grave, the artwork consists of calico sewn with silk threads, c.80cm wide and 82 cm high.

Paupers would have worked a 12-hour day of hard labour in Liverpool's *Brownlow Hill Workhouse*. Oakum picking was a tedious job. It involved separating old shipping ropes into loose fibres. Done over hours, this made hands bleed. The resulting material was blended with tar and sold for use as a watertight sealant in shipbuilding.

Another common job, in the workhouse for women and girls, was sewing. For *An Naprún/The Apron*, Nicola's group at ***Powerfull Beyond All Measure*** used needles and thread to create individual 'frames' developing a digital animation depicting the repetitive action of hands at work picking oakum. Each section of embroidered calico has taken hours of work to produce, skillfully hand-stitched by a team of 15-women. The separate pieces of fabric have been combined and sewn together to create a Victorian-style apron (complete with concealed coins), like the ones worn by paupers in the workhouse.

Comparing the experiences of The Great Hunger migrants displaced to Liverpool, with those of people living in (or new to) the city today, allowed Nicola to invite the participants' children and grandchildren to draw their hopes and dreams for the future. The children created images of families, flowers, sunny skies and the number 17 bus. The group then transferred these illustrations onto the fabric and embroidered them into the panels bearing the oakum picking hands to create a multi-layered composition, encompassing aspects of life in the workhouse as well as the future dreams for the city's youth community.

This work has a brilliant short film linked to it, that is available on our Lace Street page on the *Liverpool Irish Famine Trail* website and app. Readers are highly recommended to access it.

Above: Stills from the film *Welcome to Somewhere New* featuring Vicky Sayle and James Martin (c) Lydia O'Hara, 2024.

Lydia O'Hara, *Spider Project*

***Welcome to Somewhere New*, representing the Price Street plaque, the artwork comprises two mixed media banners each approximately 50cm x 130cm.**

The artwork, *Welcome to Somewhere New*, was inspired by a group discussion centred around the conditions – societal and political – that the original *Liverpool Irish Famine Trail* plaques were installed under. The 1990s were a different time to today. The atmosphere around Irish people, ahead of the Good Friday Agreement, could still create a good deal of tension. There was concern within the ***Liverpool Great Hunger Commemoration Committee*** that the plaques may be targeted by those affected or activated by 'The Troubles'.

Each of the Trail's plaques – and its memorial – were funded by local people who cared about The Great Hunger's commemoration. However, they were additionally protective of the work they were installing. This means that, often, plaques were placed high off the ground and without ceremony due to fears of backlash or vandalism. The group, based at the ***Spider Project*** in Birkenhead, felt its work with Lydia could function as a vigil to both The Great Hunger itself and those who engaged in the *Liverpool Irish Famine Trail* in the nineties.

Straddling secular 'Stations of the Cross' and a trade union banner march, *Welcome to Somewhere New* uses imagery and spoken text as a metaphor for the hardships endured by and coming together of two peoples.

One character represents people local to Merseyside who bore the responsibility of accommodating, feeding and supporting hundreds of thousands of people from Ireland in a short space of time with little help from the rest of the country. The other character represents people forced to leave their homes in Ireland in search of safety and security, coming to an unfamiliar land faced with further challenges and difficult living conditions on their arrival. Visually, and through the spoken text, these two groups of people blend and create a new Birkenhead, a new Liverpool, forever changed by the circumstances of the time.

In the associated film for Price Street, the banners the group made with Lydia, are marched through Birkenhead representing the two sides, discussed above. As with each of these listings, it is available on our website and app. Please do pay the film a visit.

Pamela Sullivan, *Birkenhead Library*
***A Place across the Sea*, representing the Lace Street plaque and Wirral connections, the artwork comprises of a porcelain sculpture, 35cm tall.**

Pam and the *Birkenhead Library* group undertook extensive research to make a court-house as 'real' as possible, in terms of its proportions and the materials the porcelain depicts. Court-houses were the most used accommodation for The Great Hunger poor. The group did a huge amount of research on the kinds of houses the merchants in Birkenhead were living in and the conditions of the Victorian docks and fever hospitals. Pam took all this research and brought it together, with deft hands, to form an emotive portrait of a building.

Porcelain is a very delicate substance. Making a piece as large this one holds considerable risk because the porcelain can crack, buckle or slump during the fabrication process, if it is not expertly managed. Things can go wrong during the object's firing, but the result is something stable, but fragile, like glass. Pam stated that this symbolised both the strength and vulnerability of The Great Hunger poor's plight.

As you've read, in May 2024 some of the *Liverpool Irish Famine Trail* team completed *The Walk of the Bronze Shoes* (see chapter 7). Leaving Strokestown, the walkers could not know what lay ahead or how they would feel arriving in Dublin, or Liverpool, having completed the pilgrimage. One thing the Festival was certain of was that the world had already taken a considerable amount from Strokestown. As Emma and John left the estate, they bore the weight of Liverpool's pair of bronze shoes (3kg), thus removing another Strokestown belonging.

Before the pilgrimage, the Festival had planned to gift something to Strokestown, rather than just taking from the place. When the group reached Dublin, the Festival presented the Strokestown Estate team with Pam's porcelain court-house, representative of the sort of dwelling the 1,490 may have stayed in during their time in Liverpool or on the Wirral. The artwork was intended to compliment the housing stock the ***National Famine Museum*** already has on display, showing the four kinds of housing prevalent on the original estate,

Above: Pam Sullivan's original porcelain court-house macquette.

from Palladian estate house to fourth grade turf housing. This model extended the storytelling about the 1,490 by indicating the experience they may have had outside their former home.

Pam joined the ***Liverpool Irish Festival*** on the stage at ***EPIC*** (Ireland's migration museum) to present the work and it now resides in the reflection room at Strokestown's ***National Famine Museum***, creating an exchange between the two locations, rather than another absence.

Once more, the Festival hopes readers will afford it a line or two to thank participants and artists for the time, dedication and commitment each gave to the projects and for the fantastic information and artworks developed. The team are grateful to every single member of these groups and our lead artists. Go raibh maith agat/Thank you.

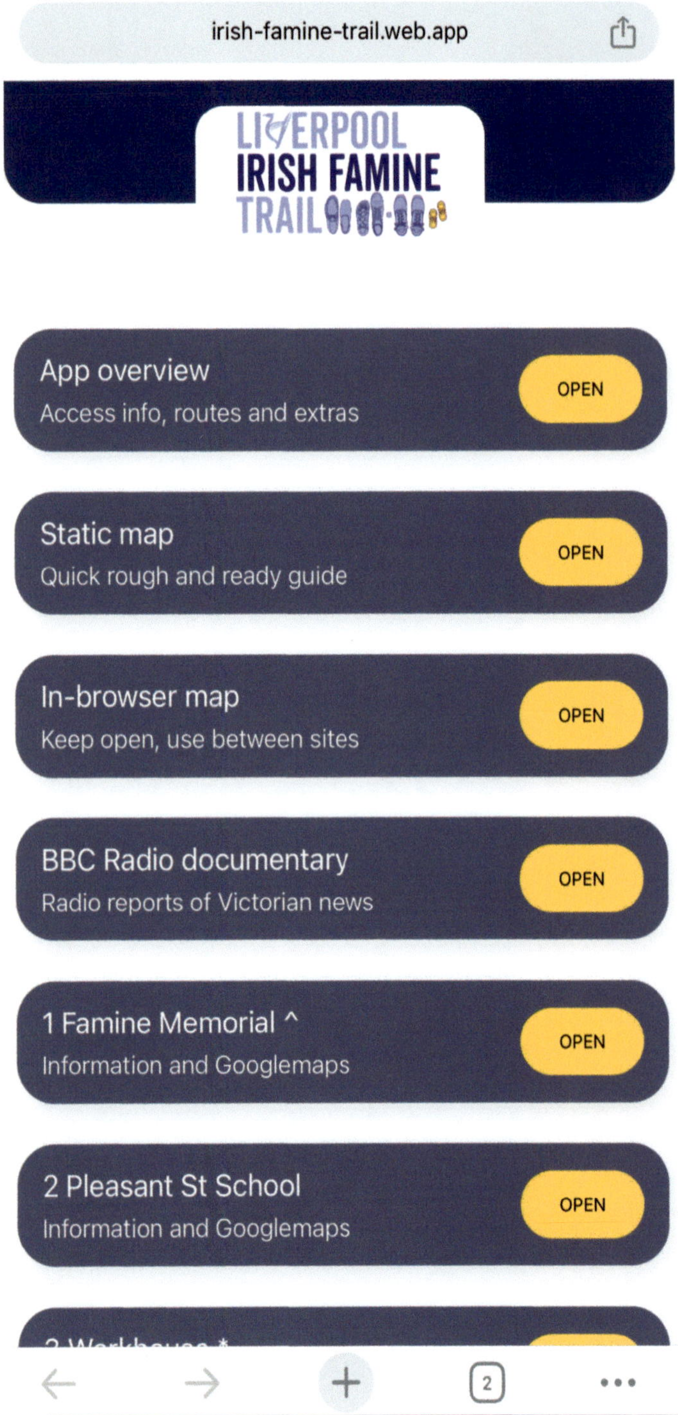

APP DESIGN AND DEVELOPMENT

Apps have fallen from favour in recent years, as they can be memory-greedy and require updating for ***Android*** and ***Apple*** formats. That said, they can also be extremely helpful. The app has been mentioned several times to date, but there will still be people asking: what is an app and why does the Trail want one?

An app is a software program designed to deliver a specific task. It can be a downloadable piece of software, or it can function within a browser, depending on the programme coding. Apps require a user interface to work – such as a device's screen – and can be programmed to use other aspects of the device they are working on, such as its camera or speakers.

The Festival worked with ***European Space Agency*** affiliated developer, ***Gazooky Studios*** and ***Second Stride***, to produce an in-browser app that users can use on any device wherever they are. With no need to download software, the *Liverpool Irish Famine Trail* app is lightweight and easy to use within an open browser.

The intention was that – however brilliant the tech might be – it would be user friendly and interesting. The motto used throughout its development was "keep it simple, stupid" (KISS) [217] to ensure it remained usable 'in the field'. Understanding what needed to be said and how creative content could continue to be added was and remains a guiding principle in its development.

Understanding what the commissioned artists would produce gave the team confidence there would be a diverse and interesting set of digital stories available to launch the app with. The app is also Global Positioning System (GPS) enabled, providing an active and interactive map of all the sites so users can navigate from any site to another, using as little data as possible.

[217] ***Interaction Design Foundation*** on the advent and application of the KISS design principle **https://www.interaction-design.org/literature/article/kiss-keep-it-simple-stupid-a-design-principle?srsltid=AfmBOopH-JI0dXdRai3JZgMhcOf_4ftyt0-K2g879bAlrs1NnhqoA5K** accessed 3 Mar 2025

It is full of sound files and associated scripts (for reading if audio is not available or beneficial to you), films, galleries and in-map guides. Whilst the advent of a new app is not by or of itself overly creative, the Festival hopes it approach in providing users with rich content is.

EXHIBITIONS AND DOCUMENTARY

Resulting from the artworks listed above, items generated by *The Walk of the Bronze Shoes* and the ongoing work of developing the Trail, the Festival was able to host two exhibitions during *#LIF2024* in partnership with ***The Docklands Trail*** and ***Baltic Creative***.

Featuring the bronze shoes, art works and a new collection plate, as well as the postcards posted daily from *The Walk of the Bronze Shoes*, the exhibitions reflected the experiences of the year, being seen by almost 1500 people.

Donated to the Trail, the collection plate (pictured below right) is a small touchstone, which will be used at future ceremonies to allow for donations to the continuing work of the Trail. Made in Liverpool and gifted by the Festival Director, its simplicity speaks to the need of The Great Hunger, with the bowl indicating the wish for nourishment. The clay, glaze and firing costs were kindly donated by local potter Attila Olah of ***Altar Pottery***.

Revealing Trails was shown at Collingwood Dock, between October and December 2024, sharing the work of the citizen research groups and the broader story of the walk. The Festival selected a piece of work from each artist group and gave a detailed outline of what the work represented, just as has been done here. Presented at Collingwood Dock, just north of Clarence Dock, visitors had a sense of the arrival of people coming in from the water, feeling the sea air on their faces. *Postcards from a Pilgrimage* provided aluminium prints of the nine postcard images and written reverses, with full message transcriptions. Shown at ***Northern Lights***, the extension to Irish philanthropist Robert Cains's brewery site, also drew connections with the past.

An addition to showing work connected with the Trail and pilgrimage, the Festival chronicled the journey from Strokestown (Ireland) to Liverpool (UK) by making a feature-length documentary, which will launch in 2025. Information on the walk is available in chapter 7, but the documentary is an exciting part of our programme, providing another way for us to engage audiences in premiers locally and possibly overseas. At the time of writing, the Festival team is still waiting – excitedly – to see the full film but know it will involve many of the people and locations they journeyed through. Emma and John are looking forward to re-meeting their fellow walkers and supporters and being transported back to the pilgrimage. Full of interviews and reflections from those that walked, it will be an honest portrayal of the evocative and sometimes difficult pilgrimage. It will also feature the events, speeches and activities that took place along the way, including our vigils and memorial events.

Sponsored by the Irish Government's *Strategic Diaspora Fund* and supported by our ***National Lottery Heritage Fund*** application there is a strong desire to submit it to international film festivals and premiering it during the 2025 Festival. Produced and delivered by local ***Overshoot Productions***, it has been locally sourced and produced, with Scouse directors, cinematographers and recordists.

OVERVIEW

What the different formats help the Festival and Trail to do is reach different people, both in their creation and their observation. Ranging from the deeply technical interface of the app and documentary; through the elemental aspect of clay for the collection plate and deep creative discussions between artists and citizens, this multifaceted approach to story gathering and relay is imperative to success. Helping people visualise what An Gorta Mór means to them, whilst also linking this with facts, helps us to develop a stronger throughline for people to connect to the emotional core of The Great Hunger story. Or, as Eleanor Lybeck asserts:

> "Art thereby emerges as a vital medium for reinterpreting and sustaining cultural narratives across generations, ensuring that particular elements of intangible cultural heritage remain relevant and resonant…
>
> "These activities have facilitated the transmission of Famine-related cultural memory, transforming it into a living heritage accessible to a wider audience"[218].

As a set of processes, the Festival has learned some meaningful lessons about connecting people with their heritage (intangible or otherwise) and how quickly empathy can form. The compassion the team have seen in the *History Research Group*, artists, citizens and spectators of the work shows that when creative expression is used meaningfully and mindfully it can draw people into complex ideas and assist people in asserting their beliefs. There is something about touch and engaging people in using tactile objects or processes that enables people to tune in to their sensory or emotional intellect, sometimes in opposition to their political self. Allowing compassion in, seems to help people to draw comparisons from yesterday to today, allowing a transformative tomorrow.

[218] Lybeck, E. and Alsalloum, A. (2025). *Tracing Intangible Cultural Migrant Heritage in the UK*. Springer. From the chapter 'Near This Place: The *Liverpool Irish Famine Trail* in Visual Art'

12/ RELIEF SOUP

Comfort and warmth... A bowl of soup nourishes and can make you feel looked after and well. In winter months, most households will have a pan of soup on the go, at one point or other. Here in Liverpool, it is generally our traditional 'Scouse', brought over hundreds of years ago by Scandinavian sailors.

With soup a lot can go around using very little. Water can be added to make it feed more people. There is an old Liverpudlian phrase, 'What won't feed will fatten'. This pertains to the lack of nutritional value in a meal of naught but hot water. Often known as 'stir about', hungry diners would stir about in the liquid hoping to find a vegetable or — even better — some type of meat.

Contemporary Ireland is littered with 'famine bowls', a staple feature of An Gorta Mór exhibitions and sometimes cast aside in yards or repurposed into flowerpots. These remain a harsh reminder of the soup relief given during The Great Hunger and the great communal need they served. Black cast iron pots were needed to provide for the millions of people dependent on soup during Black '47. These bowls are imposing. They are big enough to contain voluminous amounts of soup – tens of pints – and symbolise the plight of the hungry. During our research we have come across variations of contemporaneous soup recipes.

ALEXIS SOYER'S SELF-TITLED 'FAMINE SOUP'

One of the first celebrity chefs, Alexis Soyer (b.1810-d.1858) worked at ***The Reform Club***[219]. ***The Reform Club*** remains a private members club, owned and controlled by its members, on the south side of Pall Mall in Central London, England. This club famously appears in Jules Verne's (b.1828-d.1905) *Around the World in Eighty Days* (published 1872). In fact, the main character — Phileas Fogg — is a member who sets out to circumnavigate the world on a bet from his fellow members, beginning and ending at the club.

[219] ***The Reform Club***'s website today, which recognises its formation after *The Reform Act* of 1832, which opened its doors in 1836 **https://www.reformclub.com** accessed 3 Mar 2025

Above: Alexis Benoît Soyer. Stipple engraving by H B Hall, 1859, after E Soyer, 1843. Created 1859. Contributors: Emma Soyer (1813–1842). Work ID: pxqy767w. Credit: ***Wellcome Collection***. Detail only.

Soyer was known for his theatricality. He and his team cooked a delicious breakfast for 2,000 guests on the morning of Queen Victoria's coronation, Thursday 28 June 1838. He sold recipes and books, making a substantial income from his cookery prowess. His signature breaded lamb cutlet recipe still appears on the menu at ***The Reform Club***. During The Great Hunger, Soyer set out to provide a cheap nutritious soup on a large scale for the starving Irish.

Granted a leave of absence from ***The Reform Club***, after being approached by Russell's government for assistance, Soyer constructed a 'model' soup kitchen at Croppies Acre (Dublin, Ireland in April 1847), consisting of a large tented wooden structure with a cloth roof. At the centre of this 'pop-up' kitchen was the cooking area. Around the core kitchen were place long tables with benches. Spoons were chained down so they could not be stolen. Being a theatrical cook, he ensured there was space for spectators to gather. Soyer charged a five-shilling entry fee for the rich to witness the poor as they ate their soup (the equivalent of £20 in 2025). At the grand opening, Soyer wore his trademark red velvet hat at a jaunty angle, accompanied by the elite of Dublin society.

The Freeman's Journal heavily criticised this voyeuristic poverty safari[220]...

> 'Five shillings each to see paupers feed!...five shillings each! when the animals at the Zoological Gardens may be inspected at feeding time for sixpence!'.

Sixpence (6d) would have been half a shilling in old money, making five shillings 60d, 10-times the value of the zoo ticket! It is interesting to note that "poverty tourism" was as rife then as today. Reports show the soup kitchen fed between 5,000 and 8,000-people per day (see image on the right). Soyer sent recipes to the press which he believed were sufficient to provide nutritional value for those in dire need. Below is one recipe, which was published in various forms in the ***St James's Chronicle*** (London), ***The Morning Herald*** (London), ***The Evening Mail*** (London), ***The London Evening Standard***, ***The Era*** and ***The Times*** in 1847[221]. The following is taken from ***The Times***:

> **The Recipe for Soup No.1** (direct transcription, unexpurgated)
>
> I first put one ounce of dripping into a sauce-pan (capable of holding two gallons of water), with a quarter of a pound of leg of beef without bones, cut in to square pieces about half an inch, and two middle-sized onions, peeled and sliced. I then set the saucepan over a coal fire, and stirred the contents round for a few minutes with a wooden (or iron) spoon until fried lightly brown. I had then ready washed the peeling of two turnips, fifteen green leaves or tops of celery, and the green part of two leeks (the whole of which, I must observe, are always thrown away). Having cut the above vegetable in to small pieces, I throw them in to the saucepan with the other ingredients, stirring them occasionally over the fire for another ten minutes; then added half a pound of common flour (any farinaceous substance would do), and half a pound of pearl barley, mixing well together. I then added two gallons of water, seasoned with three ounces of salt, and a quarter of an ounce of brown sugar, stirred occasionally until boiling, and allowed it to simmer very gently for three hours, at the end of which time I found the barley perfectly tender. The above soup has been tasted by numerous noblemen, members of Parliament, and several ladies, who have lately visited my kitchen department, and who had considered it very good and nourishing.

He also published a book – selling for sixpence – *Soyer's Charitable Cookery; or, the Poor Man's Regenerator*[222] (1847) from which one penny from every sale was given to charities working with the poor. The book contained 23 'nutritious' recipes, including Oyster Porridge, Curry Fish, Meagre Pea Soup or Cabbage Stirabout, with details on how to create a 'model' kitchen. 110,000 copies were sold in 4-months. If we consider the maths from this and the known sales, 1d to charity does add up, showing Soyer would have provided £458 to charity (see table on next page), the equivalent of £40,000+ today. If he had sold 250,000 copies it would have been over £1,000 in 1847. Perhaps a question for today is: was Soyer truly philanthropic? Does 1/6 of total proceeds constitute benevolence?

[220] Quotes from ***The Freeman's Journal***, including the one cited here, **http://www.ricorso.net/rx/az-data/journals/f/Freemans/jrn.htm** accessed 3 Mar 2025

[221] ***British Newspaper Archive*** search for *Soyer's Soup No.1* recipe **https://www.britishnewspaperarchive.co.uk/search/results/1840-01-01/1849-12-31?basicsearch=soyer%20soup%201&exactsearch=false&retrievecountrycounts=false&region=london%2c%20england&mostspecificlocation=london%2c%20england&sortorder=2** accessed 4 Mar 2025

[222] ***Oxford University***'s *Bodleian Library's* digital copy of *Soyer's Charitable Cookery; or, the Poor Man's Regenerator* **https://dbooks.bodleian.ox.ac.uk/books/PDFs/590930355.pdf** accessed 4 Mar 2025

Soyer's Charitable Cookery; or, the Poor Man's Regenerator								
Price per unit (d)	**Units sold**	**Proceeds from sales (d)**	**Proceeds from 1d per booklet**	**£s to charity (converting d in to £s)**	***Bank of England* inflation calculator value for 1847 to Jan 2025**	**Deducted from gross (d)**	**£s to Soyer**	***Bank of England* inflation calculator value for 1847 to Jan 2025**
6	110000	660000	110000	£458	£40,268	550000	£2,292	£201,517
6	250000	1500000	250000	£1,042	£91,615	1250000	£5,208	£457,897

Above: Opening of Alexis Soyer's soup kitchen, 1847, *Illustrated London News*, p. 256. Date: 17 April 1847.

Receipt No. 1.—For two Gallons.

Two ounces of dripping.	0½d.
Quarter of a pound of solid meat, at 4d. per lb. (cut into dice one inch square)	1
Quarter pound of onions, sliced thin Quarter pound of turnips; the peel will do, or one whole one cut into small dice Two ounces of leeks; the green tops will do, sliced thin Three ounces of celery	1
Three quarters of a pound of common flour	1
Half a pound of pearl barley, or one pound of Scotch	1½
Three ounces of salt Quarter of an ounce of brown sugar	0¼
Fuel	0¾
Two gallons of water	0
	6

Above: Recipe from page 19 of *Soyer's Charitable Cookery; or, the Poor Man's Regenerator.*

Taken directly from page 19 of *Soyer's Charitable Cookery; or, the Poor Man's Regenerator*, the above right illustration shows how Soyer could make 2 gallons (over 9 litres) of soup for 6d. Using modern weights and measures, that's enough to serve 36 people (250ml each) on £2.20 or 6p per portion (in 2025, based on the ***Bank of England***'s inflation calculator).

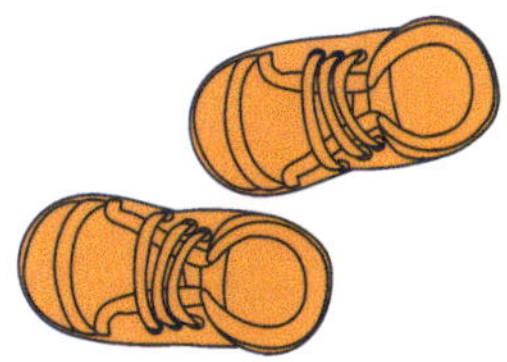

OTHER 'FAMINE' SOUPS

Today 'Famine Soup' recipes abound, mostly following the same outline as provided in Soyer's recipe above. In general, the still use low quality ingredients, such as the tops of leeks or celery leaves rather than the main body of the vegetable. The huge quantities – requiring long cooking times – need vast amounts of fuel and diminish the nutritional value. In Noel Kissane's *The Irish Famine: A Documentary History*[223] a Quaker recipe for 200 gallons of soup[224] runs as shown on the next page.

223 Kissane, N. (1996). *The Irish Famine: a Documentary History*. Syracuse, N.Y. Distributed for ***The National Library Of Ireland*** by ***Syracuse University Press***

224 PDF of Noel Kissane's book *The Irish Famine: A Documentary History*, referencing the Quaker recipe for famine soup on page 80 **http://sarkoups.free.fr/kissane1995.pdf** accessed 4 Mar 2025

Quaker recipe			**Modern conversions**		
Receipt for 200 gallons			**Stones**	**Kilos**	**Litres**
Beef	150	lb	10.71	68.0	68.039
Peas	70	lb	5.00	31.8	31.751
Oatmeal	42	lb	3.00	19.1	19.051
Scotch barley	42	lb	3.00	19.1	19.051
Ground pepper and allspice	half	lb	0.04	0.2	0.2268
Salt	1/4	stone	0.02	0.1	0.1134
Totals			**21.8**	**138.2**	**138.2**
Add water to make up to 200 gallons					**770.99**
Litres made					**909.22**
Number of 250ml servings					**3637**

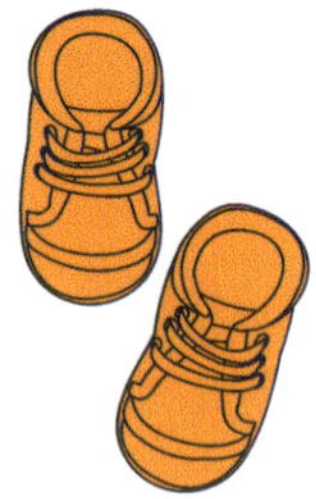

Based on feeding 18 people per gallon from Soyer's recipe, this recipe should feed 3,600, but our calculations suggest that if we equate 1-kilo to 1-litre and afford people a 250ml serving, there would be 3,637 servings, making the Quaker recipe stretch further that Soyer's. The authors will leave it up to you, the readers, to decide which is the more benevolent.

Differing in its preparation and using dried goods (peas) that require longer cooking times, the Quaker recipe does add spices. Soyer avoided using such items suggesting they actively promoted hunger because those that enjoyed them wanted more.

The Quaker recipe suggests boiling an amount of water into which you add the meat, cut in to walnut size pieces, with any bones broken small. After cooking for an hour, the cook should add the peas in 14lb bags. After 4-hours, the peas should be turned out of their bags to be mashed into a paste in a tub before being returned to the boiled meat to cook for a further 5-hours. Having blended the oatmeal with cold water, this is added to the pot and topped up with the remaining water needed to bring the volume to 200 gallons. Salt and spices should be added an hour after the oatmeal and cooked for a further hour, after which it would be ready for consumption.

Kissane goes on to talk about Irish relief committees, set up to try and administer support in providing soup to those in need.

Usually, soup could be bought for a penny (1d), but some relief committees tried to set up pools, gifted the soup to those in need under subscription by patrons who gave to the committee to set up 'soup shops'. Cloone, County Leitrim, was one such offer (see image, right[225]).

As if it were not enough to have been in the position to require the gift of a meal, from an individual or a soup shop, in Ireland those who used the soup kitchens were often derided for 'taking the soup' or being 'soupers'[226]. Although the term originated pre-The Great Hunger, the notion that 'taking the soup' meant you were a turncoat was deeply offensive, suggesting you had changed faith in your hour of need to avail of the food. This phrase is still heard occasionally today.

FAMINE SOUP LEGACY

Though there are many more 'famine soup' recipes available, they are mostly akin to the Soyer method and logic, meaning they are principally flawed in taste, health or nutrition.

[225] From the Clonbrock Papers and the ***National Archive*** *Relief Commission Papers*, 10,120 as seen in the ***National Library of Ireland*** **https://irishmanuscripts.ie/womenshistorysources/index.php?whp_function=1&whp_identifier=10120** accessed 4 Mar 2025

[226] ***RTÉ*** article on *Where the phrase 'taking the soup' comes from* **https://www.rte.ie/brainstorm/2021/1012/1253213-taking-the-soup-ireland-famine-history** accessed 4 Mar 2025

CLOONE SOUP-SHOP.

Days of Distribution:

WEDNESDAYS AND SATURDAYS,

WEEKLY.

Rule 1.—That Mrs. Hogg be requested to act as Treasurer, and superintend the management of the Cloone Soup Shop.

2.—That Soup be sold to the destitute at 1d. per Quart.

3.—That, in order to provide some Subsistence for the totally destitute, who are *wholly* without means, a copy of these Rules be sent to the Clergy, Gentry, and Farmers of the Parish of Cloone, to afford them an opportunity of supporting this benevolent object, and providing substantial relief for the Poor in their localities.

4.—That each Subscriber shall have power to recommend persons for gratuitous *weekly* supplies of Soup, according to the following order:

Subscribers of £1, to dispose of 16 Quarts of Soup, weekly, for 16 weeks, on Recommendation Tickets, to be supplied by the Treasurer.

Subscribers of 10s., to dispose of 8 Quarts, weekly, for 16 weeks, &c.

Subscribers of 5s., to dispose of 4 Quarts, weekly, for 16 weeks, &c.

Subscribers of 1s., to dispose of 2 Quarts, weekly, for 6 weeks.

The Glebe, Cloone,
December, 1846.

P.S.—Bailiffs to have power to recommend on the Subscriptions of absentee Landlords, as above.

[BRENNAN, Printer, Ck.-on-Shannon.

Image: From the Clonbrock Papers and the ***National Archive*** *Relief Commission Papers*, 10,120 as seen in the ***National Library of Ireland***.

Whilst tangible objects such as cast-iron famine pots litter museums, fields and gardens recipes fall from favour and memory, especially those that provide such little positive 'food for thought'. Though well documented in the vaults of archives, they have little lasting tangibility in and of themselves. Their influence is witnessed in etchings and paintings, plays and novellas and occasionally they will be recounted from personal memoirs scoured through by researchers, but — unlike songs or folklore stories — such recipes are unlikely to be spoken father-to-son, mother-to-daughter.

In his day, Soyer was primarily regarded as a philanthropist, without whom many more would have perished. However, even in the 1840s people raised questions about the value of his 'liquid diet' soup provisions and its nutrient values. Not to be beaten, Soyer returned with 'peas panada', a solid meal costing a quarter of the price of bread but having more nutritious value. This recipe was included in Soyer's follow up book *Soyer's Shilling Cookery for the People*, published by **Routledge and Co, London** (1854)[227]. Even so, Soyer's legacy is less widespread today than it would have been then. Could this be to do with the juxtaposition of his wealth with the very thing that brought him to fame?

As a major self-publicist, Soyer was in all the papers and was understood to be a de riguer chef, straddling the worlds of the upper classes and soup kitchens simultaneously. Today, this could be compared with Jamie Oliver (b.1975-d—) and his campaigns for school dinner reforms, sugar taxing, fair health food advertising standards and others[228]. How will those campaigns be viewed a100-years from now?

What the repeat in history demonstrates is there remain individuals with wealth working to aid those in severe need. As we see the disparity between the rich and poor grow, just as Dickens saw in Victorian England, we need benevolence in leadership to improve the lot of those least fortunate.

Perhaps Soyer's model is an in-road for this, to be applied alongside new learning about fuel efficiency, nutrition and humanity?

That said, revisiting 'famine soup' is important because it helps us see how society was looking at the individual starving. They were collectivising 'them' and hoping to deal with their needs en masse. The recipes show society asked its richest minds to create the most basic provisions, using a hegemonic structure to resolve a hegemonic issue. Conceivably, this needs to be a warning. If we listened earlier to the people at the coalface, we might prevent the need for '200 gallon' responses.

Taste and hunger, in this instance, are completely intangible cultural heritages. The reflection on the recipes used and produced at the time gives us a gateway to try to imagine what was being experienced by those in need then. However, it is this author's sincerest hope, that no one reading this will ever truly feel the lardy-slop in their two-year-hungry stomach or the texture of overboiled barley in their dehydrated mouths, eaten from a spoon chained to a table, because they cannot be trusted to leave without it, whilst someone wearing expensive cologne and a sharp suit carrying a designer bag looks on.

Below: Detail from The New Poor Law poster, 1837 (EXT 6/1), taken from ***The National Archives*** (UK). A man carries two buckets labelled 'Pea soup for the paupers', whilst a group of children pick oakum.

[227] ***Foods of England***'s *A Shilling Cookery or The People* **https://www.foodsofengland.co.uk/book1845soyer.html** accessed 4 Mar 2025

[228] Jamie Oliver's campaign trail **https://www.jamieoliver.com/campaigns** accessed 4 Mar 2025

13/ MEMORIAL MUSIC – A COMMISSIONER'S REFLECTION

What do we aim to do when we commemorate something as important and far reaching as famine? Ultimately, we strive to unite people to reflect – communally – on an event. We invite people to share in a moment of collective understanding to recognise a point of influence or change, usually in front of an official. This generates venerability, loaning weight and importance to the subject by showing society that its officials and citizens still care. However performative this gesture might be, such acts can connect onlookers with their past, their heritage and the very people that encountered or endured the point of change under reflection.

Liverpool's Irish Famine memorial events have, in recent years, primarily comprised of a set of speeches and a minute's silence gathered around The Great Hunger commemoration memorial, outside ***St Luke's 'Bombed Out' Church***. The deconsecrated church is run as a memorial to peace, following the destruction of its internal facilities during the Blitz in World War II.

'Lest we forget' is now a common commemorative idiom, primarily used about the horrors of warfare. Taken from Rudyard Kipling's poem, *Recessional* (***The Times***, 1897)[229], this phrase has become a communal call to present and future generations not to waste knowledge by repeating history. Whilst we may not wish to use a colonial term in this context, the Liverpool Irish Famine memorial (as an object and an event) is a call to action to our present and future generations that states that famine is never inevitable, whilst simultaneously marking the global importance of this single 'event'. At its core, an event like this is a recognition of intangible cultural heritage made evident through collective memory and by bearing witness. So, what are the kinds of things that will draw people together? Locations, friendships, spectacles, speeches, music… Ireland is famed for its music and its laments. It has given the world songs that reflect on leaving Ireland or on lost loves, teamed with rebel songs, murder ballads and aislings (vision poems). As an arts commissioner, it struck the Festival that song might be a way of gathering people together in reflection.

Ireland hosts an annual national famine memorial day on the third Sunday of May. As the custodians of the *Liverpool Irish Famine Trail*, it is now our honour to host a memorial. The ***Liverpool Irish Festival*** is always held in October. Being roughly six-months away from St Patrick's Day, and the competition that creates, the Festival has found its home within Liverpool's rich event calendar.

Being in October – and at ***St Luke's 'Bombed Out' Church*** – provides certain pros and cons. It is the spiritual home for the event, being that the Eamonn O'Doherty statue is there 24:7 365-days a year. It forms a significant backdrop for the live activity, having now served the community for almost 30-years. However, the site has minimal seating and being outside it means audiences and performers are always subject to the elements. Practically, this means the memorial event needs not to last more than c.30-minutes long, it being inhospitable to ask people to stand for longer, especially for those that cannot.

Asking people to reflect on the horrific ordeals of others can cause great upset. When academics, historians or researchers think about An Gorta Mór they often talk about 'collective trauma' and 'intergenerational traumatic memory'. This considers how a population of people were affected and how that experience is passed on. After World War II there fell a 'great silence' and so it was with the Irish Famine. What happens beyond these silences and how do we help people unlock difficult experiences without creating new trauma(s)? New studies into epigenetics, and how trauma is carried in the body and across generations, are underway but what we know – as of now – is that laying down markers and allowing collective memory to bear witness to events can help.

[229] Rudyard Kipling's *Recessional* was first posted in ***The Times*** (17 Jul 1897) details here: **https://www.kiplingsociety.co.uk/readers-guide/rg_recess1.htm** and poem here **https://www.kiplingsociety.co.uk/poem/poems_recess.htm** accessed 4 Mar 2025 on the ***Kipling Society*** web pages

Memorials can be a healing part of that process. At the Festival we realised that, in holding a memorial, we intended for people to recognise the historical event without taking on pain or expecting individuals to process empathy for experiences too numerable to process. Anyone who spends time researching bleak parts of history — be it political conflict, war or pandemics — will need respite from it. It is not humane to dwell in pain-recall for extended periods. As curators of the Great Hunger memorial event, it is anticipated that the event creates a bond that enables attendees to return year-on-year. This means providing something meaningful for attendees to connect with, without generating anger, too much sadness, pain or trauma.

MUSIC

In 2023, the Festival commissioned a song. Written by Úna Quinn *Those Roads* (performed by Úna and local guitar sensation Neil Campbell) closed the annual famine memorial. Following the minute's silence, the audience were deeply appreciative of the beauty, candour and hope offered by the song[230]. For that occasion, we were looking for a single piece to augment the memorial and offer something other than spoken word.

This prompted us to consider commissioning a song that reflected on and taught people about the specifics of the Liverpool Irish Great Hunger experience. A song could become a 'gift' for people to take away from the memorial. It could be offered to choirs, to perform annually, and a legacy piece that taught new generations about The Liverpool Irish Great Hunger story. Audiences could learn the lyrics between memorials and join in with singing it the following year. It would need to be able to be sung by one voice and/or many.

The Festival created an open call, inviting anyone to submit a song outline[231]. Writers were asked to provide example lyrics and suggest the style of music it would become when recorded.

[230] Úna Quinn's song *Those Roads* **https://www.liverpoolirishfestival.com/those-roads-una-quinn** accessed 4 Mar 2025

[231] ***Liverpool Irish Festival***'s open call for a song commission **https://www.liverpoolirishfestival.com/song-commission-open-call** accessed 4 Mar 2025

In all earnestness, the team thought that asking people to write a song about An Gorta Mór — to be performed and heard in October, possibly in a howling gale — would prove unpopular. How wrong we were. Entries flew in, ranging from traditional jigs to soaring ballads. People penned timeline songs and odes to the Mersey and Irish Sea. Judging became exceedingly difficult. A matrix was produced to determine values for

- what extent and how well people had responded to the brief
- how specific it was to the Liverpool Irish story
- whether we could fully envisage the end song
- if it had been written for solo and multiple voices
- a licence for free use was offered
- how people had showed they would and could work to time
- completing all obligations of the brief.

A panel was formed from within the Festival, the *History Research Group* and the ***Liverpool Irish Centre Choir*** with whom the matrix shared, completed, compared, aggregated and reviewed. The panel discussed how relevant the music would be to intergenerational audiences; appropriateness to the subject matter; clarity of purpose and other creative factors that the submissions had presented. The panel wanted to challenge conventional approaches to memorialisation that prioritise solemnity above all else. A winner was selected.

THE ULLALOO

An 'ullaloo' is a lament or coronach (funeral song).

Ian Cantwell and Marty Snape's song of the same name is perhaps a surprising choice. It has a very upbeat verse and chorus structure, whilst delivering politically critical lines and dark imagery. Nevertheless, it commemorates the pain of The Great Hunger, acknowledges Liverpool's support and brings the 'Lest we forget' quality, raised in the refrain: "Why, why in my time, To lose a million sons and daughters?". For readers with online access, we encourage you to listen to the song on our app, within the Memorial section. Asked about their experience of creating the song in September 2024, Ian Cantwell said:

Ian Cantwell, October 2024.

"I first heard the word Ullaloo on a radio programme about terms that have long since fallen out of use. It is a haunting expression that rolls off the tongue. An ancient ritual lament to the dead.

"I had been researching my family tree and learned that my great-great grandparents William and Rose had fled the ravages of the Great Hunger - or An Gorta Mór - setting sail for Liverpool in 1850. With five young children and a newborn baby, Rose and William left Rahan in County Offaly for the last time, never to set foot on Irish soil again.

"Words in the history books became flesh and blood, and the story of my great-great grandparents struggle became the inspiration for the song *The Ullaloo*.

"It is an honour and a proud moment for Marty and myself to have our song chosen and we cannot wait to hear it performed by the choir".

The Ullaloo's unexpectedly upbeat musical structure represents an original artistic choice that attempts to balance honouring tragedy whilst simultaneously offering hope. As commissioners, the panel felt this would create a legacy piece rather than a single moment of reflection.

Since commissioning, the song has been arranged, scored and shared publicly, as well as having its inaugural performance at the 2024 ***Liverpool Irish Festival***'s annual Liverpool Irish Great Hunger commemoration memorial. Anyone can access music and arrangement sheets, the song recording and lyrics, here: **liverpoolirishfestival.com/ullaloo**

In years to come, we hope to build the number of choirs that want to come and present it with us as part of the Festival's memorial event. The song is seen to transform commemoration from a passive experience into an active, participatory one that can evolve over time.

The Festival is incredibly proud of the commission and grateful to Ian Cantwell and Marty Snape for their talented and compassionate contribution. Sharing it with the ***Liverpool Irish Centre***'s choir was a brilliant way of reaching the community we serve. It is hoped more of this will happen with them — and others — in future. Everyone involved is extremely grateful to ***The National Lottery Heritage Fund***, which funded the work as part of the *Reveal* project. As a communication tool, the Festival believes this song is a valuable way of beginning to tell the Liverpool Irish part of the An Gorta Mór story. Readers are encouraged to embrace the song, share it, learn it and sing it with others at future memorial events.

The frontrunners for the *Liverpool Irish Famine Trail* vigil pass the *Liver Building* **on 26 October 2024. They include Ireland's Ambassador to the UK Martin Fraser and Consul General Sarah Mangan; Caroilin Callery; Professor Christine Kinealy, members of *The Armagh Rhymers*; citizen research group participant James Martin, walker John Maguire; Dr Jason King and Metro Mayor Steve Rotheram, among many others.**

14/ TYING IT ALL TOGETHER

What we have tried to do with *Reveal* is make a complex history, involving many of millions of stories, more approachable. Instead of writing a history of An Gorta Mór — which has been done very successfully by historians such as Quiery, McMahon and Kinealy — ours is a means by which those existing histories are overlaid and interlocked with Liverpool's geography, society and people.

As a creative organisation, we continually ask, "is this original thinking? Are we bringing something new to the table?". If not, we have an issue. What we believe *Reveal* does is share the approaches we have taken to memorial that you, the public, have paid for via funding we have been awarded. We were granted funding *because* we would return something to the public. With our app, song, free events, talks, walks, tours, exhibitions and physical assets (bronze shoes, plaques, books and artworks), we have generated a diverse range of new materials and dialogues that are unlocking intangible and contested histories, giving people access to their heritage today. The physical and digital aspects of the project combining to create multiple entry points for different audiences.

Reveal is just one of many routes people have in to discovering our findings. As the book demonstrates, we have tried to provide multiple contexts that frame An Gorta Mór as something interwoven with today's societal development and politics, showing that the history we have lain has deep crossovers our 'now'. We placed importance on personal stories and individual narratives to make history relatable and meaningful to contemporary audiences, treating them as the backbone of the project. We know theoretical and factual tomes already exist, but for some, it will take a personal connection to bring them into a complicated history such as this. We are proud that our approach has given voice to a diverse range of experiences, connections and viewpoints. The collaborative nature of the project has brought together diverse voices and perspectives involving academics, artists, community members and descendants.

Publicly funded knowledge is and should be, to our minds, publicly owned and accessible. All the facts and figures from this book, are available within our app or on our website. Selling the book as a product, which raises money towards the Festival's ongoing work on the Trail, was a difficult moral decision for us to take. When we arrived at the idea for *Revive* it came from a change of use to our funding. To take the same decision deliberately for *Reveal* meant a serious consideration of what we were doing it for and whether we were commercialising An Gorta Mór. We do not want to echo Soyer, claiming philanthropic benevolence, but keeping five-sixths of the proceeds.

The book is the product of thousands of hours of work by volunteer researchers, designers, historians, artists, photographers, citizens and archivists. Its physical manifestation cannot be made for free. It is an optional add on for readers to choose to buy, to collate the compendium of stories, to touch and hold, share and gift. It is in today's terms — we believe — a moderately priced book for its design, construction and quality. Rather than seeing this as the commercialisation of An Gorta Mór, we see it as a means of memorialisation and hope our readers do, too. As a charity, the Festival's proceeds are always reinvested in work to give to the public. This will be no different.

As we are on the subject of charity, we believe it is important to note Liverpool's humanitarian contribution in the 1840s and 50s. As a resource for good, Liverpool is often overlooked for its direct aid, being combined with the 'English' or 'British' response. We hope *Reveal* has highlighted that Liverpool's *Select Vestry* was a leading benefactor in providing relief and direct aid. The city's leaders also provided progressive and advanced approaches to medical leadership, whilst faith leaders petitioned to create tailored support for those in need. Their intervention, without governmental support, supported hundreds of thousands of lives, avoiding many more fatalities and providing a home long beyond the end of The Great Hunger.

We are not blind to the exploitation that existed; conditions were far from perfect. Nevertheless, compared with contemporary responses to far smaller migrant numbers it is impressive that Liverpool expanded to cope and that there are not many more reports of anti-establishment activities, riots and crime. The people of Liverpool have much to be proud of, when thinking about its role as a city of sanctuary and its continued life as an Irish British city today.

Internationally recognised, ***Liverpool University Press***'s HQ sits within the space between the *Brownlow Hill Workhouse* and *Paupers' Graveyard*. Established in 1899 it is the third oldest university press, after Oxford and Cambridge. Having the benefit of a ***Liverpool University Press*** peer review is invaluable, as it acknowledges that our new thinking can be evidenced and is legitimate in the pantheon of texts on this subject. Unbiased, knowledgeable and considered overviews always strengthen a work. Having the Press's approval tells us we have been successful in connecting broader conversations about migration, displacement and humanitarian responses today, whilst making historical memory relevant to current challenges. Though we want the academic rigour of the Press, we also hope that our tone and insights are approachable and accessible, helping the Press fulfil its civic mission to support the region's creative economy.

Reveal is not a full stop to this work, as we hope we have indicated. We have many plans, including the refreshment of the memorial and plaques, site additions and deeper research. There will be many more events, talks, walks and conferences and at every step we will seek community engagement with this history, because community is at the centre of all of this. We make this history available because it affects community identity and recognition, connects people to their heritage and enables people to trace their family through time. Connections make us stronger, more united and better able to make collective decisions for the greater good. Connection helps reduce isolation, improving our health and wellbeing, allowing for self-actualisation and confidence in how we locate ourselves in the world. Knowing where we came from means we can return and knowing this means we can make new pathways. Looking back, therefore, can help us to look forward, to see new beginnings, just as the An Gorta Mór survivors had to, leading to over 70-million Irish diaspora globally.

We began *Revive* — and indeed *Reveal* — with short quotes from Warsan Shire's *Home*[232]. Because it is so fitting, we'll end with another portion from the same poem:

> I want to go home,
> but home is the mouth of a shark
> home is the barrel of the gun
> and no one would leave home
> unless home chased you to the shore.

Cuimhnich. Remember.

[232] Warsan Shire's *Home*, as presented by ***Amnesty International*** **https://www.amnesty.ie/wp-content/uploads/2016/06/home-by-warsan-shire.pdf** accessed 7 Mar 2025

The Bronze Shoes bearers arrive at the Liverpool Irish Great Hunger commemoration memorial, 27 May 2024. Left to right: John Maguire, Emma Smith, Caroilin Callery and Greg Quiery.

15/ ACKNOWLEDGEMENTS

The Festival has a huge number of thanks to offer for all manner of contributions to the Trail and connected work. There are so many organisations and people to thank. Where organisations have been listed, we hope the teams there know we mean them, too.

- ***Altar Pottery***
- ***ArtsGroupie CIC***, with endless gratitude to John Maguire who has given so much to the project and to Mikey Dunne whose support is much valued
- *Birkenhead Library*
- Canada's Ambassador to Ireland, Nancy Smyth
- Ian Cantwell and Marty Snape
- Chris Matanlé-Mockridge
- ***Conradh Na Gaeilge*** with particular thanks to Tomás Ryan
- Tadhg Devlin
- *#Cultural Connectedness Exchange Network*
- ***EPIC***
- ***Gazooky Studios***
- ***Global Irish Famine Way***
- ***Government of Ireland*** with special thanks going to Ambassador Martin Fraser, General Consul Sarah Mangan and Vice-General Consuls Carina O'Brien and Deirdre O'Flaherty for their year-round support, advocacy and collaboration
- Ireland's Ambassadors to Canada, Dr Eamonn McKee and John Concannon
- ***Irish Heritage Trust***, especially Dr Jason King
- Professor Christine Kinealy of ***Quinnipiac University***, USA
- ***Liverpool BID***
- *Liverpool Central Library* with a special mention for Denise Jones and Vicki Caren
- ***Liverpool Great Hunger Commemoration Committee***, especially Greg Quiery and his sister-in-law Pamela Quiery who have both championed the cause and 'walked the walk' with ease and grace
- ***Liverpool Irish Centre Choir***, particularly Amy Housley – for assistance with *The Ullaloo* – and Maureen Royce for making the connection
- *Liverpool Irish Famine Trail's History Research Group*:
  - Lewis Braithwaite
  - Becky Clancy
  - Kieran Daly
  - Steven Garnett
  - Vicki Caren
  - Catherine Leen
  - Tricia Mackin
  - Clare McGrath
  - Richard Orritt
  - Flora Small
  - Katherine Wiseman
- ***Liverpool University Press***, especially Alison Welsby
- ***Martin's Bed and Breakfast***, Strokestown, Ireland
- ***National Famine Museum***, Strokestown, Ireland
- ***National Famine Way***, Strokestown, Ireland
- ***The National Lottery Heritage Fund***
- Nicola McGovern
- Lydia O'Hara
- ***Overshoot Productions*** and Ailsa McQueen
- ***Powerfull Beyond All Measure***
- ***Spider Project***
- ***Strokestown Estate*** and in particular Caroilin Callery
- Paul Robinson
- Pamela Sullivan
- ***Waterways Ireland.***

Our volunteer *History Research Group* have been jovially and competently led by John Maguire, Director of ***ArtsGroupie CIC***. The Festival thanks each of you, but especially John. Papi is proud.

As well as thanking those above, the ***Liverpool Irish Festival*** have key organisations and names that warrant additional attention and commendation.

For their direct investment into the project, we thank ***The National Lottery Heritage Fund***. Your trust in us has been transformative for the Trail and the Festival.

Though we have tried to make it clear throughout, the Irish Government is a true supporter of this work. Not only have they found funds to support us via *Strategic Diaspora* and *Emigrant Support Programme* funds, but they are also active advocates for our work and ensured that good people have known about us. Special thanks go to Ambassador Martin Fraser and Consul General Sarah Mangan.

For his tireless work, support, friendship and advice, we thank Greg Quiery. Greg was a member of the original ***Liverpool Great Hunger Commemoration Committee***. He is also an author of a book on this subject, *In Hardship and Hope: A History of the Liverpool Irish*, which we highly recommend.

Gone, but not forgotten, is Tony Birtill. We are indebted to Tony for his early work on the Trail and support of the Festival, alongside his community endeavours and all he did with ***Conradh Na Gaeilge Learpholl*** and ***Oideas Gael***, among additional organisations to which he gave his time and energy.

People and organisations that have provided in-kind support for the project, from *Revive* to *Reveal*, include

- Marion Acreman, ***MacDonagh Junction Shopping Centre*** and ***Kilkenny Famine Memorial Site***, Kilkenny
- ***St Anthony's Church***
- Caroilin Callery of ***Great Famine Voices Roadshow*** and ***Strokestown Park***
- ***Ainsley Gommon Architects***
- ***Liverpool Great Hunger Commemoration Committee***
- Professor Christine Kinealy, Director of ***Ireland's Great Hunger Institute***, ***Quinnipiac University***, USA
- Dr Jason King at ***Irish Heritage Trust*** and ***Strokestown Park***
- Eamonn Lavin and the team at ***The Philharmonic Dining Rooms***
- *The Institute of Irish Studies* at ***University of Liverpool***
- ***Liverpool Arts Bar***
- *Liverpool Central Library* ***and Archive***, Liverpool City Council
- ***Liverpool Irish Centre***
- Breege McDaid and the team at ***Irish Community Care Merseyside***
- The ***Mersey Maritime Museum***, ***National Museums Liverpool***
- ***National Museums Liverpool***
- Michael O'Neill, Tony McKean and Shelley Bethel of ***St. Patrick's Chapel***
- Reverend Crispin Pailing from ***Our Lady and St Nicholas's Church***
- Andrew Weatherstone, Charlie Backhouse and Sam Harrison at ***Nonconform***.

The Festival works with over 80-organisations a year, which is too many to list, but we would like to state our gratitude to each and every one of you. Last, but by no means least — the Festival's Board of Trustees, who in the last year have included Dr Ann Hoskins (Chair), John Chandler (Board Secretary), Martin Bond, Gerry Diver, Ollie Hall, Eamonn Lavin, Professor Mary Hickman, Clare McGrath, Patsy O'Connor and our Festival Coordinator, Pascal O'Loughlin, must also receive gratitude.

For funding Festival activities outside the project, we would like to offer our gratitude to

- ***Arts Council England***
- ***Culture Liverpool***
- Government of Ireland's ***Emigrant Support Programme***
- ***HM Government*** and ***#HereForCulture*** for cultural recovery funding
- Liverpool City Council
- Liverpool City Region Combined Authority
- ***Tourism Ireland***.

Great Famine Commemoration Committee (Liverpool)
Between 1845 and 1852 over one million Irish people died from starvation and disease. A further one million emigrated. Ireland remains the only country in Europe where the population today is less than it was in 1845.

16/ REFERENCES

The following text is compiled in the Harvard reference style. It is not formatted as per the house styling of the Festival, or the rest of the book. This complies with academic standards, whereas our house styling relates to other accessibility measures. If you want to access these online (including live links), you can do so using the QR code above or the URL that follows:
liverpoolirishfestival.com/reveal-reference-list

Archives Hub (2025). *Records of the National Association for the Repeal of the Contagious Diseases Acts.* [online] Archives Hub. Available at: https://archiveshub.jisc.ac.uk/search/archives/06cf0698-1f6f-3e61-b592-b3620ddbd825 [Accessed 12 Feb. 2025].

Art UK (2018). *Memorial to Captain Noel Chavasse (1884–1917), VC and Bar MC (The Liverpool Heroes Memorial) | Art UK.* [online] Art UK. Available at: https://artuk.org/discover/artworks/memorial-to-captain-noel-chavasse-18841917-vc-and-bar-mc-the-liverpool-heroes-memorial-301913 [Accessed 6 Mar. 2025].

Bain News Service (2015). E. De Valera - Public domain photograph (Library of Congress), glass negative - PICRYL - Public Domain Media Search Engine Public Domain Search. [online] PICRYL - Public Domain Media Search Engine. Available at: https://picryl.com/media/e-de-valera [Accessed 25 Mar. 2025].

Bank of England (2024). *Inflation Calculator.* [online] Bank of England. Available at: https://www.bankofengland.co.uk/monetary-policy/inflation/inflation-calculator [Accessed 8 Mar. 2025].

Barewall Art Gallery (2015). *Beatles Statue 2015 Maquette Sculpture by Andy Edwards.* [online] Barewall. Available at: https://www.barewall.co.uk/collections/andy-edwards/products/the-beatles-statue-2015-maquette-sculpture-by-andy-edwards [Accessed 6 Mar. 2025].

BBC (2022). Ireland profile - Timeline. *BBC News.* [online] 13 Dec. Available at: https://www.bbc.co.uk/news/world-europe-17480250 [Accessed 8 Mar. 2025].

BBC Teach (2024). *KS3 History: Transforming the Health of Liverpool - Doctor Duncan.* [online]. Available at: https://www.bbc.co.uk/teach/class-clips-video/articles/znfp382 [Accessed 8 Mar. 2025].

Belchem, J. (2011). *Irish, Catholic and Scouse The History of the Liverpool-Irish, 1800–1939.* Liverpool University Press.

Bevan, S. (2023). Discovering the 'Secret of Life'. *University of Cambridge.* [online] 28 Feb. Available at: https://www.cam.ac.uk/stories/DNA-structure-discovery-cambridge-70th-anniversary [Accessed 8 Mar. 2025].

Birtill, T. and Stowell, B. (2020). *A Hidden History: the Irish language in Liverpool (An Ghaeilge i Learpholl).* Liverpool, UK: G&K Publishing.

Bloy, M. (2002). *Gilbert's Act (1782).* [online] The Victorian Web. Available at: https://victorianweb.org/history/poorlaw/gilbert.html [Accessed 11 Mar. 2025].

Booth, R. (2025). *Meta to get rid of factcheckers and recommend more political content.* [online] The Guardian. Available at: https://www.theguardian.com/technology/2025/jan/07/meta-facebook-instagram-threads-mark-zuckerberg-remove-fact-checkers-recommend-political-content [Accessed 8 Mar. 2025].

Bowden, A. (2020). *Halsall Navvy Sculpture, Leeds & Liverpool Canal.* [online] Lancashire Past. Available at: https://lancashirepast.com/2020/08/16/halsall-navvy-sculpture-leeds-liverpool-canal/ [Accessed 6 Mar. 2025].

British Newspaper Archive (2025). *Search results for 'soyer soup 1' (between 1 Jan 1840-31st Dec 1849, London, England).* [online] British Newspaper Archive (co.uk). Available at: https://www.britishnewspaperarchive.co.uk/search/results/1840-01-01/1849-12-31?basicsearch=soyer%20soup%201&exactsearch=false&retrievecountrycounts=false&region=london%2c%20england&mostspecificlocation=london%2c%20england&sortorder=2 [Accessed 4 Mar. 2025].

British Online Archives (2025). *Gore's Liverpool Directory.* [online] British Online Archives. Available at: https://britishonlinearchives.com/collections/8/volumes/5/gores-liverpool-directory [Accessed 26 Feb. 2025].

Broadbent (2025). *Broadbent Studio.* [online] Broadbent Studio. Available at: https://broadbent.studio/reconciliation-triangle-casestudy [Accessed 4 Mar. 2025].

Broadbent Studio (2025). *River of Life.* [online] Broadbent Studio. Available at: https://broadbent.studio/river-of-life [Accessed 4 Mar. 2025].

Burke, P. (2024). *Those who suffer write the songs - Frank Harte.* [online] An Phoblacht. Available at: https://www.anphoblacht.com/contents/13805 [Accessed 11 Mar. 2025].

Cairde na hEireann Liverpool (2021). *Irish ethnicity.* [online] Cairde na hEireann Liverpool. Available at: https://cairdeliverpool.wordpress.com/tag/irish-ethnicity-2/ [Accessed 24 Feb. 2025].

Canon van Vlaanderen (2024). *The Potato Crisis.* [online] Canon van Vlaanderen. Available at: https://www.canonvanvlaanderen.be/en/events/the-potato-crisis/ [Accessed 8 Mar. 2025].

Cavanagh, T. (1996). *Public sculpture of Liverpool.* Liverpool: Liverpool University Press.

Central Statistics Office, Ireland (2023). *Press Statement Census of Population 2022 - Summary Results - CSO - Central Statistics Office.* [online] www.cso.ie. Available at: https://www.cso.ie/en/csolatestnews/pressreleases/2023pressreleases/pressstatementcensusofpopulation2022-summaryresults/.

Chitty, M. (2000). *Historic Wavertree, Liverpool - The Village Green and Lock-up.* [online] The Wavertree Society. Available at: https://thewavertreesociety.uk/wavsoc/dhw/page50.html [Accessed 5 Mar. 2025].

Chitty, M. and Prison History (2019). *Wavertree Lock Up House - 19th Century Prison History.* [online] 19th Century Prison History.

Available at: https://www.prisonhistory.org/lockup/wavertree-lock-up-house/ [Accessed 5 Mar. 2025].

Church of Ireland (2017). *Church of Ireland – Parish Handbook: Introduction to serving on a Select Vestry.* [online] Church of Ireland. Available at: https://www.churchofireland.org/cmsfiles/pdf/Resources/ParishResources/SelectVestry/Introduction-to-Serving-on-a-Select-Vestry-11-01-17.pdf [Accessed 27 Feb. 2025].

Clement-Lorford, F. (2019). *Alexis Soyer: The Greatest Chef of the 19th Century.* [online] Alexis Soyer. Available at: https://alexis-soyer.com/ [Accessed 8 Mar. 2025].

Cobain, I. (2025). *Sectarianism in Liverpool: The Evaporation of Hatred.* [online] Dublin Review of Books. Available at: https://drb.ie/articles/the-evaporation-of-hatred/ [Accessed 24 Feb. 2025].

Colonial Office: Land and Emigration Commission (1849). Colonial Office 384/84, 4584 Emigration, Commissioners: Merivale, 22 May 1849. Accessed by Kieran Daly.

Commonwealth Secretariat (2025). *London Declaration, 1949; issued at the Commonwealth Prime Ministers Meeting, London, United Kingdom, 22-27 April 1949.* [online] Commonwealth. Available at: https://thecommonwealth.org/london-declaration-1949 [Accessed 8 Mar. 2025].

Cooks Info (2005). *Alexis Benoit Soyer: Chef and Food Writer.* [online] Cooks Info. Available at: https://www.cooksinfo.com/alexis-benoit-soyer [Accessed 8 Mar. 2025].

Cousins, C. (2019). *Cinderella Soldiers: The Irish in Liverpool in the Great War.* Stroud: The History Press.

Crowley, J., Smyth, W.J., Murphy, M. and Roche, C. (2012). *Atlas of the Great Irish Famine.* New York: New York University Press.

Curlter, W. (2024). *A short history of English agriculture.* [online] Wellcome Collection. Available at: https://wellcomecollection.org/works/g4qaep54/items?canvas=2 [Accessed 6 Mar. 2025].

Darwen, L. (2015). *Lewis Darwen | Loughborough University - Academia.edu.* [online] Academia.edu. Available at: https://lboro.academia.edu/LewisDarwen [Accessed 26 Feb. 2025].

Darwen, L. and RTÉ (2021). *A Strange Environment indeed: Famine Irish in Northwest England.* [online] RTÉ. Available at: https://www.rte.ie/history/post-famine/2021/0204/1195102-a-strange-environment-indeed-the-famine-irish-in-england/ [Accessed 8 Mar. 2025].

Davis, P. (2023). *Legislation on the Slave Trade.* [online] Archive.org. Available at: https://web.archive.org/web/20230711152759/https://www.pdavis.nl/Legis_06.htm [Accessed 12 Feb. 2025].

Department of Foreign Affairs (2017). *Ambassador - Department of Foreign Affairs.* [online] Irishembassy.com.my. Available at: http://irishembassy.com.my/irish-embassy/canada/about-us/ambassador/ [Accessed 26 Feb. 2025].

Dobson, K. (2020). *Dignity In Poverty - Royal Liver Memories.* [online] Royal Liver Memories. Available at: https://royalliverhistory.co.uk/2020/10/04/dignity-in-poverty/kevind/ [Accessed 5 Mar. 2025].

Donnelly, J.S. (2002). *The Great Irish Potato Famine.* Stroud: The History Press/Sutton.

Duffy, P. (2008). *The Killing of Major Denis Mahon: A Mystery of old Ireland.* New York, USA: Harper, p.111.

Dunne, G. (2020). *St Anthony's Church.* [online] St Anthony's Church. Available at: https://stanthonyscotlandroad.wordpress.com/ [Accessed 25 Feb. 2025].

Dwyer, F. (2025). *Home | Irish History Podcast.* [online] IrishHistoryPodcast. Available at: https://www.irishhistorypodcast.ie/ [Accessed 12 Mar. 2025]. Specifically the episodes on 'The Story of Irish Coffin Ships'.

Echo, L. (2013). *Remembering The Ragged Trousered Philanthropists author Robert Tressell, 100 years after his death in Liverpool.* [online] Liverpool Echo. Available at: https://www.liverpoolecho.co.uk/news/liverpool-news/remembering-ragged-trousered-philanthropists-author-3386148 [Accessed 5 Mar. 2025].

Ellis, L. (2017). *Wages and Prices: A Family Story.* [online] A Family Story. Available at: http://www.afamilystory.co.uk/history/wages-and-prices.aspx#Annual-wages [Accessed 8 Mar. 2025].

English Heritage (2001). *Josephine Butler: Champion of Women's Rights (Blue Plaques).* [online] English Heritage. Available at: https://www.english-heritage.org.uk/visit/blue-plaques/butler-josephine-butler [Accessed 8 Mar. 2025].

EPIC (2018). *EPIC The Irish Emigration Museum (Dublin).* [online] EPIC CHQ. Available at: https://epicchq.com [Accessed 8 Mar. 2025].

Europa Nostra (2017). *Mr. Jim Callery - European Heritage Awards / Europa Nostra Awards.* [online] European Heritage Awards/Europa Nostra Awards. Available at: https://www.europeanheritageawards.eu/winners/mr-jim-callery [Accessed 26 Feb. 2025].

Faulkner, M. (2025). *People: Kitty Wilkinson (1786-1860).* [online] St James' Cemetery, Liverpool. Available at: https://www.stjamescemetery.co.uk/index/category/kitty-wilkinson [Accessed 12 Feb. 2025].

Fergus (2016). *Marking the 1916 Rising Centenary in Frongoch.* [online] The Irish Place. Available at: https://www.theirishplace.com/heritage/854/ [Accessed 5 Mar. 2025].

Find a Grave (2012). *St Martin-in-the-Fields Churchyard in Liverpool, Merseyside.* [online] Find a Grave. Available at: https://www.findagrave.com/cemetery/2442087/st-martin-in-the-fields-churchyard [Accessed 26 Feb. 2025].

Follow The Camino (2024). *Camino Routes.* [online] Follow the Camino. Available at: https://followthecamino.com/en/camino-de-santiago-routes/?utm_source=google&utm_edium=organic&utm_campaign=undefined [Accessed 8 Mar. 2025].

Funeral Notices (2011). *Death Notices: Frank Neal.* [online] Funeral Notices. Available at: https://funeral-notices.co.uk/notice/neal/394544 [Accessed 25 Feb. 2025].

Gargano, D.V. and Lim, T.H. (2025). *Abortion Rights in Ireland: the Eighth Amendment and the Path to Repeal.* [online] Oxford Constitutions. Available at: https://oxcon.ouplaw.com/page/705 [Accessed 8 Mar. 2025].

Gavin, P. (2000). *The History Place - Irish Potato Famine: Coffin Ships*. [online] The History Place. Available at: https://www.historyplace.com/worldhistory/famine/coffin.htm [Accessed 12 Mar. 2025].

German Patent and Trademark Office (2025). *DPMA / Aspirin*. [online] Deutsches Patent- und Markenamt. Available at: https://www.dpma.de/english/our_office/publications/milestones/brandswithhistory/aspirin/index.html [Accessed 8 Mar. 2025].

GOV UK (1867). *The Representation of the People Act 1867*. [online] Legislation (.gov.uk). Available at: https://www.legislation.gov.uk/ukpga/1867/102/pdfs/ukpga_18670102_en.pdf [Accessed 28 Feb. 2025].

GOV UK (2011a). *Holidays with Pay Act 1938*. [online] Legislation (.gov.uk). Available at: https://www.legislation.gov.uk/ukpga/Geo6/1-2/70/enacted [Accessed 8 Mar. 2025].

GOV UK (2011b). *Offences Against the Person Act 1861*. [online] Legislation (.gov.uk). Available at: https://www.legislation.gov.uk/ukpga/Vict/24-25/100/contents [Accessed 8 Mar. 2025].

GOV UK (2011c). *Probation of Offenders Act 1907*. [online] Legislation (.gov.uk). Available at: https://www.legislation.gov.uk/ukpga/Edw7/7/17/enacted [Accessed 8 Mar. 2025].

GOV UK (2018). *Civil Partnership Act 2004*. [online] Legislation (.gov.uk). Available at: https://www.legislation.gov.uk/ukpga/2004/33/contents [Accessed 8 Mar. 2025].

GOV UK (2019). *National Assistance Act 1948*. [online] Legislation (.gov.uk). Available at: https://www.legislation.gov.uk/ukpga/Geo6/11-12/29 [Accessed 11 Mar. 2025].

GOV UK (2022). *Roman Catholic Relief Act 1829*. [online] Legislation (.gov.uk). Available at: https://www.legislation.gov.uk/ukpga/Geo4/10/7/contents [Accessed 8 Mar. 2025].

GOV UK (2023). *History of Sir Robert Peel 2nd Baronet - GOV.UK*. [online] Legislation (.gov.uk). Available at: https://www.gov.uk/government/history/past-prime-ministers/robert-peel-2nd-baronet [Accessed 8 Mar. 2025].

GOV UK (2024). *Past Prime Ministers*. [online] Legislation (.gov.uk). Available at: https://www.gov.uk/government/history/past-prime-ministers [Accessed 8 Mar. 2025].

GOV UK (2025). *History of George Hamilton Gordon, Earl of Aberdeen*. [online] GOV UK. Available at: https://www.gov.uk/government/history/past-prime-ministers/george-hamilton-gordon-earl-of-aberdeen [Accessed 8 Mar. 2025].

GOV UK (Hansard) (1854). *Emigrant Ships - Hansard - UK Parliament*. [online] GOV UK . Available at: https://hansard.parliament.uk/Commons/1854-03-02/debates/f5a38f43-4a74-4261-aea5-c38ae320c7ed/EmigrantShips?highlight=1851%20select%20committee%20passenger%20act#contribution-d2ab6e80-252c-4326-a7b8-3cae5c70792a [Accessed 11 Mar. 2025].

Henry, W. (2020). *A Short History of English Agriculture*. [online] Gutenberg.org. Available at: https://www.gutenberg.org/cache/epub/16594/pg16594-images.html [Accessed 25 Feb. 2025].

Higginbotham, P. (2025a). *Outdoor Labour Test Order of 1842 (full text)*. [online] The Workhouse: The story of an institution. Available at: https://www.workhouses.org.uk/gco/outdoorlabourtestintro.shtml [Accessed 27 Feb. 2025].

Higginbotham, P. (2025b). *The 1834 Poor Law Amendment Act*. [online] The Workhouse: The Story of an Institution. Available at: https://www.workhouses.org.uk/poorlaws/1834intro.shtml [Accessed 8 Mar. 2025].

Historic England and Edwards, C. (2023). Rare Travellers' Rest Stones in North of England listed. [online] Historic England. Available at: https://historicengland.org.uk/whats-new/news/rare-travellers-rest-stones-in-north-of-england-listed/ [Accessed 24 Mar. 2025].

Historic Liverpool (2024). *1846: Plan of the Liverpool Docks, by Jesse Hartley, Dock Surveyor*. [online] Historic Liverpool (.co.uk). Available at: https://historic-liverpool.co.uk/old-maps-of-liverpool/1846-plan-liverpool-docks-jesse-hartley-dock-surveyor/#4/61.82/-54.14 [Accessed 6 Mar. 2025].

History Extra for the BBC (2021). The 1815–46 Corn Laws: your guide to the crisis and why they were repealed. *History Extra: The official website for BBC History Magazine*. [online] 7 Mar. Available at: https://www.historyextra.com/period/victorian/corn-laws-guide-what-impact-why-repealed-benefit/ [Accessed 8 Mar. 2025].

History.com Editors (2009). *Civil War*. [online] HISTORY.com. Available at: https://www.history.com/topics/american-civil-war/american-civil-war-history [Accessed 8 Mar. 2025].

Holan, M. (2018). *Ireland's Famine Children 'Born at Sea'*. [online] The U.S. National Archives and Records Administration. Available at: https://www.archives.gov/publications/prologue/2017/winter/irish-births [Accessed 12 Mar. 2025].

Hume, A. (1850). *Missions at Home; or a Clergyman's account of a portion of the Town of Liverpool*. J&F Rivington.

Imperial War Museum (2022). *What You Need to Know about The Troubles*. [online] Imperial War Museums. Available at: https://www.iwm.org.uk/history/what-you-need-to-know-about-the-troubles [Accessed 8 Mar. 2025].

Ireland Reaching Out (2025a). *Arrival of Potato Blight reported in Dublin Evening Post*. [online] Ireland XO. Available at: https://www.irelandxo.com/ireland-xo/history-and-genealogy/timeline/arrival-potato-blight-reported-dublin-evening-post [Accessed 10 Feb. 2025].

Ireland Reaching Out (2025b). *IrelandXo*. [online] Ireland XO. Available at: https://irelandxo.com/ireland-xo/history-and-genealogy/timeline/queen-victorias-first-visit-ireland [Accessed 10 Feb. 2025].

Ireland's Great Hunger Museum (2019). *Learn about the Great Hunger at Ireland's Great Hunger Museum*. [online] ighm.org. Available at: https://www.ighm.org/learn.html.

Irish Genealogy Toolkit (2023). *Irish census fragments: the surviving returns from 1821 to 1851*. [online] Irish Genealogy Toolkit. Available at: https://www.irish-genealogy-toolkit.com/irish-census-fragments.html [Accessed 12 Feb. 2025].

Irish Heritage Trust (2025). *Home.* [online] Irish Heritage Trust. Available at: https://irishheritagetrust.ie/ [Accessed 8 Mar. 2025].

Jamestown-Yorktown Foundation (2025). *The Tea Act and the Boston Tea Party | Jamestown-Yorktown Foundation, VA.* [online] Jamestown-Yorktown Foundation. Available at: https://www.jyfmuseums.org/learn/research-and-collections/essays/the-tea-act-and-the-boston-tea-party [Accessed 8 Mar. 2025].

Jefferson, T. (1776). *Declaration of Independence.* [online] National Archives. Available at: https://www.archives.gov/founding-docs/declaration-transcript [Accessed 8 Mar. 2025].

Johnson, M. (2018). *How working class writer Robert Tressell will always be remembered in Liverpool.* [online] Liverpool Echo. Available at: https://www.liverpoolecho.co.uk/whats-on/how-working-class-writer-robert-15276215 [Accessed 5 Mar. 2025].

Kelly, M. and Fotheringham, A.S. (2011). The online atlas of Irish population change 1841–2002: A new resource for analysing national trends and local variations in Irish population dynamics. *Irish Geography*, [online] 44(2-3), pp.215–244. DOI: https://doi.org/10.1080/00750778.2011.664806 [Accessed 8 Mar. 2024].

Kennedy, D. (2024). *Doctor Duncan's, Liverpool.* [online] Pub Gallery. Available at: https://pubgallery.co.uk/pubs/doctor-duncans-liverpool/ [Accessed 5 Mar. 2025].

Kerr, S. and Vaughan, M. (2024). *Changing the narrative on wealth inequality.* [online] Joseph Rowntree Foundation. Available at: https://www.jrf.org.uk/narrative-change/changing-the-narrative-on-wealth-inequality [Accessed 8 Mar. 2025].

Kinealy, C. (1990). The Irish Famine 1845 - 52. *North Irish Roots*, [online] 2(5), pp.158–161. Available at: https://www.jstor.org/stable/27696747 [Accessed 8 Mar. 2025].

Kinealy, C. (2025). *Douglass in Ireland.* [online] Frederick Douglass Ireland Project. Available at: https://www.douglassireland.org/douglass-in-ireland [Accessed 6 Mar. 2025].

Kirchgaessner, S. (2015). *UN says 800 migrants dead in boat disaster as Italy launches rescue of two more vessels.* [online] The Guardian. Available at: https://www.theguardian.com/world/2015/apr/20/italy-pm-matteo-renzi-migrant-shipwreck-crisis-srebrenica-massacre [Accessed 8 Mar. 2025].

Kissane, N. (1995). *The Irish Famine -A Documentary History.* [online] Syracuse Press. Available at: http://sarkoups.free.fr/kissane1995.pdf [Accessed 4 Mar. 2025].

Kissane, N. (1996). *The Irish Famine : a documentary history.* Syracuse, N.Y.: Distributed For The National Library Of Ireland By Syracuse University Press.

Land and Emigration Commission (n.d.). *Colonial Office 384/84, 4584 Emigration, Commissioners: Merivale, 22 May 1849.*

Lashmar, P. and Smith, J. (2023). How William Gladstone defended his father's role in slavery. *The Observer.* [online] 19 Aug. Available at: https://www.theguardian.com/world/2023/aug/19/how-william-gladstone-defended-his-fathers-role-in-slavery [Accessed 11 Mar. 2025].

Lewis, E., Farr, S.-J., Merseyside Historic Characterisation Project (MHCP), National Museums Liverpool and Merseyside Archaeological Advisory Service (MAAS), National Museums Liverpool (2011). 7 *Liverpool 7.1 Location and Administration.* [online] Available at: https://images.liverpoolmuseums.org.uk/2020-01/Liverpool-Part-2.pdf [Accessed 8 Mar. 2025].

Library of Congress (2025). *Today in History - May 24: What Hath God Wrought?* [online] Library of Congress, Washington, D.C. 20540 USA. Available at: https://www.loc.gov/item/today-in-history/may-24 [Accessed 8 Mar. 2025].

Liverpool Anti-Monopoly Association and Finch, J. (1986). *Statistics of Vauxhall Ward, Liverpool, Shewing the ... Condition of More Than Five Thousand Families ...* [online] Toulouse Press; Facsimile edition . Available at: https://babel.hathitrust.org/cgi/pt?id=chi.096401888&seq=13 [Accessed 12 Mar. 2025].

Liverpool Black History Research Group (2024). *Plaque commemorating Frederick Douglass to be revealed at the Everyman Theatre.* [online] Liverpool Black History Research Group. Available at: Plaque commemorating Frederick Douglass to be revealed at the Everyman Theatre. [Accessed 5 Mar. 2025].

Liverpool Irish Centre (2025). *About | Liverpool Irish Centre -.* [online] Liverpool Irish Centre. Available at: https://www.liverpoolirishcentre.org/about-us [Accessed 12 Mar. 2025].

Liverpool Metropolitan Cathedral (2024). *The Workhouse Site - Liverpool Metropolitan.* [online] Liverpool Metropolitan. Available at: https://liverpoolmetrocathedral.org.uk/the-workhouse-site/ [Accessed 12 Feb. 2025].

Liverpool Parish Church (2024). *Home.* [online] Liverpool Parish Church. Available at: https://livpc.co.uk/ [Accessed 25 Feb. 2025].

Liverpool University Press (2025). *Liverpool University Press.* [online] Liverpool University Press. Available at: https://www.liverpooluniversitypress.co.uk/ [Accessed 12 Feb. 2025].

Living History Library (2025). *Edward Rushton.* [online] Edward Rushton. Available at: https://www.edwardrushton.org.uk/ [Accessed 24 Feb. 2025].

Long, D. (2025). *St John's Gardens, Liverpool - Irish Guards.* [online] Imperial War Museums. Available at: https://www.iwm.org.uk/memorials/item/memorial/101601 [Accessed 5 Mar. 2025].

Lybeck, E. and Alsalloum, A. (2025). *Tracing Intangible Cultural Migrant Heritage in the UK.* Springer. From the chapter 'Near This Place: The Liverpool Irish Famine Trail in Visual Art'.

Maastricht Treaty (2025). *Maastricht Treaty.* [online] Maastricht Treaty. Available at: http://europarl.europa.eu/about-parliament/en/in-the-past/the-parliament-and-the-treaties/maastricht-treaty [Accessed 21 Feb. 2025].

MacDonagh, O. (1961). *A Pattern of Government Growth: The Passenger Acts and their Enforcement.* MacGibbon and Kee.

MacRaild, D.M. (1999). Irish Migrants in Modern Britain, 1750-1922. Basingstoke: Palgrave Macmillan.

MacPherson, H. (2020). *Back in the Day: How the potato famine hit Scotland hard.* [online] The National. Available at:

https://www.thenational.scot/news/18595351.potato-famine-hit-scotland-hard/ [Accessed 8 Mar. 2025].

Magazine, T.P. (2017). *250 Years of the Liverpool Pilotage Service: 1766 – 2016 (Part 1): Geoff Topp.* [online] The Pilot Online Edition. Available at: https://www.pilotmag.co.uk/250-years-of-the-liverpool-pilotage-service-1766-2016-part-1-geoff-topp/ [Accessed 12 Feb. 2025].

Mangan, S. (2025). *Global Irish Famine Way: The Longest Heritage Trail in the World.* [online] Department of Foreign Affairs and Trade: Ireland (.ie). Available at: https://www.ireland.ie/en/canada/global-irish-famine-way-the-longest-heritage-trail-in-the-world [Accessed 8 Mar. 2025].

Mark-FitzGerald, E. (2014). *Liverpool, England (1998).* [online] Irish Famine Memorials. Available at: https://irishfaminememorials.com/2014/01/16/liverpool-england-1998/ [Accessed 8 Mar. 2025].

Maudlin, D. and Bremner, A. (2024). Inner Empire. Manchester University Press.

Maycock, A. (2007). *Liverpool Monuments: Reconciliation.* [online] Liverpool Monuments. Available at: http://www.liverpoolmonuments.co.uk/walks/recon.html [Accessed 8 Mar. 2025].

McGowan, M. (2022). *Coffin Ship: Life and Death at Sea During the Great Irish Famine.* [online] Estudios Irlandeses. Available at: https://www.estudiosirlandeses.org/reviews/coffin-ship-life-and-death-at-sea-during-the-great-irish-famine/ [Accessed 12 Mar. 2025].

McKee, E. (2024a). *Global Irish Famine Way: Update!* [online] Eamonn C Mckee. Available at: https://eamonncmckee.com/2024/05/01/global-irish-famine-way/ [Accessed 26 Feb. 2025].

McKee, E. (2024b). *May 2024.* [online] Eamonn McKee. Available at: https://eamonncmckee.com/2024/05/ [Accessed 11 Mar. 2025].

McMahon, C.T. (2021). *The Coffin Ship: Life and Death at Sea during the Great Irish Famine.* New York: NYU Press.

McMahon, C.T. (2023). *Revisiting the Coffin Ships: emigrant mortality during the Famine.* [online] RTÉ. Available at: https://www.rte.ie/history/the-great-irish-famine/2023/1205/1420245-revisiting-the-coffin-ships-emigrant-mortality-during-the-famine/ [Accessed 8 Mar. 2025].

Mellett, K. (2024). *'No Irish, No Blacks, No Dogs': Irish Times readers recall seeing notorious signs in Britain.* [online] The Irish Times. Available at: https://www.irishtimes.com/ireland/social-affairs/2024/05/06/no-irish-no-blacks-no-dogs-irish-times-readers-recall-encountering-notorious-signs-in-britain/ [Accessed 12 Mar. 2025].

Michael, C. (2025). *Collisions Involving Early Steamship.* [online] Liverpool.ac.uk. Available at: https://www.liverpool.ac.uk/~cmi/books/earlySS/collision.html#SN [Accessed 26 Feb. 2025].

Miglierini, J. (2016). Migrant tragedy: Anatomy of a shipwreck. *BBC News.* [online] 23 May. Available at: https://www.bbc.co.uk/news/world-europe-36278529 [Accessed 8 Mar. 2025].

Moby Dick on the Mersey (2013). *Melville and Liverpool.* [online] Moby Dick on the Mersey. Available at: https://mobydickonthemersey.org/melville-and-liverpool/ [Accessed 24 Feb. 2025].

Moglen, E. (2014). *Statute of Labourers.* [online] English Legal History and its Materials. Available at: https://moglen.law.columbia.edu/twiki/bin/view/EngLegalHist/StatuteofLabourers [Accessed 8 Mar. 2025].

Mullin, C. and Weston, A. (2022). *Secrets of the crypt where thousands are buried.* [online] Liverpool Echo. Available at: https://www.liverpoolecho.co.uk/news/liverpool-news/secrets-crypt-thousands-buried-23491149 [Accessed 12 Feb. 2025].

Murchadha, C.Ó. (2020). *The Panicked Flood: Emigration and the Great Famine.* www.rte.ie. [online] Available at: https://www.rte.ie/history/post-famine/2020/0903/1163045-the-panicked-flood-emigration-and-the-great-famine/ [Accessed 18 Jun. 2025].

Murray, L. and Lotha, G. (2010). *Anglo-Irish Agreement - United Kingdom-Ireland [1985].* [online] Encyclopedia Britannica. Available at: https://www.britannica.com/event/Anglo-Irish-Agreement [Accessed 8 Mar. 2025].

Museum of Policing Cheshire (2022). *Brave police officer shot twice by terrorists but kept on the radio to HQ to guide his colleagues.* [online] Cheshire Police Museum. Available at: https://cheshirepolicemuseum.org.uk/facts-and-features/brave-police-officer/ [Accessed 3 Mar. 2025].

Mytum, H., Philpott, R., Fairley Nielsson, A., Burwood, E. and Dark, N. (2022). Collaborating with the Community: Applying Non-Invasive Archaeological Methods in the Crypt and Churchyard of St Patrick's Roman Catholic Church, Toxteth, Liverpool. *Heritage,* [online] 5(4), pp.3298–3315. DOI: https://doi.org/10.3390/heritage5040169 [Accessed 8 Mar. 2025].

Nati (2025). *William Ewart Gladstone.* [online] National Museums Liverpool. Available at: https://www.liverpoolmuseums.org.uk/artifact/william-ewart-gladstone-0 [Accessed 5 Mar. 2025].

National Army Museum (2024). *First China War | National Army Museum.* [online] National Army Museum. Available at: https://www.nam.ac.uk/explore/first-china-war-1839-1842 [Accessed 8 Mar. 2025].

National Famine Way (2023). *Did you know? – 20 interesting facts relating to the National Famine Way – National Famine Way.* [online] National Famine Way. Available at: https://nationalfamineway.ie/did-you-know-20-interesting-facts-relating-to-the-national-famine-way/ [Accessed 28 Feb. 2025].

National Famine Way (2024). *The Story of the 1,490: Remember your soul and your liberty.* [online] National Famine Way. Available at: https://nationalfamineway.ie/about-the-1490/the-story-of-the-1490/ [Accessed 21 Feb. 2025].

National Famine Way (2025). *A historic Famine trail through Ireland's villages and towns.* [online] National Famine Way. Available at: https://nationalfamineway.ie/ [Accessed 8 Mar. 2025].

National Library of Ireland (2025). *Context: Letters to John Ross Mahon.* [online] National Library of Ireland (catalogue). Available at: https://catalogue.nli.ie/Record/vtls000841471 [Accessed 11 Mar. 2025].

National Museum of Ireland (2025). *Irish Emigration to America - The Journey.* [online] National Museum of Ireland. Available at: https://www.museum.ie/en-IE/Collections-Research/Folklife-Collections/Folklife-Collections-List-(1)/Other/Emigration/Irish-Emigration-to-America-The-Journey [Accessed 12 Mar. 2025].

National Museums Liverpool (2020). *Liverpool Irish Community trail.* [online] *Museum of Liverpool.* Liverpool, UK: National Museums Liverpool. Available at: https://images.liverpoolmuseums.org.uk/2020-01/Liverpool-Irish-community-trail.pdf [Accessed 8 Mar. 2025].

National Museums Liverpool (2025a). *Legacy statue.* [online] National Museums Liverpool. Available at: https://www.liverpoolmuseums.org.uk/artifact/legacy-statue [Accessed 4 Mar. 2025].

National Museums Liverpool (2025b). *Statue of James Larkin (1876-1947) by Oisin Kelly: Labour leader.* [online] National Museums Liverpool. Available at: https://www.liverpoolmuseums.org.uk/james-larkin-1876-1947 [Accessed 12 Feb. 2025].

National Park Service (2016). *Trail Of Tears National Historic Trail (U.S. National Park Service).* [online] National Park Service. Available at: https://www.nps.gov/trte/index.htm [Accessed 8 Mar. 2025].

Neal, F. (1987). *Sectarian violence in nineteenth century Liverpool: a study of the origins, nature and scale of the Catholic-Protestant conflict.* [online] University of Salford. Available at: https://salford-repository.worktribe.com/preview/1500415/Neal.pdf [Accessed 12 Feb. 2025].

Neal, F. (1988). *Sectarian Violence: The Liverpool Experience, 1819-1914: an Aspect of Anglo-Irish history.* Manchester, UK: Manchester University Press.

Neal, F. (1997). *Black '47: Britain and the Famine Irish.* Springer/Newsham Press.

Neumann, J. and Kington, J. (1992). Great Historical Events That Were Significantly Affected by the Weather: Part 10, Crop Failure in Britain in 1799 and 1800 and the British Decision to Send a Naval Force to the Baltic Early in 1801. *Bulletin of the American Meteorological Society,* [online] 73(2), pp.187–199. doi:https://doi.org/10.1175/1520-0477(1992)073%3C0187:GHETWS%3E2.0.CO;2 [Accessed 8 Mar. 2025].

Never Such Innocence (2018). *Never Such Innocence.* [online] Never Such Innocence. Available at: https://www.neversuchinnocence.com/migration-irish-war-of-independence [Accessed 6 Mar. 2025].

New Horizon Athlone (2024). *New Horizon Athlone: Refugee & Asylum Seeker Support.* [online] New Horizon Athlone. Available at: https://newhorizonathlone.org/ [Accessed 26 Feb. 2025].

Nicholsons (2025). *The Philharmonic Dining Rooms Liverpool.* [online] Nicholsons. Available at: https://www.nicholsonspubs.co.uk/restaurants/northwest/thephilharmonicdiningroomsliverpool#/ [Accessed 12 Feb. 2025].

O'Brien, G.M. (2019). *Famine Soup.* [online] Murder, Mayhem & Shiny Things. Available at: https://gillianmobrien.wordpress.com/2019/11/05/famine-soup/ [Accessed 4 Mar. 2025].

O'Dowd, N. (2023). *Was it genocide? What the British ruling class really said about the Irish Famine.* [online] IrishCentral. Available at: https://www.irishcentral.com/roots/genocide-british-ruling-class-irish-famine [Accessed 12 Mar. 2025].

O'Keeffe, H. (2020). Peel's brimstone: the Temporary Relief Commission. *RTÉ.* [online] Available at: https://www.rte.ie/history/the-great-irish-famine/2020/1117/1178730-the-temporary-relief-commission/ [Accessed 8 Mar. 2025].

O'Keeffe, H. (2021). How the Temporary Fever Act failed to stop epidemics. *RTÉ.* [online] Available at: https://www.rte.ie/history/famine-ireland/2021/0128/1193691-how-the-temporary-fever-act-failed-to-stop-an-epidemic [Accessed 8 Mar. 2025].

O'Neill, T.P. (1950). The Society of Friends and the Great Famine. *Studies: An Irish Quarterly Review,* [online] 39(154), pp.203–213. Available at: https://www.jstor.org/stable/30099847.

O'Reilly, P. (2022). *Spore Prints, how to make and use them.* [online] First Nature. Available at: https://www.first-nature.com/fungi/~sporeprint.php [Accessed 12 Mar. 2025].

Owens, P. (2025). *Crew List Index Project.* [online] Crewlist.org.uk. Available at: https://crewlist.org.uk/about/legislation [Accessed 24 Feb. 2025].

Pedersen, E.-M. (2016a). *Star of the Sea: Acts of the Famine Years.* [online] Star of the Sea: A Postcolonial/Postmodern Voyage into the Irish Famine. Available at: https://scalar.usc.edu/works/star-of-the-sea-a-postcolonialpostmodern-voyage-into-the-irish-famine/reliefs-acts-and-policies-during-the-famine [Accessed 8 Mar. 2025].

Pedersen, E.-M. (2016b). *Star of the Sea: Diseases and Conditions Aboard Coffin Ships.* [online] Star of the Sea: A Postcolonial/Postmodern Voyage into the Irish Famine. Available at: https://scalar.usc.edu/works/star-of-the-sea-a-postcolonialpostmodern-voyage-into-the-irish-famine/conditions-on-coffin-ships [Accessed 12 Mar. 2025].

Project Gutenberg (2005). *A Short History of English Agriculture by W. H. R. Curtler.* [online] Project Gutenberg. Available at: https://www.gutenberg.org/ebooks/16594 [Accessed 26 Feb. 2025].

Promeet, D. (1998). *Land League - Irish agrarian organization.* [online] Encyclopedia Britannica. Available at: https://www.britannica.com/topic/Land-League [Accessed 8 Mar. 2025].

Public Services and Procurement Canada, Government of Canada (2002). *A register of deceased persons at sea and on Grosse Île in 1847 / by André Charbonneau and Doris Drolet-Dubé.* [online] Government of Canada (Publications). Available at: https://publications.gc.ca/site/eng/9.699659/publication.html [Accessed 12 Mar. 2025]. Accessed by Catherine Leen 27 Jul. 2024.

Pye, K. (2023). *St Patrick's Cross ~ Over 1,000 Years of Pilgrimage: Discover Liverpool.* [online] Discover-liverpool.com. Available at: https://www.discover-liverpool.com/local-history-stories-to-read/st-patricks-cross-over-1-000-years-of-pilgrimage/ [Accessed 5 Mar. 2025].

Queens University Belfast (QAB) (2025). *DIPPAM.* [online] Dippam.ac.uk. Available at: https://www.dippam.ac.uk [Accessed Jun. 2024].

Quiery, G. (2017). *In Hardship and Hope: A History of the Liverpool Irish.* Liverpool, UK: G&K Publishing.

Quiery, G. (2022). *Tony Birtill obituary.* [online] The Guardian. Available at: https://www.theguardian.com/education/2022/jan/18/tony-birtill-obituary [Accessed 25 Feb. 2025].

Ramsay, S. (2024). *Blue Plaque Unveiled Celebrating George At His Liverpool Birthplace - George Harrison.* [online] George Harrison. Available at: https://www.georgeharrison.com/blue-plaque-unveiled/ [Accessed 5 Mar. 2025].

Reilly, C. (2014). *Strokestown and the Great Irish Famine.* Four Courts Press, p.67.

Reilly, C. (2021). Where does the phrase 'taking the soup' come from?. *RTÉ.* [online] Available at: https://www.rte.ie/brainstorm/2021/1012/1253213-taking-the-soup-ireland-famine-history/ [Accessed 8 Mar. 2025].

Reynolds, A. and E. (2016). *Roscommon Solstice Choir.* [online] Roscommon Solstice Choir. Available at: https://rsc2013.wixsite.com/solsticechoir13 [Accessed 26 Feb. 2025].

RMS Titanic, Inc (2024). *Where Did the Titanic Sink?* [online] Expedition Discover Titanic. Available at: https://expedition.discovertitanic.com/where-did-the-titanic-sink/ [Accessed 8 Mar. 2025].

Routledge, C. (2009). *Social Mobility in Victorian England: The Case of Robert Cain.* [online] Chris Routledge. Available at: https://chrisroutledge.co.uk/2009/01/06/social-mobility-in-victorian-england-the-case-of-robert-cain/ [Accessed 12 Feb. 2025].

Royal Albert Dock Liverpool (2023). *History.* [online] Royal Albert Dock Liverpool. Available at: https://albertdock.com/history/ [Accessed 8 Mar. 2025].

Royal Collection Trust (2025). *Official correspondence of George IV as Regent and King 1811-1821.* [online] Royal Collection Trust. Available at: https://www.rct.uk/collection/royal-archives/collections-and-catalogue/george-iv-and-princess-charlotte-of-wales/official-papers-of-george-iv-as-regent-and-king [Accessed 6 Mar. 2025].

Royal Museums Greenwich (2025). *Queen Victoria's Visit to Queenstown, 1849.* [online] Royal Museums Greenwich. Available at: https://www.rmg.co.uk/collections/objects/rmgc-object-12123 [Accessed 10 Feb. 2025].

Save the Children International (2018). *What is happening in Yemen?* [online] Save the Children International. Available at: https://www.savethechildren.net/stories/what-happening-yemen [Accessed 8 Mar. 2025].

Sefton War Memorials (2016). *Bootle War Memorial – Sefton WW1.* [online] seftonwarmemorials.org. Available at:

https://seftonwarmemorials.org/bootle_war_memorial/ [Accessed 5 Mar. 2025].

Select Committee Passenger Acts 299-300, Q.2861-4, House of Commons 1851 (632), xix. (1851).

Select Committee Passenger Acts 299-300, Q.2861-4, House of Commons 1851 (632), xix. (1851). *Select Committee Passenger Acts 299-300.* Accessed by Kieran Daly.

Shakeshaft, A. (2025). *1800 - 2000 timeline.* [online] Time Toast Timelines. Available at: https://www.timetoast.com/timelines/1800-2000 [Accessed 8 Mar. 2025].

Shire, W. (2016). *Home, Warsan Shire.* [online] Amnesty International. Available at: https://www.amnesty.ie/wp-content/uploads/2016/06/home-by-warsan-shire.pdf [Accessed 7 Mar. 2025].

Smith, C. (2020). *Bank of England: the Gold Standard.* [online] House of Lords Library. Available at: https://lordslibrary.parliament.uk/bank-of-england-the-gold-standard/ [Accessed 8 Mar. 2025].

Smith, E. (2023a). *Song commission: open call - Liverpool Irish Festival.* [online] Liverpool Irish Festival. Available at: https://www.liverpoolirishfestival.com/song-commission-open-call/ [Accessed 4 Mar. 2025].

Smith, E. (2023b). *Those roads - a new song from Úna Quinn - Liverpool Irish Festival.* [online] Liverpool Irish Festival. Available at: https://www.liverpoolirishfestival.com/those-roads-una-quinn/ [Accessed 4 Mar. 2025].

Smith, E. and Liverpool Irish Festival (2022). *Liverpool Irish Famine Trail: Revive.* 1st ed. [online] Liverpool: Liverpool Irish Festival. Available at: https://www.smashwords.com/books/view/1152121? [Accessed 8 Mar. 2025].

Smith, E. and O'Callaghan, C. (2023). *Liverpool's football transformed by Irishman - Liverpool Irish Festival.* [online] Liverpool Irish Festival. Available at: https://www.liverpoolirishfestival.com/liverpools-football-transformed-by-irishman/ [Accessed 5 Mar. 2025].

Soyer, A. and Foods of England (2025). *Foods of England - A Shilling Cookery for The People, 1845.* [online] Foods of England. Available at: https://www.foodsofengland.co.uk/book1845soyer.html [Accessed 4 Mar. 2025].

St Luke's Bombed Out Church (2024). *The Story of St Luke's Bombed Out Church.* [online] St Luke's Bombed Out Church. Available at: https://www.slboc.com/the-story [Accessed 8 Mar. 2025].

St Luke's Church, Formby (2025). *Percy French.* [online] St Luke's Church, Formby. Available at: https://www.stlukesformby.org.uk/french.html [Accessed 5 Mar. 2025].

Stevens, R. (2020). *The Wellington Rooms.* [online] Liverpool1207. Available at: https://liverpool1207blog.wordpress.com/buildings/the-wellington-rooms/ [Accessed 5 Mar. 2025].

Strokestown Park: The National Famine Museum (2025). *National Famine Museum - Famine House.* [online] Strokestown Park: The National Famine Museum . Available at: https://strokestownpark.ie/national-famine-museum/ [Accessed 8 Mar. 2025].

The Board of the Liverpool Select Vestry Finance Committee, Minutes of Meetings from Dec 1846 and throughout 1847. (1846-7).

The Church of St Mary, Grassendale in the County of Lancashire (2025). *Lancashire Online Parish Clerk Project - District of Liverpool.* [online] The Church of St Mary, Grassendale in the County of

Lancashire . Available at: https://www.lan-opc.org.uk/Liverpool/Grassendale/stmary/index.html [Accessed 27 Feb. 2025].

The Guide Liverpool (2023). *The story of Charles Dickens and his links with Liverpool.* [online] The Guide Liverpool. Available at: https://theguideliverpool.com/the-story-of-charles-dickens-and-his-links-with-liverpool/ [Accessed 12 Feb. 2025].

The Jeanie Johnston (2024). *The families who walked 165km to board a boat to Quebec - Jeanie Johnston Tall Ship.* [online] The Jeanie Johnston. Available at: https://jeaniejohnston.ie/story/the-families-who-walked-165km-to-board-a-boat-to-quebec/ [Accessed 26 Feb. 2025].

The Jeanie Johnston (2025). *The Jeanie Johnston Tall Ship - An Irish Famine Story - Dublin Ireland.* [online] The Jeanie Johnston. Available at: https://jeaniejohnston.ie/ [Accessed 8 Mar. 2025].

The Kipling Society (2021). *Recessional.* [online] The Kipling Society. Available at: https://www.kiplingsociety.co.uk/readers-guide/rg_recess1.htm [Accessed 4 Mar. 2025].

The Liverpool & South West Lancashire Family History Society (L&SWLFHS) (2023). *Liverpool | Liverpool & SW Lancashire FHS.* [online] The Liverpool & South West Lancashire Family History Society (L&SWLFHS). Available at: https://www.lswlfhs.org.uk/index.php/Liverpool [Accessed 5 Mar. 2025].

The Liverpool Mercury (various authors) (1846). *The Liverpool Mercury,* (newspaper), from January 1847 through 'til October 1847.

The National Archives (2019). *1833 Factory Act/Muster lists of Kroomen serving in various ships.* [online] The National Archives. Available at: https://discovery.nationalarchives.gov.uk/details/r/C530143 [Accessed 8 Mar. 2025].

The National Archives (2025). *The 1833 Abolition of Slavery Act and compensation claims: Collection highlights.* [online] The National Archives. Available at: https://beta.nationalarchives.gov.uk/explore-the-collection/explore-by-time-period/georgians/1833-abolition-of-slavery-act-and-compensation-claims/ [Accessed 8 Mar. 2025].

The National Archives (2025b). The National Archives - Homepage. [online] The National Archives. Available at: https://www.nationalarchives.gov.uk/education/resources/voices-of-the-victorian-poor/have-we-underestimated-the-victorian-poor/poor-law-poster/ Forms part of The National Archives KS1-3 education pack, as found at https://cdn.nationalarchives.gov.uk/documents/education/poor-law.pdf.

The Next Generation of Genealogy Sitebuilding and Gibbs, M. (2018). *Rev. Augustus Campbell.* [online] Gibbs Family Tree (.com). Available at: https://gibbsfamilytree.com/tng/getperson.php?personID=I5139&tree=gft1 [Accessed 27 Feb. 2025].

The Reform Club (2024). *Home.* [online] The Reform Club. Available at: https://www.reformclub.com/ [Accessed 8 Mar. 2025].

The Select Vestry Register of Pauper Burials for St Mary's Cambridge Street for 17th March to 15th July, 1847. (1847). Microfilm held at Liverpool Records Office.

The Victorian Web (2009). *'Gladstone Memorial,' Liverpool, by Sir Thomas Brock.* [online] Victorianweb.org. Available at: https://victorianweb.org/sculpture/brock/30.html [Accessed 5 Mar. 2025].

The White House (President Donald Trump) (2025). *Ending radical and wasteful government DEI programs and preferencing – the White House.* [online] The White House. Available at: https://www.whitehouse.gov/presidential-actions/2025/01/ending-radical-and-wasteful-government-dei-programs-and-preferencing/ [Accessed 8 Mar. 2025].

Titanic Memorials (2025). *Memorial to Heroes of the Marine Engine Room; Liverpool.* [online] Titanic Memorials. Available at: https://www.titanic.memorial/post/memorial/engineers+memorial+liverpool/ [Accessed 6 Mar. 2025].

Torrance, D. (2025). *The Anglo-Irish Treaty, 1921.* [online] House of Commons Library. Available at: http://commonslibrary.parliament.uk/research-briefings/cbp-9260/ [Accessed 21 Feb. 2025].

Toxteth Park Cemetery (2023). *Notable People– Toxteth Park Cemetery.* [online] Toxteth Park Cemetery. Available at: https://toxtethparkcemetery.co.uk/notable-people/ [Accessed 8 Mar. 2025].

Trench, W. (1865). *Sanitary Amendment Act, 1864 : report of the Medical Officer of Health on his second presentment to the grand jury.* [online] Wellcome Collection. Available at: https://wellcomecollection.org/works/zx3c2s93/items?canvas=3 [Accessed 12 Feb. 2025].

Trueman, C.N. (2015). *Gladstone and Ireland.* [online] History Learning Site. Available at: https://www.historylearningsite.co.uk/ireland-1845-to-1922/gladstone-and-ireland/ [Accessed 8 Mar. 2025].

U.S. Department of State (2020). *Treaty of Paris, 1783.* [online] U.S. Department of State (2001-2009). Available at: https://2001-2009.state.gov/r/pa/ho/time/ar/14313.htm [Accessed 8 Mar. 2025].

UK Parliament (1572). *Vagabonds Act 1572 .* [online] UK Parliament. Available at: https://www.parliament.uk/about/living-heritage/transformingsociety/livinglearning/coll-9-health1/health-06/ [Accessed 8 Mar. 2025].

UK Parliament (1985). Anglo-Irish Agreement Volume 87: debated on Wednesday 27 Nov 1985. *Hansard,* [online] 87. Available at: https://hansard.parliament.uk/commons/1985-11-27/debates/c0c5b045-dc9d-4666-ae37-a4de4d511172/Anglo-IrishAgreement [Accessed 8 Mar. 2025].

UK Parliament (2015). *1829 Catholic Emancipation Act.* [online] UK Parliament. Available at: https://www.parliament.uk/about/living-heritage/evolutionofparliament/2015-parliament-in-the-making/get-involved1/2015-banners-exhibition/rachel-gadsden/1829-catholic-emancipation-act-gallery/ [Accessed 8 Mar. 2025].

UK Parliament (2023). *The Reform Act 1832.* [online] UK Parliament. Available at: https://www.parliament.uk/about/living-heritage/evolutionofparliament/houseofcommons/reformacts/overview/reformact1832/ [Accessed 8 Mar. 2025].

UK Parliament (2025a). *Emancipation.* [online] UK Parliament. Available at: https://www.parliament.uk/about/living-heritage/transformingsociety/private-lives/religion/overview/emancipation/ [Accessed 8 Mar. 2025].

UK Parliament (2025b). *Incumbered Estates (Ireland) Bill - Hansard - UK Parliament.* [online] UK Parliament. Available at: https://hansard.parliament.uk/lords/1849-06-11/debates/e64ee548-5ea9-4118-bde8-2971f4e40b71/IncumberedEstates(Ireland)Bill [Accessed 10 Feb. 2025].

UK Parliament (2025c). *Poor Relief (Ireland) Bill - Hansard.* [online] UK Parliament. Available at: https://hansard.parliament.uk/Commons/1847-03-12/debates/3cc8f39d-901b-4e35-af4c-c037b3aed099/PoorRelief(Ireland)Bill [Accessed 24 Feb. 2025].

UK Parliament (2025d). *The Assassin: John Bellingham.* [online] UK Parliament. Available at: https://www.parliament.uk/about/living-heritage/building/palace/estatehistory/from-the-parliamentary-collections/spencer-perceval/portrait-of-john-bellingham [Accessed 24 Feb. 2025].

UK Parliament (2024). *The 1848 Public Health Act.* [online] UK Parliament. Available at: https://www.parliament.uk/about/living-heritage/transformingsociety/towncountry/towns/tyne-and-wear-case-study/about-the-group/public-administration/the-1848-public-health-act/ [Accessed 8 Mar. 2025].

University of Essex (2004). *Content associated with: Census of England and Wales (HISTPOP.ORG - 2004-2007).* [online] Online Historical Population Reports. Available at: http://www.histpop.org/ohpr/servlet/AssociatedView?path=Browse&active=yes&mno=4001&assoctitle=Census%20of%20England%20and%20Wales [Accessed 12 Feb. 2025].

University of Nottingham (2012). *Daniel O'Connell (1775-1847; Irish nationalist leader) - The University of Nottingham.* [online] University of Nottingham. Available at: https://www.nottingham.ac.uk/manuscriptsandspecialcollections/learning/biographies/danieloconnell(1775-1847).aspx [Accessed 8 Mar. 2025].

University of Portsmouth (2025). *Vision of Britain: Context for data value and the meaning of 85,698.* [online] A Vision of Britain Through Time. Available at: https://www.visionofbritain.org.uk/datavalue/11449257 [Accessed 12 Feb. 2025].

University of Southampton (2016). *Census of Ireland 1861: Part I, Area, Population, and Number of Houses, by Townlands and Electoral Divisions Provinces of Ulster and Connaught.* [online] Internet Archive. Available at: https://archive.org/details/op1248751-1001/page/n7/mode/2up [Accessed 12 Feb. 2025].

University of Wisconsin-Madison (Department of History) (2025). *James S. Donnelly, Jr.* [online] Department of History: University of Wisconsin-Madison. Available at: https://history.wisc.edu/people/donnelly-james/ [Accessed 8 Mar. 2025].

Wahl, M. (2009). *Everton FC: history, facts and stats.* [online] Football History (.org). Available at: https://www.footballhistory.org/club/everton.html [Accessed 8 Mar. 2025].

Wahl, M. (2011). *Liverpool FC: history of the club.* [online] Football History (.org). Available at: https://www.footballhistory.org/club/liverpool.html [Accessed 8 Mar. 2025].

Wainright, M.D. (1951). *Agencies for the Promotion or Facilitation of Emigration from England to the United States of America, 1815-1861* . [online] Royal Holloway (repository). Available at: https://repository.royalholloway.ac.uk/file/6156f646-7c44-4521-97bd-5345af378b4c/1/10097845.pdf [Accessed 26 Feb. 2025].

Waite, P.B. (2013). *Confederation: The Canadian Encyclopedia.* [online] The Canadian Encyclopedia. Available at: https://www.thecanadianencyclopedia.ca/en/article/confederation [Accessed 8 Mar. 2025].

Walsh, T. (2011). *Being Irish in Liverpool.* Liverpool, UK: St Michael's Irish Centre, p.224.

Weston, A. and Carubia, E. (2025). *Secret tunnel that runs beneath famous city street.* [online] Liverpool Echo. Available at: https://www.liverpoolecho.co.uk/news/liverpool-news/secret-tunnel-runs-beneath-famous-30748328 [Accessed 5 Mar. 2025].

Wiki Commons (2025). *James Larkin gravestone image.* [online] Wiki Commons. Available at: https://upload.wikimedia.org/wikipedia/commons/4/44/James_Larkin_gravestone.JPG [Accessed 12 Feb. 2025].

Wikipedia Contributors (2019). *List of Prime Ministers of the United Kingdom.* [online] Wikipedia. Available at: https://en.wikipedia.org/wiki/List_of_Prime_Ministers_of_the_United_Kingdom [Accessed 8 Mar. 2025].

Wikipedia Contributors (2022). *Irish heads of government since 1919.* [online] Wikipedia. Available at: https://en.wikipedia.org/wiki/Irish_heads_of_government_since_1919 [Accessed 8 Mar. 2025].

Williams, T. and Neal, F. (2004). *Great Hunger Commemoration Service: St Anthony's Church Liverpool, 3 October 1997.* Newsham Press Ltd.

Yale Law School: Lillian Goodman Law Library and Henderson, E.F. (2020). *The Statute of Laborers; 1351.* [online] Yale Law School - The Avalon Projects. Available at: https://avalon.law.yale.edu/medieval/statlab.asp [Accessed 8 Mar. 2025].

You can access an interactive list of all these references by scanning this QR code or visiting **liverpoolirishfestival.com/reveal-reference-list** In addition to above, we've collated information from private archives, including census searches for Ireland, Liverpool and Birkenhead (years spanning 1801-1951); documents held in the ***Pleasant Street School Archives;*** the Great Hunger Commemoration service, 1997 and information made available by ***Merseyside Maritime Museum***, courtesy of ***National Museums Liverpool***. Please note, all information was correct at the time of writing; but websites, route planners and connections may change over time. Please plan your route.

Pebbles are often used as a memorial marker at holocaust sites, using the Jewish tradition of leaving a stone when honouring the dead as a sign of rememberance and respect. Witnessed several times along the journey, it is occasionally seen at the Liverpool Great Hunger commemoration memorial, too.

CUIMHNICH

REMEMBER